Debrief

A Complete History of U.S. Aerial Engagements
1981 to the Present

Craig Brown

Schiffer Military History
Atglen, PA

Acknowledgments

As a student of military history, the books I've always enjoyed reading the most were told by the actual participants. Along this line, I highly recommend *Crusader! Last of the Gunfighters* by ADM Paul Gillcrist (Available from Schiffer Publishing, Ltd.). ADM Gillcrist captured all 17 of the F-8's MiG kills during the Vietnam conflict, and these are told almost entirely in first person. His work was an inspiration for this publication. I have many people to thank. First and foremost are the MiG killers who contributed their time, stories, and photos for this book; it would never have happened without them. It was such a pleasure getting to know and work with them on this project, and their support was above and beyond what was necessary. Mr. Soph Moeng of Aerospace Publishing Limited and Alicia Gansz of The Washington Institute for Near East Policy graciously helped fill in gaps in several stories, and Steve Davies, author of *F-15C Units in Action* (Osprey Publications), was a tremendous source of help and advice. The support of the Naval Aviation Museum Foundation Magazine staff was fantastic. Many thanks to Robert F. Dorr for the text and photo support, as well as the great advice from a great historian / author. Thanks to all who contributed photos: Stefano Antoniazzi of the 31st Aviano Tail Spotters Group; Michael Baldock; Chris Blommendaal; David F. Brown; Gary Chambers; USAF MSgt T. Collins; Gary L. Coots; USAF SrA Greg L. Davis; USAF MSgt John Deshetler of the 1st FW History Office; Robert F. Dorr; Pete Fitzsimmons; Ed Groenendijk; Lieuwe Hofstra; USAF Lt Col Bran McAllister; Ian Nightingale; Jeff Puzzullo; Tony Silgrim; Bas Stubert; Pieter Taris; and especially Don Logan. Any of Don's books are a "must read" for the aviation enthusiast, and can also be obtained through Schiffer Publishing, Ltd. Various works of art were supplied by Ronald Wong, Price Randel, William Lacy, and Jim "Max" Qualls; my thanks go out to all these fantastic aviation artists. I could never have thanked BGen Robin Olds enough for taking the time to write the foreword for this project. We lost Robin in June 2007. He was a consummate warrior, a truly inspirational leader, and my friend. Godspeed, Robin. And a special thanks to my "senior editor," my wife, Tina. Her encouragement, guidance, and grasp of the English language are the only reason you are reading this book. Thank you.

Book Design by Ian Robertson.

Printed in China.
ISBN: 978-0-7643-2785-8

We are interested in hearing from authors with book ideas on related topics.

Published by Schiffer Publishing Ltd.
4880 Lower Valley Road
Atglen, PA 19310
Phone: (610) 593-1777
FAX: (610) 593-2002
E-mail: Info@schifferbooks.com.
Visit our web site at: www.schifferbooks.com
Please write for a free catalog.
This book may be purchased from the publisher.
Please include $3.95 postage.
Try your bookstore first.

In Europe, Schiffer books are distributed by:
Bushwood Books
6 Marksbury Avenue
Kew Gardens
Surrey TW9 4JF
England
Phone: 44 (0) 20 8392-8585
FAX: 44 (0) 20 8392-9876
E-mail: Info@bushwoodbooks.co.uk.
Free postage in the UK. Europe: air mail at cost.
Try your bookstore first.

Contents

Preface

Welcome to my first book! Over the years I found myself going to several different books to read accounts of the post-Vietnam MiG kills. I quickly realized that there was no "single source" to go to, and many of the accounts were not recorded outside of classified documents. Hence, the idea for *Debrief: A Complete History of U.S. Aerial Engagement 1981-Present* was born. I wanted to capture all 56 engagements that ended in an official kill by United States aviators since the end of the Vietnam conflict. These are their stories, largely in their own words.

Aerial kills are unique in contemporary history for several reasons, but the primary reason is volume. There simply are not the numbers of aircraft airborne in a modern conflict that there had been in the past. This is a symptom of technology and precision capability. And even when there are major conflicts, the opposition may not choose to fly their fighters and engage in aerial combat to contest their airspace. This means the odds of even seeing an enemy aircraft in ones' career rival the odds of winning the lottery. While a strike pilot *will* drop bombs on every combat mission, there is no guarantee that escort or sweep air-to-air missions will see any action. The amount of air-to-air, and subsequently kills, has declined in every conflict since WWII. During Operation IRAQI FREEDOM, more MiGs were buried in the sand than flown!

The MiG killers in this book will be the first to acknowledge that luck had a large stake in putting them in the right place at the right time. What makes their kills a unique achievement is that, when presented with the opportunity, they executed their mission under incredible stresses and lived to tell about it. They will also be the first to acknowledge that the mutual support of their flight members and ground crews made their kills possible. While one aircraft scored the kill, the entire flight accomplished the mission. It is ingrained into every U.S. pilot and aircrew member that teamwork is the only solution; "Lone Wolves" fail and die.

The accounts in this book were collected in several ways. I never wanted to "write history"; therefore, I made every attempt to interview each participant, or at least have them refresh a previously given account. For many of the pilots this is the first published account of their kill. To the maximum extent possible, these accounts are a true oral history told in first person. In the cases where a member was deceased or could not be contacted, previously published accounts are reprinted here and the source acknowledged.

I can only hope you enjoy reading this book as much as I enjoyed putting it together.

Regards,
Craig Brown

Foreword
BGen Robin Olds, USAF (Retired)

After agreeing to write this foreword I was sent three of the combat reports to be contained herein. Nothing I have read or experienced in my eighty-odd years has ever brought home so vividly what vast changes in aerial warfare have evolved over just a few decades. As I write, I can't help feeling that a description of my position relative to the adventures of today's fine young American fighter pilots would best be told as that of a veteran of the Battle of Gettysburg asked to comment upon the Battle of Britain.

But never mind. Just bear with me as I draw comparisons, and marvel at those changes brought before me in these accounts.

To begin, let me say briefly that I was privileged to be a fighter pilot for thirty years. I flew out of England in World War II, and over Hanoi some twenty-odd years later. I learned very early the fervor and the essence of being a fighter pilot culminates when he is thrust into an air-to-air combat situation, particularly when he returns home a victor. From encounters often against odds, from having downed the foe, the fighter pilot gains respect in his calling, and becomes something more as a person than he ever dreamed possible.

That reaction is the similarity of the young and the old that runs through these accounts. But it stops there. We were comparatively primitive in my day. We went, we attacked, or we were attacked, and each of us was alone, even in a sky full of churning planes. We fought with fury. Sometimes we lost, often we won. Every day evoked changes within ourselves scarcely recognized, and certainly not thought about. Those who survived quickly evolved into battle hardened warriors, thankful to survive this day and never mind tomorrow. What we did, we did virtually alone, depending upon our individual talents and skills for success and survival. Our machines were a thrill to fly and we loved them, but as machines of war they were Model-T Fords in comparison to the beauties of today.

I hope in reading these reports you will gain respect for those who brought about the changes that make today's air battle a choreography of integrated technology, communication, and of coordination of land, sea, air, and space. Above all, give thanks and your respect for the highly trained young people in each of those spheres of action who make possible America's success in the battles we must fight in the future.

Robin Olds
2006

Major Robin Olds pictured in 1945 with his P-51D, "*SCAT V.*" During WW II Olds scored 13 victories while assigned to the 434th Fighter Squadron flying first the P-38 then transitioning to the Mustang. Note the 10 kill markings on the canopy. This photo was sent to me by Gen Olds specifically for use with this forward. *USAAF via BGen Olds.*

Brigadier General Robin Olds
14 July 1922 - 14 June 2007
Then-Col Olds seen while commanding the 8th Tactical Fighter Wing, Udorn, Thailand, in 1967. Col Olds scored four official kills over North Vietnam, and is regarded as the finest combat leader of the conflict. We lost Robin this year (2007), and he was laid to rest on the grounds of the USAF Academy. There will never be another like him, Gods Speed General Olds.

Glossary of Terms

The accounts in this book are told fighter pilot to fighter pilot, and as you'll quickly find, fighter pilots speak their own language. It is filled with abbreviations and catch phrases, quotes from stupid airplane movies, and is often crude. None of this is by accident. Fighter Squadrons are closed shops, and these pilots enjoy being an insular group. I make no apologies; it's just the way it is.

While most books relegate the glossary to the end of the text, the nature of this work dictates that I place the glossary at the beginning. I've only included terms that were used by the individuals in their accounts. My intent was not to recreate a tactics manual, and I'm sure many of the terms here have changed, and might have different meanings to different branches of the service. While the scope is narrow, here is most of the "speak" you will need to know to really appreciate this oral history:

3-1:	Joint manual that spells-out standard comm. terms and phrases.
AAM:	Air-to-Air Missile.
AA-2:	Soviet-built copy of the AIM-9B, NATO codenamed the Atoll.
AIM-7:	500 lb radar missile carried by the F-15C, F-15E, and F/A-18s in this book. The Sparrow is not a "fire and forget" weapon; the launch aircraft must stay locked to the target throughout the time of flight (TOF) of the missile. This was the only radar missile available during DESERT STORM to all fighters, except for the AIM-54 equipped F-14s. Associated radio call at launch is "FOX 1."
AIM-9:	150lb class heat seeking missile, officially named the Sidewinder, and nicknamed "heater." Once the missile sees the heat source it will "growl" in the headset, and the pilot will then un-cage the seeker head to ascertain the proper heat source and fire and forget the weapon. Any heat seeker is susceptible to decoy by flares or guiding on the sun. It is carried by all fighter aircraft. Associated radio call at launch is "FOX 2."
AIM-120:	300lb class "fire and forget" radar missile designed to replace the AIM-7 series, although the Sparrow is still mustering on in service. This weapon entered service in the USN and USAF after the first Gulf War, and opens up incredible flexibility and tactics with its fire and forget capability. The missile is officially named the Advanced Medium Range Air to Air Missile (AMRAAM), and is nicknamed the "Slammer" by USAF pilots. Associated radio call at launch is "FOX 3."
AMRAAM:	See AIM-120.
Angels:	Altitude expressed in thousands of feet, ie "Angels 10" is 10,000 feet.
AOR:	Area Of Responsibility. Defined geographical area in which the aircraft are responsible to complete their mission.
APG-63/65/68/70:	Hughes-built Air-To-Air radars used by the F-16, F-15C, F/A-18, and F-15E, and later the F-15C, respectively.

Aspect: The number of degrees as measured from the targets dead six o'clock; ie, if you are looking up the target's tail pipe, that is a 0 aspect. Looking directly down the nose is a 180 aspect, however, the zero is always dropped, making it an "18" aspect. If you were looking at the right side of the target it would present a "9R" or "9 Right" aspect. All aspects greater than a 9 are considered "Hot" as you are in front of the target, while behind the "9" are "Cold" aspects.

AWACS: Airborne Early Warning and Control. The E-3 Sentry aircraft is based on the C-135 airframe, and provides a dramatic increase in radar coverage over ground-based radar sites.

AWG-9: Radar used by the F-14A.

Bandit: Term for a contact or visual sighting of a known enemy aircraft.

BDA: Battle, or Bomb Damage Assessment.

BE: Bullseye. One of two ways to express the position of a radar contact. In this case it is in relation to a fixed point on the ground called the Bullseye, which becomes a virtual VOR station. This establishes a common point of reference between the fighters and controllers. There may be several BEs in use at one time, and they will then be given different names. A sample radio call to define a radar contact 50 nm south of the BE would be "call sign, Group Bull 180, 50." The other way to define position of a contact is called Bearing-Range-Altitude (BRA).

Beam(ing): Term used to define a target maneuver that is showing either a 9L or 9R Aspect, ie "group beaming south" means you see the side of the target.

BFM: Basic Fighter Maneuvers. One-on-one (1 vs 1) dog-fighting.

Bingo: 3-1 brevity term for a fuel state that dictates returning to base (RTB).

Bitchin' Betty: Slang for the audio warning in most fighters that will warn of critical malfunctions and also Bingo fuel.

Bogey: Term for a contact or visual sighting where there has been no "Hostile" or "Bandit" declaration made. Unknown identity.

BRA: Bearing, Range, Altitude. This format for calling the position of a radar contact references the fighter's nose, so is usually only useful for radio calls within the flight. If the fighters are flying north and the radar contact is north of the fighters by 50 nm at 20,000', the call would be "call sign, group BRA 360, 50, 20 thousand."

BVR: Beyond Visual Range.

CAOC: Central Air Operations Center. Regional command and control of air assets.

CAP: Combat Air Patrol. Usually a race track pattern flown to defend an area from enemy fighters. The leg pointed at the suspected threat azimuth is called the "hot" leg, and the leg spent aimed the other way is "cold." There are various kinds of CAPs, such as HVAA CAP (High Value Airborne Asset), which protects assets such as an AWACS. There are TAR CAPs in the target area and BAR CAPs, or Barrier CAPs, which establish protection for borders or coastlines.

CAS: Close Air Support. Direct support of troops by air-to-ground sorties.

DCA: Defensive Counter Air. The official terminology for most air-to-air missions, such as Sweeps, Combat Air Patrols, and Escort.

ELT: Emergency Locator Transmitter. Transmits a beeper on the guard frequency when activated, often automatically upon ejection.

FAIP: First assignment instructor pilot. Generally a recently graduated student pilot that graduated very high in his class, and hence was retained to be an Instructor Pilot (IP).

FOX 1: See AIM-7.

FOX 2: See AIM-9.

FOX 3: See AIM-120.

Frame: The time it takes the radar to run though its set search volume in azimuth and elevation, or altitude coverage.

FTU: Fighter Training Unit. Also see RTU.

FWIC: Fighter Weapons Instructor Course. Formal name for the USAF Fighter Weapons School. The course lasts almost six months, and produces doctorate level instructors and weapons system experts.

GCI: Ground Controlled Intercept. A ground radar station whose purpose it is to direct fighter aircraft in a tactical setting.

Group: 3-1 term for a radar contact, but does not denote how many aircraft are in the group.

Guard: Term for any emergency frequency.

HARM: High Speed Anti-Radiation Missile (AGM-88). The primary weapon of the Wild Weasel mission, this weapon seeks out the radar transmissions of SAM sites, tracks to the site, and destroys the SAM radar.

HUD: Heads Up Display. Common now on all fighters, this clear glass allows flight, radar, and weapons data to be projected in front of the pilot's eyes so that the pilot does not have to look down into the cockpit for all information.

ID: Identification. Every target must be ID'd before it can be destroyed. There are three primary means of ID'ing, or "labeling" a contact. VID is visual identification. Other platforms can ID, such as AWACS. There are also classified electronic means that most fighters can use to ID a contact. PID is Positive ID.

IFF: Identification, Friend or Foe. Almost all military aircraft are equipped with this system, which will display to any radar with an IFF interrogator the identification of the IFF-equipped aircraft.

Joker: Fuel state that dictates stopping the current activity and moving on with either the mission or recovery.

LANTIRN: Low Altitude Navigation Terrain following Infrared Night. A two-pod system used by the F-15E and Block 40/42 Vipers with one pod (NAV Pod) for night low altitude navigation, and a Targeting Pod for the laser designation of targets.

MEZ: Missile Engagement Zone. Range within which Surface to Aim Missiles can engage an aircraft.

Naked: 3-1 term used to let other flight members or AWACS know that you do not show anything on the RWR scope, ie I am not targeted. Opposite of "Spiked."

NAS: Naval Air Station.

nm: Nautical Mile. The standard distance used for military measurements.

OCA: Offensive Counter Air. Official term for strike sorties that are not engaged in CAS. Usually a strike package going against a strategic target.

Pure: One of three pursuit curves. Going pure means to point directly at the target, pulling lead means to point in front, and lag, or lagging, means to point behind.

PCS: Permanent Change of Station.

RAG: Replacement Air Group. Naval training squadron for a specific aircraft.

Radar modes: Modern A/A radars have many modes, and the details and capabilities of these modes are highly classified. However, here is a very generic run-down: RWS - Range While Search. Normal search or sweep mode. STT - Single Target Track. Used to lock only one contact. Necessary for an AIM-7 shot. TWS - Track While Scan. Used to track multiple targets at once; the primary track is called the Primary Designated Track (PDT). There is a sub-Mode called High Data Rate (HD) TWS with a faster refresh rate. Mini-raster - Used when commanding a lock. Auto Guns - an Auto Acquisition (Auto Acq) mode where the radar is sweeping in short range and will lock the first contact it sees.

Red Ball: Maintenance term used to denote last minute fixes to an aircraft that has already started engines.

RIO: Radar Intercept Officer. A Naval Flight Officer specially trained to fly the back seat position on the F-14 Tomcat; primary duty is to run the radar.

RIVET JOINT: RC-135 reconnaissance aircraft. Everything about this aircraft and its mission are classified — that helped, didn't it?

ROE: Rules of Engagement.

RTR: Range Turn and Run. The range at which a target, if fired upon, could not turn and out-run a missile. Displayed on the WEZ staple on the radar and HUD.

RTU: Replacement Training Unit. Responsible to train new pilots on a particular USAF fighter aircraft. Later re-named FTU for Fighter Training Unit.

RWR: Radar Warning Receiver. A small scope in the cockpit that displays whether an enemy radar is hitting the fighter. A very sophisticated "Fuzz Buster."

SEAD: Suppression of Enemy Air Defenses. Mission of the Wild Weasel and jammer aircraft.

Sorted: Term used to let the flight lead know that you can see your target, either visually or on radar, and can maintain this responsibility.

Spiked:	opposite of "Naked." I have an enemy radar looking at me, as shown by the RWR scope. "Spiked Mud" is commonly used to refer to SAM radars.
Target:	Direction by the flight lead to take responsibility for a particular contact, ie "ZIPGUN 2, target southern group."
TD box:	Target Designator box. When locked, the radar will display a small box in the HUD to look through. The contact will be in this box, which makes it an amazing tool for visually acquiring contacts even at longer ranges.
TFR:	Terrain Following Radar. An on-board radar system that looks for and follows the terrain in front of the aircraft.
TFS:	Tactical Fighter Squadron.
TFW:	Tactical Fighter Wing.
TOF:	Time of Flight. The time for any weapon from launch until impact.
UPT:	Undergraduate Pilot Training. Basic T-37 and T-38 training for all USAF pilots.
VID:	Visual Identification. Also see ID.
Viper:	The most common name used for the F-16. The F-16 has several sub-variants built in "Blocks." The most common are the Block 40/42s with a primary bomb-dropping mission, and the Block 50/52s with the Wild Weasel mission.
Vul:	Vulnerability period. The time you are responsible to cover in your AOR.
WEZ:	Weapons Engagement Zone, displayed to show if a shot is "in range."
WILD WEASEL:	Designation of any USAF aircraft dedicated to the counter-SAM, or SEAD, mission. During DESERT STORM the F-4G was the sole Weasel; after the F-4G was retired, the F-16CJ (Block 50/52) assumed the role.
WSEP:	Weapon System Evaluation Program. Considered a "good deal" by any squadron, units are rotated through Tyndall AFB and put through their paces firing missiles at drones using various scenarios.
WSO:	Weapons System Officer. USAF Navigator specially trained to fly the back seat position of any USAF fighter.

CDR Henry "Hank" Kleemann (USN)
Lt Dave "Inlet" Venlet (USN)
Lt Larry "Music" Muczynski (USN)
Lt(jg) Jim "Amos" Anderson (USN)

VF-41 "Black Aces," F-14A
Gulf of Sidra
2 x SU-22 Kill
19 August 1981
Call-sign: FAST EAGLE 102 / 107

Larry Muczynski graduated the United States Naval Academy at Annapolis in 1976, and did his primary flight training in the T-28 at Corpus Christi, Texas, then proceeded to Kingsville for T-2 and A-4 advanced training. He received his wings in August 1978, and was assigned to VF-101 for F-14 Replacement Air Group (RAG) training. "Music" reported to VF-41 for his first fleet tour. At the time of this engagement "Music" was a section leader with just under 1,000 hours in the Tomcat. The following account was written by "Music" for this publication.

I arrived in VF-41 as they were working-up for what would be the first of three fleet cruises for me in the "Black Aces." The first cruise was to the Med, and we had been there a few months when the Iranians took the hostages in Tehran. Since we were aboard the nuclear powered *USS Nimitz* (the lead carrier of the *Nimitz* class), it was decided to send us to the coast of Iran for a show of force. We left the Med via the Straight of Gibraltar on 2 January 1980 and made a speed run around Africa. We had our "Shell Back" ceremony at the equator, which was quite an experience. We were the launch platform for the helicopters that attempted the rescue of the hostages, which ultimately failed. We ended up spending 144

days at sea without a port call on that cruise. This pretty much set the tone for my active duty career, in that we spent a lot of time at sea with VF-41.

We returned to the States in May 1980, and it seemed like we immediately started work-ups again for our summer 1981 cruise back to the Med. We sailed for Rota, Spain, and "chopped-in" to the fleet. Our first event for this cruise was to sail to the Gulf of Sidra for the freedom of navigation exercise. I don't think any of us thought anything would come of this, but President Reagan had just been sworn in (January 1981), and he was playing hardball. Libya was not recognizing either the three or twelve mile territorial

F-14A 'FAST EAGLE' 107, the Tomcat crewed by Muczynski and Anderson on the ramp at NAS Oceana. A silhouette of a SU-22 has been painted under the front canopy rail. *Robert F. Dorr.*

waters limit, but instead was claiming all of the Gulf of Sidra. This would be similar to the United States drawing a line from Key West, Florida, to Brownsville, Texas, and then claiming all the Gulf of Mexico as its territorial waters. We were to ensure the free use of international airspace / waters for all.

Our task force had put out Notices to Airmen and Mariners (NOTAMS) announcing our intentions to conduct an open ocean missile shoot exercise on 18 and 19 August. The area of the Med NOTAMed for the shoot was roughly the shape of home plate, and it extended into the Gulf of Sidra. Even though it was a hundred miles out to sea, it did extend into the waters claimed by Libya south of N32.30, or the infamous "Line of Death"—in which they claimed they would shoot anyone down that entered their "internal waters"—so we expected them to challenge the exercise in some way.

The rules of engagement (ROE) up until this exercise were very specific. We could *not* shoot without permission. Even if we were fired upon, we still had to call back to the ship, describe the situation, and get permission to shoot. Any fighter pilot knows that this is just WAY too long. In any engagement that lasts more than 60 seconds, your probability of getting shot increases exponentially. However, prior to this exercise we were briefed on a new ROE. We could now be pre-cleared by our controllers to engage a specific target, and most importantly, if we were fired on we could return fire, no questions asked. They developed the first ROE due to the fact that during this exercise EP-3s, EA-6Bs, E-2Cs, and other hi-value assets would all be present. We were concerned about two scenarios where the Libyans might try to target these assets. The first was the possibility of launching a MiG-25 Foxbat up to 70,000 or 80,000 feet, and then diving it down to take a shot and run back to Libya. The second would be for MiG-23s to come out on the deck and pop up to attack the assets.

The exercise started as scheduled on the morning of the 18th. Both ships and aircraft were involved in shooting missiles

Part of the *USS Nimitz* battle-group in the Mediterranean Sea during the August 1981 exercise. From left to right are the *USS Nimitz* (CVN-68), *USS Mississippi* (CGN-40), *USS Texas* (CGN-39), and the *USS Biddle* (CG-34). *USN photo by PH3 Cruz.*

at drones and other targets. There were two carrier battle groups involved; the *Nimitz* was positioned northwest of the shoot area, and we had two F-14 squadrons on board: VF-41, and our sister squadron VF-84. About a hundred miles to our east was the *USS Forrestal* with two F-4 squadrons embarked. The *Nimitz* fighters were responsible to man three CAP (combat air patrol) stations, one to the south of the open ocean shoot area and two to the west. The *Forrestal* had two CAPs to the east of the shoot area. Both air wings also maintained a CAP over their respective carrier. The ship ran a "flex-deck," as we rotated duty from the alert fighter on deck to the CAP over the ship, then we would move out to fill in any one of the CAPs until you either ran out of gas, had an aircraft maintenance issue, or just needed a break.

We had been briefed that the Libyan pilots did not like to fly at night, and didn't much care for flying over the water, so our initial plan for the first day of the exercise was a pre-dawn launch, a quick refueling from the A-6s or A-7s over the boat, and then be on station when the sun came up. This would let us be in position should they decide to come out and play. And they did. On the first day of the exercise all three of our CAPs were engaged. The perception was that the two western CAPs were getting most of the action. When we were all back on deck that night and compared notes, we felt that their Mirage pilots were the most aggressive, but we saw just about all of their aircraft over the period of the first day to include MiG-25s, MiG-23s, SU-22s, and Mirage F-1s. Half of the time we would intercept them and they would let us join right to the wing—you know, Blue Angel stuff!! One Tomcat would stay in a mile trail, just in case, while the wingman would take pictures, inspect the MiGs visually, and sometimes make rude hand gestures to the Libyan pilots! It was pretty surreal to be a couple of feet from two MiG-25s that up to now had only been a picture in a book, and now here it was next to my jet. And when he lit those huge afterburners on that Foxbat, wow! His motors were HUGE! He could really move in a straight line, but couldn't do much else. So, the first day we had a lot of fun and plenty of excitement for all involved. We had no reason to believe that the second day wouldn't be a carbon copy of the first, but of course it wasn't.

Day two started just like the first, with a dark launch and getting our gas. The E-2 sent us to the southern CAP, but so far I had no wingman. With covering all these CAPs, the E-2 would just match two jets from the same squadron in the same CAP—it didn't matter if it was two flight (or section) leaders or two wingmen. After going 30 or 40 miles to the south I realized they had forgotten about me, and I asked if anyone was coming down to join us on the CAP, and that is when they sent "Hank" Kleemann to join us. Even though we were both section leads he was the squadron commanding officer, so I naturally passed the lead to him and flew the wingman position for him.

One thing we had learned over dinner the night before was that the southern station was the dead CAP of the three; only one or two intercepts had occurred on that station on the first day. So we talked it over, and "Hank" decided since the southern CAP was so far from the ship, we had better raise our bingo fuel for an early return to the boat. What this would really do for us was get us out of this dead CAP quick, get back to the tankers, and then get to the western stations for some more action. Sure enough, we started hearing some of the VF-84 guys out in the west engaging bogies, so we knew we just had to get out of there and get our tails out west.

At about 0715 we are in our opposite direction racetrack CAP, basically oriented north-south, and the Girdibayah Airfield was the one we were watching to the south. Its single runway was north-south also, and with the Pulse-Doppler radar in the F-14 it made it possible to monitor anyone getting airborne. Sure enough Dave Venlet, in the back seat of "Hank's" airplane, gets contacts coming off the runway at about 800 feet AGL heading north towards us. They climbed right up to 20,000 feet and accelerated out to 540 knots, still heading right for us. So we're thinking this is great, and we might actually see something on the south CAP, but we still didn't think anything different than the day before might happen. As "Hank" was heading south in the CAP, we turned and joined him and set up for a "shooter-eyeball' intercept, where "Hank" would be the eye and take them close-aboard for the ID. I would hook them and be the shooter as necessary.

It became pretty obvious that they had GCI control, because as we would check 30 degrees right for some offset, they would turn and point at us. We'd go left, and they would follow suit. So we knew that this engagement was going to start with a beak-to-beak pass. Even without the free angles, this offered a couple of advantages. It is hard to see an aircraft that is pointed right at you, even a big one like the F-14. Also, our motors would smoke a little in military power, but if we went to min burner, the smoke went away. So we say what the heck, lets point at them and go get 'em! I wanted to be at "Hank's" two o'clock, slightly hi, so that when "Hank" merged I would be coming down and be 90 degrees out to these guys, and in a really good offensive position. With all the maneuvering I ended up back at his four o'clock and about 5,000 feet above him. At about seven to eight miles lead calls "Tally-ho," but since I'm looking down into the early morning haze I can't see them yet. At about four miles I finally get a tally-two on them, and they are in a right echelon formation with about 200 feet between the aircraft. Just then our radar dies. We didn't know it at the time, but the short range function had died, and there was nothing we were going to be able to do about it. "Amos" in the back seat is trying to lock them back up, and I'm yelling at him, using expletives that you use when you're in your 20s.

With "Hank" inside a mile to these guys with 1,100 knots of closure, I'm now in a big nose-low left turn and with 4,000 feet to lose. I'm screaming downhill so much that I'm at idle with the speed brakes out to keep from overshooting the merge. As all this is going on, I see the whole left side of the lead SU-22 light up. The brain is an amazing computer, because in this nanosecond I think that he has just caught fire, then I could see the missile come off the rail and the smoke trail, and I realized that they were shooting at us! "Hank" is less than 1,000 feet from the Fitters when the missile goes under him, then kind of comes up towards us before clearing off behind us. It sure got my full attention. This is where the old adage of "train like you fight 'cause you'll fight like you trained" came into play. After the thousands of intercepts in training,

Libyan SU-22 Fitter identical to the aircraft engaged and destroyed by the VF-41 Tomcats. *USN.*

everything now just became automatic. Break turn, chaff, and flare all just happened. I roll back and keep a visual, and instinctively pull right to the 6.5g limit of the aircraft while coming down on the intercept. The SU-22s split, with the leader (the guy that shot the missile) climbing and turning left to a northwest heading, and the wingman starts a hard right turn back through east like he is going to bug-out for home.

I think it was natural that both of us wanted to engage the guy that shot at us, and "Hank" is also in a left turn. As I ramp down with so many knots I spit out in front of him, and he gets on the radio and says, "Where are you going and what are you doing?" I come back with "I've got the lead and the guy that shot at us." "Hank" said, "Roger, I've got the wingman." "Hank" reverses his turn back to the right, and is very quickly in a firing position on the wingman. This is due to the incredible superiority of the turn rate and radius of the F-14 over the SU-22, especially since we had the F-14A Block 95 model with the auto-maneuvering slats and flaps, which worked phenomenally well. This allowed us to run the wings in the auto mode, and the wing sweep was automatically managed to maintain the best maneuverability for any speed. "Hank" has his guy locked with a good tone but, unfortunately, they are heading east in this right-hand turn and pointed right at the rising sun. He told me later his plan was to use the AIM-9L heat-seeking missile, which you can't employ while pointed at the sun, or it will guide on the sun! So "Hank" has to wait a few seconds before he can squeeze the trigger on his guy. Once clear of the sun, they were about 40 degrees off his tail at about a mile pulling five g's when "Hank" squeezed the trigger. The "Lima" came off their jet and pulled its lead turn, which the missile must have realized was too much, because it reversed back, and when it hit the SU-22 it was 90 degrees out to the target. It impacted in the tail section of the aircraft, knocking off most of the vertical stab and deploying his drag chute, which the Sukhoi used for landings. The pilot immediately ejects, gets a chute, and is drifting down.

While this was going on we had gotten behind and below our guy, and I'm trying all kinds of things to get a radar lock, which was never going to happen. Finally I decide to pull the nose up and get a boresight AIM-9 seeker lock. I'm just getting all this done when Jim in my backseat says, "Someone's been hit, someone's been shot!" So I ask, "Who is it?" He says, "I can't tell." Because of the split of the two bandits we were several miles from the other engagement, and Jim said all he could see was flame and smoke. I again begin to berate him for his uselessness. Ah, youth! But since I've got my bandit trapped at twelve o'clock I have the time to take my eyes off the bandit and look over to the east. Sure enough, Jim was right!! All I could see was smoke and a black dot.

There are a lot of thoughts that go through your mind at a time like this, very quickly. Thoughts like: even though we know the ROE, we are not at war. And, what if I shoot my guy and "Hank" decides NOT to shoot his guy. Boy, would I be in a world of hurt if the skipper holds off and I don't. Also, since Qadhafi is an absolute lunatic, this could start World War Three. So I'm wrestling with all this in a nanosecond, and I get on the radio and ask "Hank" "What should I do with this guy?!!" "Hank" had flown a little at the end of Vietnam, and the veterans of that war had ingrained in him that the MiG that gets you is the one you don't see. As they are shooting their bandit, they had lost sight of us and the other bandit temporarily. Now they can't see either of us. They surmised my bandit may have switched back onto them and they were at risk. So instead of responding to my question or getting into a discussion, "Hank" makes the most clear, brilliant radio call I have ever heard, simply saying, "Shoot, shoot, shoot!" This cleared up every question running through my mind, as well as telling me three things. First, it told me they were the shooter (not the shot), second that they were okay, and lastly, the skipper just told me to shoot, so things are GREAT now!

I've got the master arm on, and am just about to squeeze the trigger on this guy when he starts a hard, maybe five to six g turn to the right. I don't think he knew we were there; we were below and behind and didn't have a radar to trigger his warning gear. Maybe he too saw the fireball and decided it was time to bug-out back for home? So as he starts his right turn, and it's no problem staying with him, but I do have another issue. I only have one Sidewinder on board. Our starboard AIM-9 station was found to have an electrical problem on deck, so they launched us with only one Sidewinder (on station 1A under the left wing). We still have our radar missiles (Sparrows and Phoenix), but they are of no use since the radar died, and we have a full gun. So if this Sidewinder doesn't work, I'm going to have to go in and gun this guy. So with about five g's on my jet I squeeze the trigger, and out of my peripheral vision to the left, I see the missile come off the rail. However, since I'm turning right and the missile goes straight for 1,000 feet after launch, it appears to be going away to the left. I'm dumbfounded by this; here I have only one missile, and it has gone stupid! So I switch to guns and glance back to the left at the missile just as the fins unlock and it pulls 45g's and heads back to the right straight for the bandit. You don't think that makes a fighter pilot happy, do you?!!

As fast as I can get my eyes back to the right the missile tracks right up the tail pipe, and the explosion is just like a WWII gun camera film. There is a massive explosion, with smoke, parts, and tanks flying everywhere. My immediate thought is, "Oh God, I've just shot myself down!" We were inside half a mile when I shot, and now I'm closing on all this debris at 500 knots, so I take both

hands on the stick and pull for all I'm worth, because if there's one thing the Tomcat will do it's pitch like a son-of-a-gun. Both of us lost vision down to a soda straw with the Gs, but we didn't black out. I was just waiting to hear debris hitting our jet, but I don't. So I jam the stick forward and roll to the right. Now we're upside down looking up through the canopy at the ocean, and right below us is the SU-22. I can still see this picture in my mind; the SU is blown in half at the wing-root, and the forward half is tumbling end over end. There is fuel streaming out and smoke and fire everywhere, and parts and tanks are still falling away. Just then I see his canopy come off and the little rocket under the seat as it clears the wreckage. He gets seat-man separation, and I'm thinking this is just like a Pensacola training film. I'm expecting to see a chute any second, but he's just falling. So maybe it will open at 10,000 feet or something...but nothing. I lose sight of him and never see a chute open, so maybe it just wasn't his day at the office. Like I said about our training, we always preached to be out of the fight in 60 seconds, or bad things will probably start to happen. If you hack the clock at the first "Engaged" call and stop it at my "Fox 2 kill from Music," the whole event took 44 seconds. Takes me forever to tell the story, but the whole thing was done in 44 seconds! Time compression is an amazing thing.

We start calling back and forth to each other to figure out where we were, and since the ship's TACAN (call-sign Mother) was radiating, I could see that we were due south of the mother for 125 miles, and they were about 132 miles south. So there is about seven miles between us. We're still in hostile territory as far as we are concerned, and we need to get back together RIGHT NOW, so I tell "Hank" that I'll do a slow left 360 degree turn to let him join, and then we'll both bug-out north. I'm slowing and doing this casual 3g turn when I pick up "Hank" coming north, and he is screaming. The wings are full back, the blowers are lit, and he's going the speed of heat! So now I'm about to become a straggler if I don't step on it. I tell him to pull it back to let me join on his left side and that his six was clear.

When this thing started we both made some radio calls on fleet common that we were under attack and engaging. This caused all kinds of confusion, and both the E-2 and the battle group commander thought we had said, "My leader's been shot!" So they explode on the radio, and we have to tell them to shut up, we're busy! They vector four more Tomcats out of the overhead CAP our way, and we pass them heading south while we're heading north, and they too tell us we're clear, so we throttle back and join up in close formation. We check each other out for damage, and then I settle back into parade formation on "Hank." This is when all the adrenalin that I didn't realize was in my system left. I got the shakes in both hands. "Amos" in the backseat is a proverbial Wildman! He's whooping and screaming and beating the canopy so hard I can feel it. He's just loving life.

Getting back aboard was interesting. Normally we come over the ship for the break at 800 feet and descend to 600 feet in the break. From there we come around and land on the ship, just like in the movies. But today the ceiling was at about 500-600 feet, but we still wanted to do the overhead, and since we were both experienced, and "Hank" had a lot of confidence in me, he just briefed the pattern as a flat, non-descending pattern. I roger'd this, and in we go in close parade formation. "Hank" pitches, and I take my normal 17 seconds and break level. When we get to the 180, or abeam the landing zone, we're watching "Hank," who is one of the best "ball flyers" in the wing. Just then he bolters! We were dying laughing—I mean, he NEVER bolters, and now he does today! So he's back off the bow to come around for another pass. He later told me what happened. His Vietnam instructors had always told him that if you even see a MiG, let alone shoot one down, you should just do a three mile straight-in to the boat. You'll be so pumped up that all your corrections on the ball will be gross, and you'll need plenty of time to settle down. So "Hank" knew all this and took us to the overhead anyway. I don't find this out until much later over a few beers.

I roll out in the groove and the ball is dead-center. I'm thinking this is cake—I mean, I'm a Landing Signal Officer (LSO), I know what I'm doing. Next thing I know the ball is going up and gets to about two balls high, and it goes off the lens at three. So I've got a pretty big correction to make, and pull some power off. Just like that, the ball just drops! In the center the ball is yellow, but now it's getting lower and turning pink to orange. Red means you're dead, you could hit the back of the ship. So I've made this beautiful correction from two balls hi to almost two balls low, and I'm thinking "Holy crap, what's going on here!" So I'm adding all this power, and now the LSOs are on the radio saying, "Easy with power," which is their polite way of saying, "Settle down, you're

Kill marking located on the tails of the two VF-41 F-14s. This was 'FAST EAGLE' 102 during the engagement and was later given the new side number of 101. *Don Jay.*

an idiot." As we touch I give it full power, and we caught the four-wire on the fly. You can tell you caught the four-wire (the last of four), because when you come to a stop the nose is almost over the water, and I couldn't see any deck off the nose!

They spin us out and marshal us towards the island after safeing the missiles. As we're parking, here comes "Hank" in on his second pass. We're seeing lots of smoke from big power changes, the LSOs are making power calls, and next thing we know, he bolters again! Now we're really laughing our asses off, because we made it. I didn't care what grade those LSOs were going to give me for my pass, I'd just got a MiG kill! (For the record – the LSOs were VERY generous with us both. The grades were both OK – no comment, oh yeah – a little too much MiG all the way). So the skipper comes around for his third pass, and this one is basically an LSO talk-down, and he gets aboard. While he is getting spun-out we are getting chained and chalked, and I'm getting ready to shut down the starboard motor (I had already secured the left) when I get a master caution light. I look down at the warning light panel to see what's causing it, and I have a "LADDER" light on, meaning the boarding ladder is down. So I look to the left, and there is my plane captain looking me in the eye. He's banging on the canopy just like in the movies. I start waving at him to get down when he shakes his finger at me and gestures "wait." He reaches in his back pocket and pulls out a can of spray paint and some sort of MiG or aircraft stencil, and sprays on the MiG kill marking before we've even shut down! He was that proud. So we finish shutting down and pop the top. When you shoot a missile the umbilical, or "pig-tail," stays on the jet. When I get to the bottom of the ladder one of our "Ordies" is standing there, and very matter-of-factly hands me the pig-tail and just says, "Sir, I believe this is yours." I thought that was pretty cool.

The four of us get together in this huge crowd, and there's lots of hi-fives and handshakes, just like the end of the movie "Topgun." Funny how sometimes movies really do emulate real life. Then the Admiral's aid comes up to us and says, "Guys, come with me." We were parked right under the island, which you normally NEVER do. This is like Presidential parking. So we go right in the island, get out of our gear, and he takes us to the bridge. The commanding officer of the *USS Nimitz* was Capt Jack Batzler, and he was an F-8 pilot during Vietnam, so he wanted to hear the story RIGHT NOW. "Hank" did all the talking, and then he got a picture with the four of us. Then the aid took us down to Combat—actually to the spy shack in Intel. They separated us into four separate rooms with a pencil and paper, and told us each to write what we saw and what we did. I thought that was pretty amazing; they were making sure we were on the level, and there was no collusion or anything. After we all finished we hung out in Intel, and the aid took the accounts to the Admiral next door. We had our first chance to compare stories for about 15 minutes when the aid said the Admiral wanted to see us. We gave him the three minute version, and he basically said, "Congrats, now go get something to eat and get back to your ready room to go again."

All this took several hours before we got back in the squadron areas. I had not had a chance to do a maintenance debrief or anything with all the excitement, but then I was approached by

Left to right; Lt(jg) James Anderson, Lt Larry Muczynski, Lt Dave Venlet, CDR Henry Kleemann (Commanding Officer, VF-41) at a press conference following the 1981 engagement. *USN.*

one of our senior maintenance Master Chiefs. He pulled me aside and asked if I thought I might have over-G'd the airplane. After thinking about it for a second I told him that I might have. He asked by how much, since it would make a difference on the inspection. Since we were used to pulling 6.5g's I told him that I might have pulled seven, maybe eight g's tops. I really thought that was the top. There is a tradition that if you over-g the jet, you help the mecs pull panels and do the inspection. So I asked if they wanted me to help right away. He leaned in and said quietly, "Well sir, it was 10.2 g's, and I'm gonna give ya a free one for doing a hell of a job today." It happened when I snatched the stick to miss the debris I'm sure. But when you've got the "Iron Works" building airplanes, they work just fine!

We had multiple press conferences, and I received mail from all over the world congratulating us. This was the first time for the F-14 to prove itself in combat, and I think it was a big boost for the morale of the community, Grumman, and the country as a whole. President Reagan's image as a "tough guy" was set, and for the first time in a long time, Americans knew that the U.S. would not take it lying down. You saw on theater marques, "USN-2; Libya-0" and all kinds of things. But we just did what we were trained to do, and the training and the equipment worked as advertised. As I have repeatedly said, any of my squadron mates could have done what we did. We just happened to be there at the right time, in the right place, with the right results. I'm just proud to have been part of history.

After completing his VF-41 tour "Music" was assigned to the Training Command teaching T/A-4s at NAS Meridian, Mississippi, for a year with VT-7. As a reservist, he later instructed at NAS Oceana in the F-14 RAG with VF-1486, a squadron augment unit attached to VF-101, the east coast F-14 RAG. After three years he joined VF-201 at NAS Dallas as they transitioned to the Tomcat. Before retiring in 1996 "Music" went on to command VF-201, and attained over 3,000 hours in the Tomcat. He now flies for a major airline. A few years after this engagement Commander Kleemann took command of VX-4, and was killed when his F/A-18 flipped on landing at NAS Miramar. Lt(jg) Anderson is also deceased, killed in a freak skiing accident. Lt Venlet later went to pilot training, and is currently a Rear Admiral serving in the Naval Air Test program.

VF-32 "Swordsmen"
Names withheld

VF-32, F-14A
Gulf Of Sidra
2 x MiG-23 Kills
4 January 1989
Call-sign: GYPSEY 207 / 204

The following account is a recreation of the engagement using the cockpit tapes and existing unclassified material. Due to terrorist concerns, the crews wish to remain anonymous. While a first person account of this engagement was not possible, sources close to this engagement have helped the author clarify the major points of the fight.

Roughly eight years after the VF-41 kills, the *USS Kennedy* Battle Group was tasked by the 6th Fleet to conduct "Freedom of Navigation" exercises in and near the Gulf of Sidra. These are routine exercises conducted in the Mediterranean and the Gulf of Sidra to challenge Libya's claim to the entire Gulf, and not the accepted 12 mile limit to territorial waters. Manning one of the CAP stations this day was a section of VF-32 (Tactical call-sign GYPSY 207 / 204) F-14s from the *USS Kennedy*. During their routine patrol they detected, intercepted, and subsequently destroyed two Libyan MiG-23s. The Libyan pilots were observed in their parachutes, but were reported as lost at sea by the Libyan government.

The Navy immediately released an excerpt of the cockpit tapes from the two "Swordsman" Tomcats, detailing the communication between the E-2, the Combat Information Center aboard ship (CIC), and the F-14s. At the end of the tape, the view through the lead F-14's TCS (Television Camera System) is displayed showing a glimpse of the second MiG about to be downed by dash-1's (or flight leader's) AIM-9. The Navy was quick to point out that the MiG was carrying AAMs (as verified by the TCS film), thus supporting the "hostile intent" claim by the F-14 crews.

The controversy surrounding these kills continues, fired mostly by the misunderstanding of a radio call during the intercept from the CIC Tactical Action Officer stating, "Warning yellow,

F-14A GYPSY 207 (the lead aircraft during the engagement) on the ramp at NAS Oceana on the day of it's return from cruise, 31 January 1989. *David F. Brown.*

weapons hold, I repeat, warning yellow, weapons hold." This was interpreted by most in the media that the F-14s were not cleared to fire. This is not the case. Only "weapons tight" restricts the fighters from firing in any circumstance. A "yellow, weapons hold" call simply alerts the fighters that there is a possible threat to the battle group (warning yellow), and "weapons hold" is more of a reminder that peacetime rules of engagement (ROE) still apply, and the fighters must assess hostile intent or threat, or act in self defense in order to shoot.

This is where the second part of the controversy springs forth. In the case of the VF-41 kills, the intruding aircraft fired first and made the engagement/shoot decision very easy. Many believed that this "shoot first" act by the threat aircraft was the one and only requirement that would permit the GYPSY F-14s to fire. Again, this is not the case. In the peacetime ROE at the time, there were many acts that could have been construed as hostile intent, such as locking onto the fighters with fire control radars in preparation to fire, and also repeatedly "hot-nosing," or pointing at the fighters. As we go through the communications and the geometry of this engagement, you will see the latter is the case here. While the engagement was investigated and scrutinized, the actions of the F-14 crewmembers were not found to be in violation of any standing ROE.

During the engagement, the lead Radar Intercept Officer (RIO) in the back seat of GYPSY 207 detects the MiGs south of the CAP. He directs collision steering to the southeast to cut-off the MiGs. The MiGs are tracking northwest, with several jinks to the north during the intercept to point at the F-14s. At thirteen miles GYPSY 207 fires an AIM-7, and follows with a second Sparrow

USS John F. Kennedy (CV-67) underway in the Mediterranean Sea, 27 June 1982. USN.

at eight miles, but both missiles fail to engage the MiGs. GYPSY 204 fires an AIM-7 at approximately four miles, destroying the wingman MiG (the MiGs are flying in an echelon right formation). The lead MIG commences a left turn directly in front of the Lead GYPSY (207), who falls in about a one mile trail. After several attempts to acquire the MiG with both the radar and the AIM-9 seeker, GYPSY 207 finally downs that MiG with an AIM-9.

Below is a transcript from the engagement. Inter-cockpit communications are annotated, otherwise all transcribed communications are actual radio transmissions. Here is the cast of characters:

VF-32 "Swordsmen" F-14A, along with a sister-squadron VF-14 Tomcat (backround) on the deck of the *USS John F. Kennedy* in 1986. *USN photo by PH1 Phil Wiggins.*

207 Pilot – Lead pilot
207 RIO – Lead RIO
204 Pilot – Dash-2 (or wingman) pilot, call-sign "Munster"
204 RIO – Dash-2 RIO
CLOSEOUT – E-2C Hawkeye
ALPHA BRAVO – Battle Group Commander aboard *JOHN F. KENNEDY*

Tape begins.
207 RIO- "GYPSY 207 contact at 175, 72 miles, looks like a flight of two, Angels 10."
CLOSEOUT- "Closeout concurs, showing 78 miles."
204 RIO- (inter-cockpit) "Throttle back just a little bit here."
CLOSEOUT- "Closeout shows 25 mile separation for an inbound"
207 RIO- "Contacts appear to be heading, ah, 315 now, speed 430, Angels approximately 8,000."
CLOSEOUT- "Roger ACE, take it north." (Authors note: ACE was the call-sign for USS Kennedy A-6 Intruder aircraft)
207 Pilot- (inter-cockpit) "Looks like we'll have to make a quick loop here."
204 RIO- "Come starboard, ah, I need to give ya collision here. Yeah, come starboard about 40."
(Authors note: The MiGs are south of the Tomcats for 72 miles heading 315 degrees (northwest) at 8000 feet. The F-14s turn right about 40 degrees to create cut-off.)
207 RIO- "207 ah, 61 miles now, bearing 180, Angels 8, heading 330."
207 RIO- "Steady up."
CLOSEOUT- "Alpha Bravo this is Closeout."
207 RIO- "Come back port, ah, 20 degrees here, he's jinkin' (*or turning hard*) now."
207 RIO- "Bogies appear to be coming, ah, jinking to the right now, heading north, speed 430, ah, angels 5,000 now in the descent. So lets take her down now, we're goin' down."
204 Pilot- "Concur."
207 RIO- "Closeout, 53 miles now. Bogies appear to be heading directly at us. I'm coming towards. Steady up 150 for 33 offset, 50 miles. 49 miles now, speed 450, Angels 9, I'm goin' down to 3."
(Authors note: The look-down capability of the MiGs radar and weapons is nowhere near as good as the F-14's, hence, the Tomcats wanted to get below the MiGs altitude.)
204 Pilot- "I am crossing back over"
207 Pilot- "Roger."
207 RIO- "Roger that, 30 degree offset now. Bogies heading 340, speed 500, let's accelerate."
207 Pilot- "Okay, it looks like they are at 9,000 feet now."
207 RIO- "Roger, bogies have jinked back into us now, now lets come starboard 30 degrees the other side."
204 Pilot- "Coming starboard, say their Angels."
- "(unintelligible) VF-14 Camelot aircraft setting up station."
207 RIO- "Roger, Angels now 11, steady up."
ALPHA BRAVO- "Closeout, ah, Warning yellow, weapons hold, I repeat, warning yellow, weapons hold. Alpha Bravo out."

CLOSEOUT- "Roger, Gypsies, passing up, Alpha Bravo directs warning yellow, weapons hold."
207 Pilot- "35 miles here."
207 RIO- "Roger that. Bogies have jinked back into me now for the third time. Noses is on at 35 miles, Angels 7"
CLOSEOUT- "Alpha Bravo, Closeout, did you copy?"
207 RIO- "Okay, I am taking another offset, starboard, starboard, ah, 210."
204 RIO- "The guy, I'm locked up here 30 miles, Angels 13,000, he's the trailer"
207 RIO- "Roger that, level off here, bogie jinked back into me for the 4th time. I'm coming back starboard. I'm back port now. Port 27 miles, bogie is at 7,000 feet."
207 Pilot- "We're at 5."
Camelot CAP- "(garbled) bogies 135-50, Angels 16, heading 340."
Unknown- "Okay."
CLOSEOUT- "Roger, same bogies."
207 Pilot- "Okay, you're in collision now, steering."
207 RIO- "Okay, bogies have jinked back at me again for the fifth time. They're on my nose now. Inside of 20 miles"
(207 internal comms - Radar altimeter tone sounds at passing preset altitude of 5000 ft MSL.)
207 RIO- "Master arm on, master arm on"
204 Pilot- "Okay, good light"
207 Pilot- "Good Light"
207 RIO- "Okay, centering up the T, bogie has jinked back into me again, 16 miles, center of the dot."
204 Pilot- "Say your Angels."
207 RIO- "I'm at Angels 5, nose up."
204 Pilot- "No, his Angels."
207 Pilot- (inter-cockpit) "Now, wait a minute."
207 RIO- "Angels are at 9!"
207 Pilot- "Alpha Bravo from 207."
207 RIO- "13 miles. Fox 1! Fox 1!"
207 Pilot- (inter-cockpit) "Ah Jesus!"
204 Pilot- "Jinking right."
207 RIO- "Roger that, 10 miles, he's back on my nose. Fox 1 again!"
207 Pilot- "Watching 'em up."
207 RIO- "6 miles, 6 miles."
204 Pilot- "Tally 2, Tally 2! Turning into me."
207 RIO- "Roger that, 5 miles... 4 miles."
207 Pilot- "Okay, he's got a missile off." (Authors note: 207's pilot sees his wingman firing an AIM-7.)
204 Pilot- "Breakin' right."
207 Pilot- "Good hit, good hit on one!" (Authors note: This is 204's AIM-7 hitting the first MiG-23.)
207 RIO- "Roger that, good kill, good kill!"
207 Pilot- "I've got the other one."
207 RIO- "Select Fox 2, select Fox 2!!"
207 Pilot- "I've got Fox 2."
Garbled- "...the trailer."
204 Pilot- 'Comin' hard starboard."
204 Pilot- "...f**kin'!"

F-14A GYPSY 204 (wingman, or dash-two, aircraft during the engagement) touching down at NAS Oceana on the day of the return from cruise, 31 January 1989. *David F. Brown.*

207 RIO- "Shoot him!"

207 Pilot- "I don't got a tone."

204 Pilot- "I've got the second one."

207 Pilot- "I've got the second one on my nose right now."

204 Pilot- "Okay, I am high cover on you."

207 Pilot- "Get a Fox, get a, lock him up! Lock him up."

207 RIO- "There! Shoot him, Fox 2!"

207 Pilot- "I can't! I don't have a f**king tone!"

207 Pilot- "Tone's up!"

- (AIM-9 Sidewinder lock-on tone heard on inter-cockpit comms)

207 Pilot- "Fox 2."

207 Pilot- "Good kill! Good kill!"

204 Pilot- "Okay, good kill."

207 RIO- "Pilot ejected."

Garbled- "The pilot's ejected out of the second one."

207 Pilot- "Okay 'Munster,' let's head north, head north."

204 Pilot- "Okay. Port side high, comin' down hard."

207 RIO- "Roger."

207 RIO- "Roger that. Let's revert. Blowin' north, let's go down low, on the deck, unload, 500 knots, let's get out of here."

204 Pilot- "Okay, two good chutes."

204 RIO- "We're showin' two good chutes in the air here, from 'Munster.'"

207 RIO- "Roger that, I see the, ah--."

207 Pilot- "I've got the splash, one splash."

207 RIO- "One splash."

207 Pilot- "Take that down to, ah, 3,000 here 'Munster.'"

204 Pilot- "The, ah, splash 160 at 96."

207 RIO- "Let's go, 'Munster.' down to 3,000 and let's get outta here."

204 Pilot- "Running North, on your right side"

207 Pilot- "Roger, the other chute is high up, just to the right of the first splash...."

Tape ends.

View from below of a MiG-23 Flogger loaded with two drop tanks, two AA-7 radar missiles, and two smaller AA-8 heat-seeking missiles. *USN.*

Captain Jon "JB" Kelk (USAF)

58th TFS "Gorillas," F-15C
Operation DESERT STORM
MiG-29 Kill
17 January 1991
Call-sign: PENZOIL 63

Jon Kelk received a commission in the USAF via Officer Training School (OTS). After graduating Undergraduate Pilot Training (UPT) at Vance Air Force Base (AFB), Oklahoma, "JB" completed F-15 training at Luke AFB, Arizona. His first Eagle assignment was at Holloman AFB, New Mexico, on the F-15A. Capt Kelk had following tours at Bitburg Air Base, Germany, and also graduated the F-15 Division of the Fighter Weapons School in 1987. While assigned to Eglin AFB, Florida, he served as the Chief of Weapons and Tactics for the 58th Tactical Fighter Squadron (TFS) until just prior to deploying for DESERT SHIELD. After handing the Weapons shop over to Rick "Kluso" Tollini, he remained one of the designated mission commanders for the first wave of DESERT STORM, and had close to 2,000 Eagle hours going into the war. This kill marked not only the first of Operation DESERT STORM, but also the first kill by a U.S. F-15. The following account is taken from a telephonic interview with Col Kelk.

When Iraq invaded Kuwait, our squadron was immediately tasked to prepare to deploy to Saudi Arabia. We took 24 aircraft all the way across from our home base at Eglin AFB, Florida, to Tabuk Air Base in Saudi Arabia. We took almost every 58th TFS pilot, plus a few pilots from our sister squadrons, the 59th and 60th TFSs. I had been the squadron Weapons Officer, and had just given the shop over to our recent Fighter Weapons School Graduate,

Rick "Kluso" Tollini. As we prepared over the months leading up to the first night of DESERT STORM, it was decided that within our paired four-ship, Rick and I would alternate between leading the flight and flying the number three position. Once we received our tasking for the first few days of the war we worked out the final schedule for the first night, and "Kluso" would lead this first flight. "Cherry" Pitts would be on his wing, and I had Mark Williams on mine.

"JB" Kelk's F-15C, 85-0125, seen at Eglin in October 1993. *Ben Knowles via Don Logan.*

As we prepared, the big unknown was the capability and response of the Iraqi Air Force. If you just look at it on paper, it was a formidable force in terms of total numbers of fighter aircraft. If they had decided to launch their entire fleet, well, this was our big unknown. We knew a lot about their air defense capabilities, and we had no intention or desire of flying through known SAM sites. As pure air-to-air guys, our role was to engage anyone that got airborne and attempted to challenge the "surprise attack" of F-117s and F-15Es. The game plan was for the Stealth guys to go in high and the F-15Es to go in low first, accomplish the surprise attack, and be out of Iraqi airspace before we pushed in to take on any enemy fighters that flew to attempt to run them down. But when you look at the size of Iraq, that's a lot of area to cover with a few Eagles. From west to east you had Eglin in the west, Bitburg covering the middle of the country, and Langley covering the east.

Our flow, along with "Cheese" Graeter's four-ship (CITGO), was to flow through western Iraq, covering all the MiG airfields. We knew that H2/H3, Al Asad, Al Taq, and a few others had a compliment of MiG-29s and MiG-25s to contend with. They also had a few forward deployment airbases, such as Mudaysis, to worry about.

At about 0300L the F-117s were to hit command and control (C2) targets in and around Baghdad, while the F-15Es were to bomb SCUD and air defense sites in the west, mostly out of political constraints to help pacify the Israelis. This was the plan, and as it was to be a surprise it was un-escorted, so they pushed in first. The theory was that the F-117s would be invisible, and the F-15Es would be below the Iraqi radar coverage. This would trigger a response by the Iraqi air defense, so as the strikers were leaving Iraq, about fifteen minutes later we would sweep into the west with eight Eagles and shoot down all the bad guys.

Launch was uneventful, and each four-ship headed to separate air refueling tracks. After months of seeing almost no weather, the storms and turbulence during the air refueling were tremendous. It was the scariest part of the mission! So there we were in the middle of the night, with fully loaded jets getting hammered with turbulence and trying to refuel. I couldn't wait to get off the tanker and climb up and out of that stuff. In fact, as a rule of thumb I spent the entire war above 30,000 ft.

We marshaled well south of the border so as not to telegraph our intentions. We had given ourselves plenty of time, so we were just hanging out waiting for things to happen and our push time. "Cheese's" four-ship was still well south of us, so our forces were split. About this time (0300L, or "H-Hour") AWACS came up on frequency and basically said, "Go NOW!" They were seeing MiGs airborne in with the strikers. Our plan of pushing with eight Eagles in a hundred mile wide wall was done, since "Cheese" was still over one hundred miles south of us.

"Kluso" pushed us north in a wall formation, with one and two on the left and three and four on the right. There was no initial "bogey dope" from AWACS, just the "fly north" command. The radios got very busy on the strike frequency, and it was getting hard to get a word in edgewise. My first indication of enemy presence was a spike on my radar warning gear, just before I locked a contact

40 miles north of me at about 7,000 feet. It was a very cluttered radar picture with the strikers still being north of the border. My biggest concern was that 0300L equaled midnight ZULU, which is when all aircraft are required to change, or "roll," their mode 4 IFF setting. So here I am right at "midnight madness," worried that a striker may have forgotten to roll his mode 4. I kept checking for proper mode 4, and even made a couple of radio calls to "Check mode 4" in the hopes of reminding all strikers to roll.

I was able to determine that this contact met hostile criteria, and I also still had a spike correlated to this position. I tried to get AWACS to confirm the declare but had no luck. I was still very concerned about frat, but even without AWACS's help I was getting confident that this was a bad guy. He was heading south towards me and climbing. By the time I pickled my first missile, he was up to 17,000 feet. Number four was spiked and notched to the west, and after I shot I maneuvered to the east. As far as I know, one and two off to our west continued north with the flow. They needed to keep looking at other airfields, and I only had the one contact, so they pressed.

Once I was in parameters for the shot I fired a single AIM-7. I closed my eyes and hit the pickle button, so as not to destroy the night vision I had built up. We had flown a lot of nights during our pre-war time in Saudi and were very good at flying nights in the pre-NVG era, and I didn't want to risk it. As it turns out, it's not that big of a factor. There was no doubt when the 500 lb AIM-7 left the aircraft. After I shoot and feel the "klunk" I start to maneuver to the right (northeast), since I still have the spike. This is when the confusion starts. I try to jettison my tanks; they hang on the aircraft. I keep taking it down and putting out chaff, and somewhere around 20,000 feet the spike goes away. Now, adding to the confusion, I look down at the weapons panel, and it shows that I still have all four missiles. Total sensory overload. So now I'm thinking, do I have this right? I know I felt the missile come off, but the panel shows all missiles on board. I know I tried to jettison my tanks, and they did not come off. What else could possibly go wrong? But I guess if I learned anything in the previous ten years of flying, it was not to rely completely on just one piece of information, and to stick with the plan.

As soon as I lost my spike, which was about 10 miles from the bandit, I turned hot back into him, which put me on a heading of about north. At the time that the missile should be timing-out, I look out the front and I see a purple-blueish light on the horizon. It's not the orange fireball that you think about, but this was bright, it was a streak, and it had some line-of-sight to it. After about three to five seconds it fades. I wasn't quite certain what it was, since it wasn't the classic orange fireball that I expected, but I figured it had to be something like that. I guessed it was either him blowing up, or maybe shooting missiles or dropping flares. At night you can't judge distance, so I just wasn't certain. I did a radar search of the area, and the radar was clean. I would guess we were about 75 miles south of Baghdad at this time. I didn't call the splash for several reasons. The radios were still real busy, and I was more concerned with the next merge than making a radio call. Also, with the conflicting cockpit indications I had been getting, I didn't feel that I was in a place to make that call.

Iraqi MiG-29 Fulcrum seen abandoned in 2003. After DESERT STORM the surviving Iraqi Fulcrums were plagued with a lack of spare parts. Few Fulcrum sorties were ever flown. *USAF.*

Even though Mark and I were now split by about five miles, we had flown a tremendous amount together, and we stuck with our briefed flow and altitude deconfliction plan. As we continued north, I could tell from the air-to-air TACAN that he was getting back towards a mile and a half from me. I gave him a "flash lights" call, and there he was, perfectly line abreast at 1.5 miles. We continued north, well behind "Kluso" and "Cherry," and since I was the only member not able to jettison my tanks, I was kind of holding up the show speed-wise. We get just short of Baghdad and turn west for a bit, then continue south behind one and two towards the border. Of course I'm still dragging my bags around, and I didn't want to use afterburner and highlight myself.

After we crossed the border and safed-up I couldn't stand it any longer, and I called my wingman in and told him, "I gots to know." He looks my jet over and, sure enough, one of my AIM-7s is missing. So we drive the 300 miles back to Tabuk, land, and write-up the jet. I make a kill claim, but claim it as a "probable." We were to fly again in about six hours, so I wanted to get the hell out of there and get to the hootch. I just laid there and replayed the events a thousand times, and after a couple of hours I got up and went back to Ops. I decided, after going over and over the events, that I would change my claim to a "confirmed." The squadron commander is there when I walk in, and I let him know that I've thought it over and wanted to make the change. He said, "Sorry 'JB,' it's too late, you can't do that." I asked him what he meant. He then tells me that AWACS had already called and confirmed the kill!

"JB" finished STORM with over 50 combat missions and over 2,000 hours in the F-15. He would go over 3,000 hours on a subsequent deployment to Saudi. In 1992 "JB" left active duty and joined an F-15 Air National Guard unit. He has held the positions of Operations Officer, Squadron Commander, and Operations Group Commander, and is currently Director of Operations. Most importantly, he has been allowed to fly the Eagle the entire 24 years, and has just gone over 4,000 hours at the time of this publication; a truly remarkable event to cap a tremendous career.

Captain Rob "Cheese" Graeter (USAF)

58th TFS "Gorillas," F-15C
Operation DESERT STORM
2 X Mirage F-1EQ Kills
17 January 1991
Call-sign: CITGO 51

Rob Graeter joined the USAF in 1979 after graduating East Texas State University and their ROTC program. He went to UPT at Laughlin AFB, Texas. After completing F-15 training, his first Eagle assignment was at Kadena, Okinawa. Capt Graeter had following tours at Nellis AFB, Nevada, in the 65th Aggressor Sq. and the 422 Test & Evaluation Squadron, and also graduated the F-15C Division of the Fighter Weapons School. "Cheese" joined the 58th TFS in 1989, and was one of the designated mission commanders for the first wave of DESERT STORM. The following account was written for this work by Rob Graeter.

This mission was part of the "D-Day" package. We had done a lot of mission planning for this mission; in fact, we had put in a lot of planning for the first three days of the war. Our mission commander for the eight-ship was "Kluso" Tollini with PENZOIL flight, and I was the flight lead of CITGO. We were the western eight-ship in a twenty-ship sweep package that was to go in after the F-15Es, F-117s, and F-111s finished their first strike, which was supposed to be a surprise strike to go in and wake them all up. My responsibility was the western-most lane, which gave us Mudaysis and H2/H3 to look at. Our plan was to press due north

at Mudaysis, then check the flight about 45 degrees to the left and set up a BARCAP oriented northwest-southeast to look at those bases. "Kluso" was going to start off to our east, pressing due north towards Al Assad and Al Taq. His flight would flow counter-clockwise to the west towards the Syrian border to our north, then swing south to exit Iraq to our west.

We got the news from headquarters at about noon on the 16th that it was on, with an "H-Hour" of 0300 on the 17th. That was right at mode four change-over time, which was a concern for us, but turned out to be a non-event. The mission planning was already

"Cheese" Greater's F-15C, 85-0105 of the 58th TFS seen after DESERT STORM. *Gary Chambers.*

pretty much taken care of; we still were ironing out the details, and we put our data cards together, since now we had the times. By early afternoon we went into crew rest so that we could try to get some sleep. We were using the GO/NO GO drugs, and I took one around five pm and still maybe got only a couple hours of sleep. I was up by ten or eleven to get ready, and we briefed at midnight.

My flight was the first off the runway. We took off at about one am, which was still two hours till H-Hour, but we had a long haul over to the tanker track. We were stationed at Tabuk, which is way out in the western part of Saudi Arabia, so it took us a good 45 to 50 minutes to get over to the tanker tracks, which in our case were in central Saudi Arabia up on the northern border. The closest town was probably Ar Ar, and it was one of the "fruit" tracks. As you can imagine, it was pretty crowded with activity. It was oriented northwest-southeast, and had between six to eight tankers in it, as well as some EF-111s when we got there. We were in and out of the clouds, and this was one of the most stressful parts of the mission, and one of the most stressful times in the air for me was finding the tanker in the track using the radar; then getting on board with him in and out of the weather was pretty difficult. We had closed all the way down to break lock minimum range on the radar and we still couldn't see the tanker. Then we would break out of the weather and see him and try to get joined visually before we went back in the weather. We went through several iterations of this before we got together; in fact, it took the better part of a complete lap in the track to get all the guys settled on the wing of the tanker. As stressful as it was for me, I felt worse for the guys on the wing, since they had been in fingertip for almost an hour. It was not a whole lot of fun, but we got there. Once we were on the tanker, everyone did a fantastic job of getting their gas. It was very rough, in and out of the weather, and dark. Most of the lights were off so it was a challenge, and the guys did a really good job. "Kluso" later told me that when he arrived at the tanker, my number four was just finishing up. He swore that it looked like our whole flight was doing barrel rolls, his internal gyros were that messed up.

We rejoined to fingertip, exited the track out the side, and once clear descended. We got out the bottom of the weather in the teens, and I got everyone spread out and off the wing so that they could get a breather and let go of the death grip on stick. We set up a holding CAP about 60-80 nm south of the Iraqi border, as we weren't supposed to get to close to it at first. All of our planning was set up with push time of 0310L. This gave us about 45 minutes after the tanker—plenty of time to relax and get set up. We had slowed to a max conserve speed and just kind of took it easy. By the time "Kluso" came off the tanker it was approaching 0300.

What happened next was a change of plan from "Hammer," who was a Colonel and the on-scene commander on board the AWACS. He didn't like the picture he saw, and asked for an early commit from us, from our eight-ship. He could see several MiG-29 CAPs airborne, and was concerned about the safety of the F-111s and F-15Es that were in western and central Iraq. So he wanted CITGO and PENZOIL to push early. We got very little heads-up, but once we did we started running north, getting spread out and getting our speed up. "Kluso" with PENZOIL was already 60-80 miles to our northeast, so instead of being an eight-ship,

line abreast wall, we were really in more of a 60 mile echelon southwest formation. It was just a few minutes after three, so we were pushing about seven to eight minutes early.

As we ran north, we set up our comm. In the main radio we had the eight-ship, AWACS—in fact, the whole war. In the Aux radio we had our four-ship common. Not much to really report on the push, but we did get our speed back up, and climbed on top of the weather, up into the 30s. We were all using mil power in the climb and push so we got a little spread out. "Tonic" Teal, our squadron commander, was my number three, and he was about 15 miles to my southwest. He had L.A. Brooks on his wing. My wingman, Scott "Papa" Maw, who's now Colonel Scott Maw, was offset on my right to the southeast.

The initial picture being called was a MiG-29 CAP well to the north of Mudaysis, and was still not on our radars yet, since they were well beyond a hundred miles north of us. As we pressed north across the border we started to detect the friendly IFF of the egressing F-15Es. There was a whole train of them, and that was the problem with the early push; they were just clearing their target areas. We had kind of a muddy picture, with good guys mixed in with bad guys. The whole idea of the sweep was to have a clear picture, and be able to shoot BVR with a very clean picture. This meant that we had to rely on a very ponderous ROE for identification using the IFF interrogator. Checking for squawks while you're getting ready to shoot was not what we wanted to be doing.

I was starting to see the original MiG-29s out there at 60 miles, and they didn't seem to be very interested in running on anyone. For a while it looked like they were running south behind the Strike Eagles, but the F-15Es were on the deck doing their TFR thing and the MiGs were at altitude, so I really didn't think they had much of a chance of finding them at low altitude and aspect. As it turned out they didn't, and the CAP I was looking at kind of turned into a non-factor, and they never got into any of the fights, which was probably good for them.

As we got further north we were getting closer to the F-15Es, and we had a really good picture of their whole train headed southeast towards their egress point. Unfortunately for us, and moreso for us than PENZOIL, was that we had to drive right at their egress corridor and try to pick threats out of that picture. This route took them pretty close to Mudaysis, which was this little field with a couple of "Christmas trees" at each end for alert birds, but not much else there. We knew they had forward deployed some MiG-23s and Mirage F-1s earlier, so we had to consider aircraft from the field. As we approach this field I get a low altitude, low aspect (7 Left) contact at the same time that AWACS calls out a pop-up threat that correlates to this position. He was about 22 to 25 miles off of my nose heading northwest. I was pretty confident that this was the same guy. Almost immediately he starts a left turn to point south, about right at us. I broke lock and picked up a second contact. At this time I didn't know what we had, but I had at least two guys there. I came back off of that contact at the same time that "Papa" Maw called out a contact that I thought was the second contact in line, but it turned out to be a third guy. I broke lock with what I had and went back to the leader and locked him

F-15C 85-105 seen at Eglin AFB after the war, note the two green stars denoting "Cheese's" two Mirage F-1 kills. *Alec Fushi via Don Logan.*

at about 17-18 miles. He had crossed my nose from left to right heading southeast, and I was now looking at a 15 right aspect, and he was climbing to about 5,000 feet. He was generally heading towards the track of the F-15Es. We'll never know exactly what he was doing, but my guess was that he had been scrambled on the E models. If they had any kind of radar they would have known there were aircraft in the vicinity, but what kind information or data that he had airborne, we'll obviously never know.

The contact had stabilized his altitude at about 7,000 feet MSL, or about 6,000 AGL, and I was ramping down significantly to try to cut down some of the radar look-down angle, which was getting significant by this point. I went combat one on the jettison panel and jettisoned my tanks in the descent. I didn't call it on the aux until after I had shot. I asked for a bandit declare from the AWACS controller, but he was getting pretty excited by this point. I talked to him in a bar later and he apologized, as did I, because we were both getting pretty excited. Unfortunately he wasn't much help. He had declared him a bandit right off the bat, but I never correlated this to meet my requirements. The last thing in the world I wanted to do was shoot a good guy—I would never want to ever go through that. So I went through my ID requirements, which took about five miles, so I was finally ready to shoot at about 10 miles. I was down to the mid- to high teens by this point, and had just broken out of the weather when I shot. Even though in academics we had always discussed not looking at the missile when you shoot to preserve you night vision...I looked. From the time I pickled and felt the thump and then heard the motor fire seemed to take forever. I heard

the rocket motor fire out to the right side of the jet, and watched the missile accelerate away. I could see the plume out the back and the rear fins of the missile. Our shot doctrine was "shoot-look-shoot," so I shot and watched the missile and it looked true, and since the missile appeared to be guiding and doing what I wanted it to do I just shot once. I immediately maneuvered left to a heading of about 320 degrees and kept descending, since I was still concerned with radar gimbals limits, as he was at about 30 degrees look-down, so I kept it coming down to keep him illuminated.

Through all that, it didn't take long for the missile to get there, time-of-flight wise. By the time I came back out of the cockpit I could no longer see the missile—it was gone. The rocket motor had timed out and I could not see it, but I was looking at the right spot at the right time just as the missile went off. I have a vivid memory of the warhead going off and getting that bright yellow, conical blast as the missile detonated. It looked just like a cone because of the airspeed of the missile taking the flame forward. So it was pretty neat to see, and right through the middle of that cone, the airplane flew and it just disintegrated. There were burning chunks of airplane going in every direction. The eerie part of all this is that there is no noise, obviously, so you get all this in visual only. It lit up the ground below and cloud deck above, so it had an eerie look to it. This all occurred at my right two o'clock for about four miles.

I watched that for a second, then I went back inside, went to AUTOGUNS, and rolled the search area down. I was probably at about 13-14,000 feet heading due north again. One thing I had not really done very well was to tell my wingman where I was and what I was doing, but he had seen the missile shot and the end-game explosion, so he kind of knew the general area where I was. I did call a heading to check to, and this whole time he is locked to a trailer who never turned hot. Timing wise, he had locked this guy up during the time of flight of my missile, and he monitors this guy, but he never really gives us a hot aspect to shoot at. We eventually end up chasing him out of there, but prior to that as I'm coming off the initial explosion, I'm pretty confident that there is another guy down here. I'm looking with AUTOGUNS, and I have no indications on the RWR. Even though I get no returns, I'm looking for what I assume to be a wingman in trail out here somewhere and I don't find him. What I do see about 10 seconds after the missile detonated is a second explosion. I look back over my shoulder, and what I see are the big chunks of the airplane I had just blown-up hitting the ground. They were exploding again; obviously this guy was full of gas, so there was a lot to burn. That lit up the sky again, and as I came back out the front of the airplane, looking out front, within a couple of seconds there is another explosion at my right two o'clock for about two to three miles. It's tumbling across the ground going south, so it's going from my left to my right off to my right. This lights up the sky again and the desert around it, as I can see the airplane tumbling across the desert floor, and this was really weird. Not having him on the radar, but knowing about where the guy was, and this was not the guy that Scott was locked to. He was in there pretty close to me, but 10,000 feet below me. I did not know exactly who he was at the time, but the assumption was that he was part of this group of guys that got scrambled from Mudaysis. Timing wise, he would have been the second guy airborne. They weren't really in a visual formation, but were about five miles apart as they scrambled off the runway there at Mudaysis. Timing wise, this would have all made sense as we reconstructed it later.

I was pretty close to Mudaysis—I could see it to my right three o'clock for about five or six miles. About the same time, I got an RWR indication of a Roland that corresponded to Mudaysis

Sitting in the pilot dorms in Tabuk, left to right facing camera; Jon "J.B." Kelk, Robert "L.A." Brooks, Scott "Sparky" Antolak (back to camera), Rob "Cheese" Greater, Cesar "Rico" Rodriguez. *Tony Murphy.*

at my right three o'clock. I tried to shuffle through all my memory recollections of ranges and such for that kind of weapon. I wasn't too concerned about being in his envelope, but I didn't want to get any closer. I told Scott to check and follow the guy he was locked to, and he came back that he was heading 330. I checked to that heading also. My air-to-air TACAN showed that we were separated by about nine miles, so we had gotten separated a bit during the maneuvering, but at least we were now going in the same direction. The threat that he was calling out was eleven miles off of his nose, so what I was thinking is that I was pretty close to this second guy. But I couldn't find him. In hindsight, if I had descended and been more thorough with AUTOGUNS I might have been able to find him and get in a WEZ, I don't know. But as it turns out I don't see him, and I'm not too interested in going down to low altitude to look for him. So we pushed him for a while, and he continued on to the northwest at high speed. We followed him until he got close to the WEZ of the SA-2s that were in the area of H2/H3, and I did not want to go in there after him. We ended up following him for a good 35-40 miles to the northwest, and then we came off of him and popped back up to altitude. We get back into our BARCAP with three and four. During this whole time, three and four had leaned off to the west to check-out H2 and H3 to make sure that nothing was launching from those fields. So as we were coming off our engagement, they were just setting up in the CAP. We joined them in our counter-rotating CAP at altitude, and sat there for about another 30 minutes in the CAP, but nothing ever came back up.

I was still concerned about that original MiG-29 CAP to our north, so we took a real hard look up there and never saw anything with a hot aspect. AWACS never called anything of interest, and "Kluso" with PENZOIL was up there, since that was their primary responsibility. "JB" Kelk got his kill up there about 75 miles northeast of Mudaysis, out there in no-mans land. Anyway, we sat there in the CAP, and the guys did a great job in our counter-rotating CAP, until we got down to our no-tanker bingo. With nothing going on we decided to go ahead and egress. We had two bingos: one that would not require going to the tanker, and another assuming we would have to refuel before our long drive home. "Kluso" was calling for an egress also, so we started heading southwest towards the border.

After we got back across the border we got our lights on, and we were not that far from "Kluso's" flight. We got our battle damage checks done and headed for home. We landed at about 0515, and it was still dark. Once we got on the ground everyone was very excited, because they could see the umbilicals hanging where we had jettisoned our tanks, and I had an umbilical cord hanging from my right-aft weapons station where I had fired the AIM-7. I gave that umbilical to my crew chief, and he was pretty happy about that. We were met by "Fast Eddie" Boyle, our chief of Intel. He had already pieced together what had happened with the engagement, that they were F-1s, and that they had been scrambled on the F-15Es. So he was able to put all the information together that we didn't have in the air. A pretty big lesson-learned for me was why we didn't have the capability to get that kind of information out. It all runs down to our ability to communicate

Iraqi Mirage F-1EQ seen taxiing. Note Magic IR missiles on the wingtip stations. While it was rumored that the Iraqis had captured Matra radar guided missiles from the Kuwait Air Force it was not known if the Iraqi pilots were trained and equipped to employ them. *USAF.*

and cross those lines of communication to connect those different sources. I think we're still probably having those growing pains, but nothing like it was back then.

The big lesson learned for us, and for me, was the early push, which really screwed us up. We would have had a much better picture if we had waited, since the whole idea was to get MiGs airborne off their alert pads chasing the strikers. We would have then had a clean picture to come in and clean up these guys. I think that Hammer screwed the plan when he pushed us early. "Kluso's"

flight ended up being the first Eagles across the border by about 10-15 minutes because of the skewed push.

That's about it for CITGO flight. We got a quick debrief and breakfast, went into crew rest, and flew again later that day. We fell into eight hour rotating shifts for the next two weeks or so. About halfway through the war the powers that be started reviewing the intelligence, and determined that the second F-1 was reacting defensively to the loss of his leader; hence, I was credited with the second kill.

"Cheese" went on to fly a total of 43 sorties and 247 combat hours during DESERT STORM. He returned to the Weapons School for a stint as an Operations Officer, and held staff positions with Pacific Command. "Cheese" was the Operations Officer for the 44th FS and the Commander of the 67th FS at Kadena. He was the Assistant 18th Operations Group Commander when he retired. He currently flies for a major airline.

Captain Steve "Tater" Tate (USAF)

71st TFS "Ironmen," F-15C
Operation DESERT STORM
Mirage F-1EQ Kill
17 January 1991
Call-sign: QUAKER 11

Steve Tate graduated National University, and after commissioning was assigned to Reese AFB, Texas, for UPT. He completed F-15 training at Luke AFB, Arizona, and was assigned to the 1st Tactical Fighter Wing, 71st Tactical Fighter Squadron in 1987. "Tater" had attended TOPGUN, and was a wing STAN/EVAL check pilot at the time of the DESERT STHIELD deployment. He had attained roughly 1,200 hours in the Eagle at the time of the engagement. The following account was penned by "Tater" for this publication.

First, I'm thankful for the opportunity for each of us to tell our story in our own words. As I have read other accounts of my "quotes," I don't remember saying most of that...it's too eloquent for this country boy. There was "some confusion" on my kill in regards to it being the first of DESERT STORM. I could never figure out what difference it would make, but in the "confusion" of war I guess some facts get mixed up. An example of this is when I read my aircraft assignment was aircraft 3017. I was actually assigned aircraft 2009. I had a mechanical problem and had to jump jets at the last minute, and I took 3017, which was Major Mark "Brewski" Brugh's jet.

Oh well...so much for the facts...let's strap on the g-suits and do a quick review (debrief) of the first strike mission of DESERT STORM into Baghdad. And now the real story...15 years later.

Before we deployed to Saudi Arabia (that's like trying to remember how life was before 9-11), the entire military was given the tools needed to train effectively, so that in the "unlikely" event that we ever went to war, we would be ready. This philosophy came from President Ronald Reagan, and followed with President George Bush. I remember first getting in the Marine Corps, and was assigned to HMA-39, MAG-39, 3rd MAW, a Cobra Squadron at Camp Pendleton. The squadron had to shut down for months at a time because there wasn't enough funding to buy gas for the helicopters. That was at the end of the Carter Administration. The lack of funding and training culminated in the overdue, embarrassing failure of the attempted hostage rescue in Iran. However, 10 years later the military would be ready this time.

After Saddam invaded Kuwait, we started getting intelligence reports and messages from Higher Headquarters to start planning. There was going to be an initial "show of force" by sending eight F-15Cs from the 71st Tactical Fighter Squadron, 1st Tactical Fighter Wing. I was one of the lucky ones. The "lucky eight" were sent

Capt Steve Tate seen after his return to Langley AFB, Virginia. *USAF via I FWIPA.*

My four-ship outside of the squadron briefing tent in Saudi Arabia, left to right; Mark "Snake" Atwell, Damon "Darryl" Harp, "Bo" Merlack, and myself. *via Steve Tate.*

home to get crew rest for 36 hours while the maintainers got the jets ready and the planners put the flight plan together. I was called at home the next day, and was told to come to the squadron the next day. When I arrived at the squadron and looked at the line-up board, the entire squadron of 24 jets was on it. We were all going! Our support crew did a great job in getting the jets ready. It was a 17 hour non-stop flight from Langley to Dhahran, refueling eight times. This was the most demanding 17 hours of my life. You can't imagine all the physiological issues/stresses that it put on our bodies. However, the motivation of what we were undertaking carried us through this task.

My ex-father-in-law, USN Capt F.A.W. "Bill" Franke, was a POW for 7 ½ years in Vietnam. He was declared KIA and put in solitude for three years while being tortured. He always told me how incredible the human body can adapt, and how ingenious the American Warrior is to overcome any obstacle. Now those guys are real heroes and the greatest of the American Fighting Men. That would be a book worth reading. So I guess I'll take those 17 hours any day.

The only thing that happened that was worth remembering was when we were abeam the Libyan coast. They launched two fighters toward us. I was number five out of six in the first cell. My Skipper, Lt Col "Pip" Pope, was the Squadron Commander, and was leading this cell. He dispatched two of us to point at the Libyans, and they immediately turned around and landed. Smart move. As we crossed the Mediterranean Sea we headed down the Red Sea to take a southerly approach into Dhahran and stay away from the Iraqi boarder. I've never seen so much sand, and an area of nothing but brown.

The days were long. If you weren't flying, you were studying or writing letters...no internet in those days. Can you imagine that? The hardest thing was living on an emotional roller coaster. When was this thing going to start, or when were we going to get to go home? A lesson learned from those eight months of "nothing" was to take advantage of every minute in the day. We could have been

so much more productive, which was a leadership issue. During this time we did pair up into our four-ships.

The four-ship ate, slept, flew, and did everything together. My number two was "Big Bo" Merlack. "Bo" was enlisted in the Air Force as a boom operator. He is a graduate of Ohio State. He was a new wingman in the squadron, and had the respect of everyone as a solid wingman. My number three and four that I was first assigned were temporary. Number three was LtCol Carl "VP" VanPelt. He just came from the Pentagon, and was an assistant to none other than Air Force Secretary Don Rice. He was assigned to me to get him up to speed so he could be a flight lead. His number two and my number four was 1Lt Louie "Dildo" Defidelto. Louie is an Air Force Academy Grad, and had been in the squadron about the same time as "Bo." He also had great respect as a solid wingman. After giving a tactical check ride to "VP" he was signed off and picked up his own four-ship, with Capt Dan "Hole" Booker as his three and Capt Mark "Lurch" Miller as four. I then got my number three and four, which were Capts Damon "Darryl" Harp and Mark "Snake" Atwell. Damon's an 'ol country boy from Texas, and "Snake" is an Air Force Academy Grad, and was also our entertainment. I could not ask for a better group of men to watch my back.

To this day I love them to death, and would give my life for any one of them. This brotherhood/camaraderie is one thing that develops in times of war, or I guess any situation where you are faced with life/death choices. We had a group that called ourselves the Bros. We talked the talk and walked the walked. In a fighter squadron everyone knows where they fit in. It is an environment of tremendous competition. Everyone is trying to be the big dog, and the big dog has to have his best game on to stay on top.

There were a handful of pilots from each weapon system that were involved in putting a Secret SAR (Special Access Required) plan together. The plan changed slightly as new weapon systems were brought into theater, and as intelligence came in on different targets. I would like to say that the direction came down from the Commander-In-Chief (President George Bush) that the mission commanders who would be flying these missions would put the

1st TFW F-15C prepares to launch during DESERT STORM. The 27th TFS and the 71st TFS both deployed from the 1st TFW during SHIELD/STORM. *USAF via 1 FW/PA.*

plan together, and not a bunch of Staff Officers sitting in the Pentagon. This was a big lesson that was learned from the Vietnam War.

"Men, you are going to War!" Those were the words from Gen "Buster" Glosson, who gave us the war brief on behalf of Gen "Chuck" Horner. About two weeks prior, I was able to give my four-ship the details on the mission we were going to be tasked for. I was to be the Air-to-Air mission commander for the first strike package into Baghdad. We were tasked to do a pre-strike sweep/escort mission for a squadron of F-4G Wild Weasels, a squadron of F-111s, EF-111s, F-15Es, and B-52s. We tried to get some sleep that day but failed. We sat around and reflected on life as the butterflies grew in our stomachs. We just wanted to get started. The sitting around waiting was driving us crazy. Not that we were eager and wanting war, but we wanted to get it over with.

After stepping to our jets and starting the engines, I had to switch jets due to a mechanical problem I had with mine (2009). 3015 was my backup, and I scrambled to get it going and be on time. So off we went. As we flew toward the tankers you could see all the lights from all the planes going to the tanker refueling points. While on the tanker, I checked in with AWACS and the Hammer, who was the officer in charge of the entire package from Higher Headquarters. I told him we were on the tanker, on time, and ready. After getting fuel, we turned the lights off and went Master Arm – "On." It was a short drive to the push point, and then a 10 minute wait before we headed north to Baghdad.

It was a beautiful moonlit night. The fires in Kuwait were still burning off to the east, and the Tigris and Euphrates Rivers were easily discernable with lights. Baghdad seemed like a "peaceful" city until we were about 80 miles south of Baghdad, when the F-117s dropped their bombs and continued on north. At that moment the sky over the city sparkled with twinkling lights, which were light AAA (Anti-Aircraft Artillery). Then you could see the "snakes" extending out of the sphere of lights, which were larger AAA. It was certainly the best Fourth of July fireworks display I will ever see. Our attention quickly returned to ensuring that the area was clear of any enemy aircraft. The first look towards Baghdad was clear.

In the right hand turn to the south I locked up an unidentified contact about 30 miles, very close to the ground and moving fast. I directed "Bo" to follow me as we engaged this contact. We immediately jettisoned our external fuel tanks and started interrogating the contact to determine friend or foe. It happened to be the F-111s, who were very early for their time on target. When we locked up the F-111s they turned on their mode 2 transponders and started a climb to mid-altitude. After identifying them as friendly we came off them and returned to the CAP (Combat Air Patrol).

We call it "hot" and "cold" in the CAP to indicate which direction we are heading. "Hot" is flying towards the target area. On the next turn "hot" I locked a contact that was just below my altitude (8,000' AGL) and 16 miles in front of me. AWACS did not have the contact on their radar. I directed "Bo" to use his radar to look for any wingman this contact would have. I made a positive

hostile ID and a lack of a friendly, so it met the ROE. It was a Mirage F-1, the Iraqi's front line fighter. The ID happened at 12 miles, and I shot an AIM-7 radar missile. I made the call "Fox 1 on an F-1." At the same time I was getting "lit up" by enemy SAMs (Surface to Air Missiles). The F-4G Wild Weasel Commander and I exchanged radio calls. I let him know that I had a missile in the air on the F-1 who was going towards them, and he let me know that they had shot their HARM missiles into the SAMs that were targeting us. What teamwork!

The AAA was so intense you could visually avoid it, as it was a solid sphere of tracer bullets. After shooting the missile I checked away from the F-1 to try to generate as much separation between us as possible, and to avoid the SAMs and AAA. After what seemed like an eternity I checked back to the F-1 to shoot another missile, since I still had the contact and didn't see anything. The F-1 was now three miles on my nose. I looked out to see if I could pick up the missile. At that time the AIM-7 impacted the F-1 in the left wing root. It was a huge fireball that illuminated the entire jet. It immediately broke into four large pieces. Then the aircraft just broke into millions of burning pieces. It stayed on fire all the way until it hit the ground. "Splash on the F-1" was my next call, and I then directed "Bo" to follow me south back to the CAP point. We continued in our CAP for the next 20 minutes while all the Weasels and bombers came in waves dropping their ordnance. We flew back to the tanker, refueled, and then flew back to Dhahran. Needless to say it was a long, quiet flight back to base. It was a time to "let the dust settle" on what just took place, and to gather our emotions.

After returning to base, my first concern was to make sure all the strikers made it back okay, and to see how effective they were at putting their bombs on target. The air-to-ground mission commander who led the F-4Gs and I thanked each other for doing a superb job respectively. The next attack wave was getting ready to go. It was led by Capt Russ "Job" Handy, who was the 71st Weapons Officer. I gave a quick debrief on what to expect once getting into Baghdad.

My next battle was the media, which is a story in and of itself. As I look back, I realize that I could not have done this mission without:

1. TRAINING/TEAMWORK that I received from Flight School to the current training we did in the 71st. I was privileged to have had instructors/friends/brothers like:

Russ "Job" Handy	Dan "Hole" Booker
Dave "Satchel" Page	Loui "Dildo" Defidelto
Mark "Brewski" Brugh	Carl "VP" VanPelt
Don "Karbo" Kline	Howard "Pip" Pope
Dan "Grif" Griffen	Mike "Padre" Flannagan
Brent "Nuts" Beecham	Mark "Lurch" Miller

Gen Richard Myers (Chairman Joint Chief of Staff, Retired) who was the 1st TFW Wing Commander, and Col "Jumbo" Wray, 1st TFW DO (Director of Operations).

Along with a Squadron of dedicated Fighter Pilots.

My four-ship immediately after the mission, left to right; "Bo" Merlack, myself, Damon "Darryl" Harp, Mark "Snake" Atwell. *via Steve Tate.*

Capt Tate with F-15C 83-0017. Tail number 3017 was originally Maj Mark "Brewski" Brugh's assigned jet. *USAF via 1 FW/PA.*

Finally, I owe so much to my four-ship, who put their lives in my hands and mine in theirs: number two, Paul "Bo" Merlack; number three, Damon "Darryl" Harp; and number four, Mark "Snake" Atwell.

2. LEADERSHIP is what it is all about. I have had the honor of great leaders like Col Drake Trumpe, when I first got in the USMC, to Gen Richard Myers, who was my Wing Commander. Unfortunately, I have been exposed to the worst of leaders as well. All one can do is take the best from the best, and not repeat the mistakes of noneffective/poor leaders. This is not just a military issue, but is a huge factor in business. I look up with great respect to business leaders like Truett Cathy, founder of Chick-fil-A. Truett leads by example, and has cultivated a "family-like" environment with all his employees.

Thanks for your interest in this story. When you watch football players (like Reggie White) who had a significant role in the outcome of a game and would offer thanks and recognition, I would like to end "My Story" the same way. The most important thing for all of us after getting back from war was none other than our family. I am blessed with two great kids, but even the love I have for my kids is second to the personal relationship with my God.

Capt Tate went on to fly a total of 40 combat missions during DESERT STORM, and after returning to Langley, left active duty and currently flies for a major airline.

Capt Tate after the mission shown next to an AIM-7M. Note the size of the Sparrow, nicknamed the "Great White Hope" due to its 500lb size. *via Steve Tate.*

LCDR Mark "MRT" Fox (USN)

VFA-81 "Sunliners," F/A-18C
Operation DESERT STORM
MiG-21 Kill
17 January 1991
Call-sign: QUICKSAND 64

This engagement marked the first air-to-air kill by the F/A-18 Hornet, and still stands as the only kill by this aircraft type in U.S. service. This account is reprinted from an article "STIRRING UP A HORNETS NEST," written by CDR Fox for the Naval Aviation Museum Foundation, Inc. FOUNDATION magazine, Vol. 17 Number 2, in Fall 1996. RDML Fox has edited this article, reprinted with the kind permission of the FOUNDATION staff, and the author has personally interviewed RDML Fox to create this account.

Every year in mid-January I find myself thinking about the tumultuous and seemingly unbelievable events of the same month in 1991. This is a personal account of my MiG kill engagement from a Hornet pilot's perspective.

I joined the VFA-81 "Sunliners" in March 1990 during work-ups for the first F/A-18 deployment aboard *USS Saratoga* (CV-60). The deployment, scheduled to begin in early August 1990, promised to be a true love boat cruise to the Mediterranean, with great liberty ports, highlighted by a 10-day pier-side visit to Marseilles, France, during Christmas and New Year's. Little did I know how this was all to change!

After word of Iraq's invasion of Kuwait, Old "Super Sara" made what must have been a record setting transatlantic crossing for a 34-year-old carrier. We arrived in the Red Sea by mid-August, relieved *USS Dwight D. Eisenhower* (CVN-69), and prepared for the worst.

Our original contingency plans were pretty sketchy, and basically reactive. For those of us who grew up in the 1980s, our focus had been on countering the Soviet threat, either matched directly against the Soviet Navy, or indirectly against surrogates, such as Cuba, Libya, or Syria; from my perspective, at least, there wasn't much Navy corporate knowledge about Iraq. We envisioned our participation to include suppression of enemy air defenses (SEAD) in support of USAF B-52s, and some sort of battlefield air interdiction (BAI) or close air support (CAS) in support of the Saudi Army. Given the paucity of information with which we had to plan, it's a good thing Saddam didn't attack the Saudi oil fields in August or early September.

During Operation DESERT SHIELD the *Saratoga* made a port-of-call in Haifa, Israel. During this time a ferry carrying 100 American sailors back to *Saratoga* sank, killing 21 young men in a terrible tragedy.

LCDR Mark "MRT" Fox (left) and Lt Nick "Mongo" Mongillo. *USN via RADM "MRT" Fox.*

F/A-18 "Sunliner" 401 on the deck of the USS *Saratoga* during DESERT STORM. This is the same jet, in the same configuration as flown by "MRT" Fox on his MiG-kill sortie. Note MiG kill marking, a MiG-21 silhouette, above the "401." *RADM "MRT" Fox.*

The new year found us back in the Red Sea, putting finishing touches on the four carefully planned sequential strikes that would open the campaign, as well as making other contingency plans. The 15 January 1991 U.N. deadline for Iraq to withdraw from Kuwait drew steadily closer, with no diplomatic progress toward a peaceful resolution.

By now, the lineup of who was flying on each of the first four strikes had already been determined. I was scheduled as a spare on the second strike launched from the Red Sea against H-3 airfield in western Iraq, led by VFA-83's C.O. My primary mission was as the HARM element lead for the third strike, also against H-3 airfield, led by VA-35's X.O.

Although dissatisfied not to be on the first strike—a night SEAD attack against a target near Baghdad led by my C.O., CDR. Mike "Spock" Anderson—the lineups were locked in place by the

time I took over Ops, and I couldn't shuffle my name into the first attack. I just hoped it wouldn't be a one-strike war.

We received the execute order late on the 15th; the first strike would launch late the next night, with a time on target (TOT) of 0300, Thursday, 17 January 1991. I watched the launch and silently lifted up a prayer as each aircraft took off. LCDR Scott "Spike" Speicher, flying AA 403, was the last "Sunliner" airborne. The spare didn't launch.

After a short, restless night, I woke early and called the ready room to find out how the first strike had gone. From my journal:

17 Jan 1991: The first strike from Saratoga *is complete, and Scott Speicher in 403 is the only guy who did not return. No mayday call, no comm. – I can only pray that he diverted, or in worst case, ejected, and is now hopefully to be picked up.*

VFA-81 F/A-18Cs line up with an A-6E to refuel from a USAF KC-135R over northern Saudi Arabia. The HARM missiles denote the "Sunliners" are in the SEAD role for this mission. *USN via RADM "MRT" Fox.*

A distant sense of dread of losing a friend—small things hit me as being suddenly presumptuous—putting my laundry out this morning, for example, presumes I'll be back to get it back.

I am ever so aware—now more than ever—of my total dependence on God's grace. I am choosing to be strong and courageous.

I manned-up the spare for the primary flight of six Hornets that would fly right up the middle of the strike to drop four 2000 lb. MK-84s on H-3 airfield. Also included in this strike were F-14 MiG Sweep, EA-6B jammers, HARM shooters, the E-2, and decoys. My Hornet, Sunliner 401, was loaded with two AIM-7Ms, two AIM-9Ls, and a centerline fuel tank, as well as the four bombs. The six designated "go" aircraft carried the same missile load-out, but substituted an ALQ-67 jamming pod designed to suppress the SA-6s in the target area for the fourth bomb.

Soon after launching (and with four MK-84's, it's an impressive cat-shot!) I realized I was going to fly on the strike. "Ammo" Minnis lost his mission computer and had to abort right after the launch, so I filled in as "Dash-3," or the second section lead of our six-ship element.

Once we got to the tanker track, my new wingman, "Coop" Cooper, couldn't get his centerline to transfer fuel, so he was also forced to abort. Our lead and squadron X.O., "Maggot" McKee, moved his wingman, LT Nick "Mongo" Mongillo, into a closer TAC-wing position, and made me, in effect, Dash-2, flying combat spread line-abreast off of McKee and Mongillo as if they were one aircraft.

Just prior to crossing the Iraqi border "Cajun" Trahan, in the rear element, lost his cockpit pressurization and aborted. Another formation shift, but by now my ability to flex was diminishing. McKee directed me to drop back to become "Bouncer" Osborne's wingman. Even though we planned on being in a "2+2" element trail formation, "Bouncer" and I continued to creep forward until, by the time we pushed, we were essentially a wall of strike-fighters headed north with, from left to right, Mongillo, McKee, myself, and Osborne each spaced about a mile apart.

A couple of important points: The air-to-air rules of engagement were necessarily restrictive to prevent fratricide. We had to VID an Iraqi aircraft to kill it, with two important exceptions: first, we always retained the right of self defense; second, we could fire at an enemy aircraft beyond visual range (BVR) if it had been identified as a bandit by the E-2 or AWACS, and correlated by the engaging fighter. Also, every flight briefs radar search responsibilities for each aircraft. Half the flight searches primarily high and the other half low, but due to the many changes in the formation we only had one Hornet searching high, while the rest of us were in the low block. This would have a large impact on our air-to-air awareness during the push.

We crossed the border just below the contrail level at 30,000 feet, going as fast as possible without afterburner—approximately 0.9 Mach.

Our command and control was provided by our own E-2 instead of the USAF AWACS. The common Bullseye for western Iraq was located just north of our target, and was called "Manny." It was clear that the Iraqis were airborne. Snatches of the E-2's bandit calls referencing "Manny" crowded into my mind as I tried to keep a mental picture of where the strike package was and where the bandits were. This was very difficult, as the Hornet was not yet mechanized to display this information in Bullseye format without many switch changes. I chose to focus on getting to the target and watching out visually for SA-6 plumes. Unconsciously ignoring uncorrelated bandit calls, I reverted to the basics: keep sight, keep quiet, fly good wing, and find the target and bomb it. Working hard to stay ahead of the jet, I selected air-to-ground (A/G) master mode about 35 nm south of the target. I immediately noticed the 100-knot westerly jet stream affecting my HUD, and made a mental note to correct for this on my bombing run.

Seconds after selecting A/G the E-2 controller, Lt John Joyce, made the call that finally registered, "400, that bandit's on your nose, 15." Now that was a call I understood! I immediately went back to the air-to-air master mode by selecting a Sidewinder, thumbed an auto-acquisition mode, and almost instantly locked a head-on, supersonic Iraqi MiG-21 about nine miles away. I kept un-caging the AIM-9 until I got a good tone, and squeezed the trigger once just as I saw the speck of the MiG in the HUD. This first shot was a 6.5 nm Fox-2. McKee's "400 has a Bogey on the nose" and subsequent, "306s stand by for VID" radio calls occurred while I was employing forward quarter missiles, and did not impact my actions, as I was certain of the Bandit status from the E-2 radio call. The missile fired like a passing train off of my right wing-tip... then simply disappeared, which I wasn't prepared for. Previous shots at drones produced missile trails that I could always follow, but with these new smokeless motors, this one just vanished!

Things were happening really fast; our closure was over 1,200 knots, and the MiG was getting bigger. Assuming the Sidewinder wasn't working, I thought to myself as I selected a Sparrow, "Well, he won't get away from this," and squeezed the trigger. This missile came off at 4.2 nm. This time I clearly watched the missile streak toward him. While the Sparrow accelerated, the MiG briefly disappeared in a bright flash and cloud of black smoke, then emerged, still nose-on, but trailing flame and smoke. The Sparrow hit the doomed fighter with yet another explosion, but incredibly there was still an airplane there, albeit clearly burning, decelerating, and descending. As he disappeared under my nose, I rocked up on my left wing to watch him pass about 1,000 feet

Formation at push

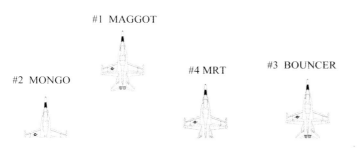

#1 MAGGOT

#2 MONGO

#4 MRT

#3 BOUNCER

Relative formation position (not to scale) of the flight at the start of the engagement. *via Mongillo.*

"MRT" seen flying F/A-18 side number 410 over Iraq during a later DESERT STORM sortie. *via RADM "MRT" Fox.*

below me. The front of the Iraqi MiG-21 was intact, with the rear half enveloped in flames. The pilot didn't get out. I passed through the black smoke from the first missile impact as we continued toward the target.

"Mongo's" excited "Splash one!" shifted my attention to the left, where his kill was marked by a huge smear of flame and smoke. This was the first that I realized that there were two MiGs. "Bouncer's" much calmer "Splash two" gave me the impression that the first explosion on my MiG was caused by one of his missiles. "Oh well, 'Bouncer' beat me to the draw.... At least I'm still alive and didn't jettison my bombs. Maybe I'll get an honorable mention for shooting a burning MiG." As I did not call my shots (my bad!), I thought that maybe "Bouncer" had shot without any comm also and caused the first hit.

There was no time to savor the kills. We were entering the heart of H-3's SAM defenses, and I was still aware I wasn't carrying the ALQ-67. Almost immediately, we got radar locks on another

group of contacts slightly west of the target that were initially nose-on, but slowly turned to the east, or beaming us. The peculiar thing about these bogeys (we never got an ID on them, though later intelligence proved them to be MiG-29s) was they were extremely slow, about .4 Mach, (or about 200 knots) at 23,000 feet! I didn't like this situation at all. There was no ID—were they bait for a trap? I started checking six constantly while we closed the distance, thinking of an ambush. I refocused my attention out front, and had a no-escape Sparrow shot as I ran down the unknown contact in a tail chase.

But at my right two o'clock was H-3! To chase the bogey down would mean I'd have to fly past the target in a predictable stern conversion to VID him, and I was still lugging around 8,000 lbs of bombs! Not the perfect VID scenario.

"Well, I came here to drop bombs on the target," I thought, as I reluctantly broke lock and switched back to A/G mode. I could not see my original target, as the sun angle precluded picking out

A fantastic shot of "MRT" about to trap aboard *Sara* after his MiG-killing sortie. Note the missing AIM-7 off the port fuselage station and AIM-9 missing from the right wingtip station. *USN via RADM "MRT" Fox.*

"MRT" Fox debriefing the *Saratoga* deck crew after the hop. *via RADM "MRT" Fox.*

Commander Fox seen later while commanding the 'Sunliners.' *via RADM "MRT" Fox.*

a dirt-on-dirt bunker. But I could see my secondary target, a large white hangar. I flew the sweetest dive bombing run of my life.

The last thing I wanted to do was get shot down "spotting" my bomb hits, so I did a series of jinks and caught a glimpse of my bombs falling together, jinked some more, and then saw them hit the hangar. The whole airfield was alive with guns and missiles being fired. Time to get out of dodge!

We got back together and headed south as fast as we could make our jets go. As we passed the area where we had shot down the MiGs there was a final reminder of our encounter; two columns of black smoke rising up from the desert in the same relative formation they'd been when we shot them down.

Still convinced "Bouncer" or someone else had put that first missile into my MiG, my hopes began to rise when we checked each other over for battle damage and I saw that only "Mongo"

was missing a Sparrow. I was more certain that it must have been my Sidewinder that caused the first explosion after all, but I put it out of my mind for fear I'd bolter when I got back to the ship, as one of the Libyan MiG killers had in the 80s.

The return to the ship was normal, and my upbringing in the Light Attack "quiet professional" school precluded me from anything like a victory roll. After losing "Spike" the night before it didn't seem like the thing to do. I did manage to get aboard with an OK-3 wire, ending the most eventful and demanding flight of my life. What a hop!

The post-strike debrief was like the locker room of a winning team in a championship football game. *Saratoga's* C.O., CAPT Joe Mobely, gave me some good-natured ribbing about firing a Sparrow into an already burning airplane. I shrugged and smiled, "I just wanted to be sure, Skipper."

LCDR Fox flew a total of 18 combat sorties into Iraq and Kuwait, including four as Mission Commander. Fox later returned to VFA-81 as Executive Officer (X.O.), and then Commanding Officer (C.O.). He subsequently served as CAG-2 aboard USS Constellation (CV-64) from 2001-2003, and led the opening "shock and awe" strike of Operation IRAQI FREEDOM on 21 March 2003. He is currently a Rear Admiral serving as Deputy Assistant to the President, and Director of the White House Military Office. As far as I can determine, this is the only engagement in recent history by a strike fighter during which the engaged aircraft went on to bomb the target after a successful air-to-air engagement. Like Mark said, "What a hop!"

LT Nicholas "Mongo" Mongillo (USN)

VFA-81 "Sunliners," F/A-18C
Operation DESERT STORM
MiG-21 Kill
17 January 1991
Call-sign: QUICKSAND 62

After receiving his "Wings of Gold" in 1987, "Mongo" served as an Instructor Pilot on T-2s for his first tour. He was subsequently assigned to the F/A-18 community, and reported to VFA-81 in August 1990, just in time to cruise on the "Super Sara" for what turned into the DESERT SHIELD/STORM cruise. This account is reprinted from an article in the Naval Aviation Museum Foundation, Inc. FOUNDATION magazine, Vol. 12 Number 2, Fall 1991. CDR Mongillo has personally edited this article, reprinted with the kind permission of the FOUNDATION staff, for this publication.

As we crossed the Saudi-Iraqi border, I performed my combat checklist for the third or fourth time. "Master Arm" was in the armed position. The thought of the target and the sophisticated SAM system (SA-6) protecting it were constantly filling my mind. Would I make it? Would I see a wingman explode? Would we destroy our target? I was scared, and I am certain the others in the strike were scared, too.

I decided, regardless of what happened, that my bombs were going to be on target. There were four of us carrying iron bombs, and we were the only ones in the strike actually flying directly into the heart of the protective SAM systems. I was the wingman of the division lead, CDR Bill "Maggot" McKee. My position was to fly off the left wing of "Maggot" in a line-abreast position.

Keep sight, stay in position, and keep my head on a swivel were my priorities. I was also trying to keep the "big picture"

Lt Nick "Mongo" Mongillo in front of F/A-18 side-number 410 after the kill. *via Mongillo.*

VFA-81 F/A-18C 410 over the *USS Saratoga* in the Red Sea during Operation DESERT SHIELD. Photo was taken by LT. Mongillo prior to the break, pilot in 410 is unknown to "Mongo." *Mongillo.*

Forward view of the *USS Saratoga* (CV-60) underway. *USN.*

in my head, assimilating the many radio calls of the other strike aircraft and the E-2. The comm was confusing, not allowing me to accurately follow exactly what was happening out in front of us.

Additionally, all bogey calls were made in reference to "Manny," a bulls-eye point located twenty miles from our target. Correlating these calls to our position was difficult, as our early model Hornets were not set up to display positions relative to a bulls-eye point. We normally worked with the E-2 using BRA format. At some point, I started blocking out the majority of the comm, concentrating exclusively on my main task of being a good wingman and putting my bombs on target.

Thirty-five miles south of the target I collapsed to a fighting-wing position, or about 45 degrees aft of line-abreast. I also selected air-to-ground master mode. All my thoughts were now directed toward my target. Every switch was set. I was ready. Seconds later, the E-2 alerted us to bandits on the nose at fifteen miles. A shudder went through my body as I selected the air-to-air master mode of my Hornet.

I peered out in front of my jet, looking for a telltale smoke trail headed for me. I knew I was well within the range of an Iraqi MiG-29's radar guided missiles. "Maggot" got a lock and called it as a bogey. This turned out to be the lead MiG. Our second section, consisting of LCDR Chuck "Bouncer" Osborne and LCDR Mark "MRT" Fox, was also locked to this MiG. I got a lock at eight miles on what turned out to be the trailer. At this point "Maggot" was pulling ahead of me for a VID pass, and I was attempting to electronically identify (EID) the contact, although I was not required to do so by the ROE.

Some thoughts on the ROE, PID, my actions, and decisions. According to DESERT STORM ROE we were cleared to fire on a correlated Bandit (the term Hostile was not in use in 1991). Thus, the E-2's call "400 bandits on your nose at 15" correlated to me as a bad guy 15 nm away, closing. By the time I selected air-to-air and locked the bandit he was at 8.6 nm, and in my mind correlation was made. However, "Maggot" at the same time was calling for a VID, so I became confused. Why did he want to VID? Did he miss

the "bandit" call? Was he not sure the "bandit" call was accurate? Thus, I delayed shooting from 8.6 nm until 2.6 nm. The EID was not part of our ROE and PID. It made me feel better when I attained the EID, but it was not a requirement to shoot. I shot because I heard "bandit," although I delayed my shot 20 seconds or so, as I thought about my impending actions, the VID call by "Maggot," the "what if" scenario if I shot down a good guy ("Maggot" told us in the brief to roll inverted and eject over Iraq if we have a Blue-On-Blue (BOB), or fratricide), and because I was new with low hours. Today I'm sure I would have acted the same, but much quicker. Heck, today our division would have had 6-8 kills that day. We wouldn't be in air-to-ground mode at 35 nm, we would correlate via bullseye, sanitize with our radar, assign targeting, and sort and kill them BVR. Additionally, I received the EID at 4.6 nm and still waited until 2.6 nm to shoot. As the gears were turning in my head I knew crunch time (min range) was quickly approaching. I knew I had seconds to shoot, or I would never be able to shoot. I thought about the "bandit" comm call one last time, I thought about the correlation one last time, I thought about the EID that eased my fears of a BOB, and then in my mind I said to myself, "I'm right to shoot and I'm following ROE." I pulled the trigger at 2.6 miles and called, "FOX-1." From the time of the first bandit call to fireball was 45 seconds.

Unbeknownst to me, "MRT" had already shot and killed the lead MiG-21 seconds before I squeezed the trigger. My Sparrow pulled to the right as soon as it came off the rail—so much that I thought the missile had gone stupid. It became obvious that the missile was working fine when it guided to a spectacular direct hit on the Fishbed, causing it to disintegrate in a sheet of yellow flame.

I made a very excited "Splash One!" call, and "Bouncer" followed with a very calm "Splash Two" to alert the entire flight and the E-2 to the actual outcome of the engagement. "Maggot"

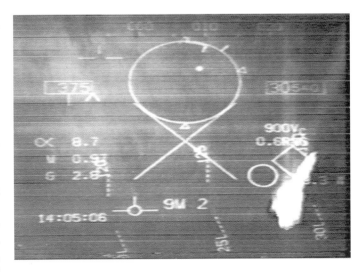

Still frame from "Mongo's" HUD tape at the moment the AIM-7 impacts the MiG in the lower right corner of the picture (note TD box on flaming wreckage). The HUD shows Mongo is in a 90 degree right turn, 22 degrees nose-low. He has already selected AIM-9 (note the "9M 2," meaning AIM-9M is selected, two remaining), and closing velocity is 900 knots at a range of 0.6 miles. *Mongillo.*

VFA-81 "Sunliners" (left to right) Front row: Tony Albano, Mark Fox, Bill McKee (squadron XO), Mike Anderson (squadron CO), Scott Speicher (KIA), and Steve Minnis. Middle row: Dave Newcom, Ed Callao, Jim Ellis, Nick Mongillo, Tom Hoffman, Bob King, Craig Bartolett, Phil Gardner, Chris Colon, and Dave Harrod. Back row: Donnie Bodin, Marc Scaccia, Mike Meyers, Chris Adams, Barry Hull, Doug Cooper, Conrad Caldwell, and Bob Wildermuth. *via Mongillo.*

had quite a sight, as two burning MiG-21s went down both sides of his canopy!

We continued toward the target, gaining separate locks on two more bogeys from about twenty miles. We weren't entirely sure if these aircraft were Iraqi, so we continued inbound without firing, working hard to sort them on radar while maintaining a good visual lookout.

Without another bandit declaration from the E-2, we had no choice but to hold our missiles and press on to the target. We could have continued the VID of these bogeys, but our mission was to bomb the target; to have pursued them could have prevented us from successfully accomplishing our assigned mission. I rolled in, easily identified my aim point, and delivered all my ordnance on target. I egressed south, quickly joining my lead and heading for the safety of the border.

A number of conclusions can be drawn and lessons learned from Operation DESERT STORM, most of which are not new or exotic:

One: our technology works. The versatility, reliability, and accuracy of the Hornet was remarkable, surpassing even our highest expectations. The idea of having one aircraft capable of performing more than one primary mission area is sound—as long as the investment in training for each area is made.

Two: consistent, realistic training paid handsome dividends. The "Sunliners" of VFA-81 (along with our sister squadron, the "Rampagers" of VFA-83) were making their first cruise since Hornet transition. Over half of the aviators in the squadron were first tour/cruise pilots. In fact, I had only been in the squadron for a week prior to this cruise. The results from combat speak for themselves.

Three: prior combat experience is not a prerequisite for success in combat. Except for our CO (CDR Mike "Spock" Anderson), there were no Sunliner aviators who had expended ordnance in anger. Again, the value of good training and mental preparation was evident.

On the other hand, having a couple of combat hops under your belt made it much easier to go back and do it again. The fear of the unknown on the first strike was immense.

LT Mongillo went on to fly a total of 25 combat sorties into Iraq and Kuwait. He later served as an adversary pilot in VF-45, and both attended and taught at TOPGUN. He has also taught on the Hornet Replacement Air Group (RAG), earning Instructor of the Year in 1996. He recently took command of his own squadron, equipped with the new F/A-18E Super Hornet. "Mongo" has over 4,600 hours and 550 arrested landings under his belt.

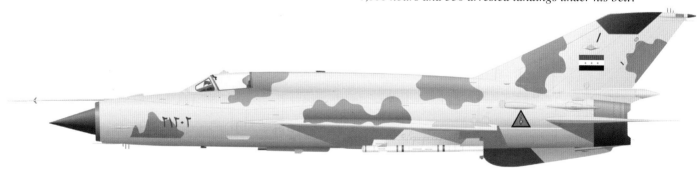

MiG-21bis Fishbed in Iraqi paint, custom art supplied specifically for this book by former USN F-14 Tomcat pilot Jim "Max" Qualls.

Captain Rhory "Hoser" Draeger (USAF)

58th TFS "Gorillas," F-15C
Operation DESERT STORM
MiG-29 Kill
17 January 1991
Call-sign: CITGO 3

Capt Draeger was assigned to the 59th Tactical Fighter Squadron ("The Golden Pride") of the 33rd Tactical Fighter Wing, Eglin AFB, Florida. However, due to his solid experience, the 58th TFS "shanghaied" him to fly with the "Gorillas" during DESERT SHIELD and DESERT STORM. This was Captain Draeger's first kill of the war, he would also kill a MiG-23 on 26 January 1991. Unfortunately Captain Draeger is now deceased, and the article below was originally published in the title Gulf Air War Debrief, *and is reproduced by permission of the author, Robert F. Dorr, and Aerospace Publishing Limited, 2006 © Aerospace Publishing Limited. In this first publication, "Hoser" mistakenly gave his call sign as UNION 3; however, on this day he was actually CITGO 3, and the author has corrected this for this publication. His wingman, "Kimo" Schiavi, has added comments at the end of this piece for this publication.*

I graduated from the University of Wisconsin in 1981, and went to OTS (Officer Training School). First, I went to the flight screening school at Hondo, Texas, and before that, a 3- to 4-week course in the Cessna T-41, which was actually the roughest part of pilot training for me. I went to pilot training at Laughlin Air Force Base in Del Rio, Texas. I got an F-15 assignment out of there, and went to fighter lead-in school in the AT-38B Talon; a two- to three-month indoctrination in fighters, followed by F-15 RTU (replacement training unit) at Luke Air Force Base, Arizona.

I had 18 months at Kadena Air Base, Okinawa, and was a flight lead when I left there. I went to Langley Air Force Base, Virginia, as my follow-on assignment, also flying F-15s, during which period I went to the Fighter Weapons School. I came to Eglin in November 1988.

I'm actually a member of the 59th Tactical Fighter Squadron "Golden Pride," which did not deploy to the Persian Gulf; I was an augmentee with the 58th "Gorillas" during that squadron's stay at Tabuk, Saudi Arabia.

What's it like to sit in the F-15C and fly it? From the standpoint of just going up and down, feeling forces on your body, it's the worst rollercoaster ride you've ever been on, multiplied by about a hundred.

All those sensations that you get with your stomach going up and down, the G-forces that you feel at the bottom of a loop—if it's not a hundred times that bad, it's ten times. In our normal flying, we deal with high G forces all the time, throughout the flight. On a regular basis here I'll pull regularly nine Gs, right to the limit of the aircraft. It's not uncommon for guys to come back with eight

F-15C 85-0119 seen in 1992 at Tinker AFB, OK, sporting "Hoser's" kill marking.
Jim Geek via Don Logan.

to nine Gs on the jet. During the combat missions we flew over in Saudi Arabia, no. I would say the most I ever pulled over there was seven Gs, which was not much.

Because we've got a bigger wing than other fighters we've got increased lift out there, and we're not going to bleed off energy as quick as other aircraft will. Take, for example, an F-105 Thunderchief. Now that had real thin wings, very high wing loading—but for flying down at low altitude, real fast, that's what you want to have, because it's going to be a real smooth ride. But when you're trying to make a turn with it, it's such a high wing loading it's going to bleed off energy at an extremely fast rate. With an F-15, we've got a big wing and low wing loading—but since it's got all that lift, it's going to be a bumpy ride out there.

It handles well on the ground, like driving a car, except you don't have a steering wheel, so you steer it with your rudder pedals. You have plenty of visibility. In fact, I think that's why a lot of people get sick—there's so much visibility, and there's a sense that when make a turn, you're kind of falling out of the jet, as opposed to a normal airliner, where you're looking out a window and feel secure in your little bubble. The F-15 kind of goes down to your shoulders, and you get the sensation of falling. It affects people, especially those who fly in the back seat for the first time.

I was credited with two kills. On one of these, my wingman Tony Schiavi also got a kill.

My other kill, the first of the two, was on 17 January. We were sweeping out in front of a strike package. We were a four-ship. The strike package consisted of F-16 Fighting Falcons, F-4G Wild Weasels, EF-111s Ravens, and other F-15s, some of which were with us, and some of which were with the strike package.

It was a morning mission. The actual strike was around noon. It was our first combat mission. We had taken off from our air base at Tabuk, tanked, and heard AWACS calling MiGs airborne while we were on the tanker: "CITGO flight, bandits southwest, Baghdad, medium altitude."

The actual strike package is going to an airfield just west of Baghdad. As we head up there, the bandits are still there. They end up being MiG-29s. They're in a CAP (a combat air patrol) just southwest of Baghdad, around that southern lake—there are three lakes on the west side of Baghdad, and right just southwest of that southern lake is where they're CAPing.

We start out at about 13,000 feet, doing a couple of turns. During that time period we'll run—we'll close the distance from about 80 miles down to 40 miles, when they're coming back hot. As they turn back cold one more time, now we're thinking that they're out of gas, because they've been airborne so long, so we're kind of saying, "Oh, man, they're heading back towards their airfield now."

While CITGO flight presses in on the MiGs, the F-15s come under heavy surface-to-air missile and gunfire, make evasive maneuvers, jettison wing tanks (while retaining centerline tanks), and dive to lower altitude. We dump our tanks off at about halfway in on the intercept. We're closer than we wanted to be to a SAM site. We've got indication that they're launching on us.

They get just west of their airfield now, and it looks like they're turning back into it, but in reality they turn back towards us. During this time period we close it from 40 miles down to 17 miles. And so, when they make their turn back in, at about 17 miles, I'll lock up the western man and shoot him with one AIM-7.

"Sly" Magill locks one up and shoots at him with two AIM-7s. Capt Charles J. "Sly" Magill, a Marine Corps exchange officer with the 58th Tactical Fighter Squadron ("Gorillas"), is leader of CITGO flight, with 1st Lt Mark J. Arriola as his wingman. I'm in the number three position accompanied by my wingman, Captain Tony Schiavi.

We're using AIM-7Ms. I see the missiles from the time they leave the aircraft until the time they hit. That's unusual. You normally don't see that because the rocket motor will burn out.

Because of the environmental conditions, I see it all —even though we don't have them visually when we start shooting. Very shortly after firing I pick them up. They descend. They're at 13,000

This MiG-29 Fulcrum was discovered near Al Taqqadum airbase, Iraq in 2003. Notice the plastic that had been placed over the cockpit section to protect it while buried. *USAF.*

Interior cockpit of the buried MiG-29 Fulcrum. Most of the instruments had been removed prior to burial and the aircraft was obviously not serviceable. *USAF.*

Left to right: "Mama" Kass, "Kimo" Schiavi, and "Hoser." "Kimo": "The three of us sitting alert at Tabuk. Notice 'Hoser's' ever-present golf club over my left shoulder, and our 'hi-tech' black-out curtains on the window!" *via Schiavi*.

feet. Now they're at 500 feet of altitude separation from us. When I actually shoot I don't see them, but at about twelve miles or so I start to pick them up. They're at low altitude, flying in echelon formation about a mile between them. And I see the missiles go right into impact. I call "Splash two."

This means we've got two fireballs out there, and the two MiGs are dead. There are no Iraqi shots. Our missiles hit them head-on, and they just drop out of the sky. These are real small fireballs because they're real low on gas.

From what we can tell they never locked us up. They may have been attempting to, but we didn't get any indications of it.

From what I can see, the MiG-29s have a camouflaged paint scheme. It's kind of in shadows so it's hard to tell.

When we get done with our mission and we're claiming a kill, we fill out paperwork that says, "This is what happened." Each guy in the flight fills out the paperwork. Even if they didn't shoot, they verify it, so you've got witnesses. A wingman will say "We did see a fireball," or, "We did see his missiles track to the target," and that's used to try to verify the kill. There are other means, too. The paperwork is sent up to headquarters and a board meets. It's decided at a higher level than just a captain. They go through all the data and say either, "Yes, it was a kill," or "No, it wasn't." Both

of my kills were pretty straightforward, and there wasn't any doubt about who was shooting at what, or what happened.

No, the F-15 isn't perfect. If I had my way, I'd say bigger engines, better radar—but the F-15C is the best in the world today. I want the ATF (Advanced Tactical Fighter, later called the F-22 Raptor) tomorrow. Realistically, compared to any other aircraft in the world, it will be real hard to improve on the F-15.

Comments by "Kimo" Schiavi:
The one thing that was also impressive about this particular engagement was what was happening while we were on the tanker, and then post-tanker while we were marshalling. During this time, we had information that there were MiGs airborne and CAPing right where we were supposed to be taking the strike package; well, "Hoser's" radar locks up, and the antenna will not sweep. So the whole time we are waiting to push across the border he is turning the radar on and off, pulling Gs up and down trying to get the thing working. Of course, I am on his wing thinking if he doesn't get his radar operational, I will most likely end up having to take his targeting responsibility—but no kidding, right as we are beginning our push, his radar starts sweeping again and, well, the rest is history. That was "Hoser," never give up, never say die, it ain't over 'til it's over.

Captain Charles "Sly" Magill (USMC)

58th TFS "Gorillas," F-15C
Operation DESERT STORM
MiG-29 Kill
17 January 1991
Call-sign: CITGO 1

The only Marine Corps Officer to score a kill since the end of Vietnam, Capt Magill was on an exchange tour with the 58th TFS after having flown the F/A-18 in the Corps. "Sly" was a graduate of both the Marine Corps Weapons School (WTI) and the USN Fighter Weapons School (TOPGUN), and had about 1,200 hours in the Hornet. He had one overseas WESTPAC (Western Pacific) deployment under his belt, and even had the opportunity to mock-dogfight against Egyptian MiG-21s during a training deployment to Egypt. This account was written by "Sly" for this publication.

I got to Eglin in the winter of 1989 after a short TX course (transition) to the F-15C. I got there just in time to fly "Paco" Geisler's wing over Panama for Operation JUST CAUSE, and then it was about eight months later that we deployed to Saudi Arabia. By that time I was the A Flight Commander, an IP, and Mission Commander in the squadron. Because I had about six ocean crossings under my belt in the Hornet, and had spent some time in Egypt, I was a designated cell leader for our 15.5 hour deployment from Eglin AFB, Florida, to Tabuk. Our routing was to

take us over Egypt, and they didn't want anyone to know they were letting us use their airspace, so it was all comm-out. We crossed the Red Sea and pressed into Saudi Arabia, and our new home for the next eight months, Tabuk.

We started 24 hour operations as fast as we could turn the jets. Our weapons officer, Rick "Kluso" Tollini, and some others had gone over about three days ahead of us on a KC-10 so they would be good-to-go as soon as we landed. We went into crew-rest, or tried to, as we acclimated to the 13 hour time difference. "Kluso"

Seen at Eglin AFB in 1996, "Sly" Magill's F-15C 85-0107. *(Don Logan)*

"Sly" Magill still in the cockpit of his F-15C immediately after the 15.5 hour non-stop flight from Eglin AFB, Florida, to Tabuk, Saudi Arabia. *(via "Sly" Magill)*

and his guys started flying CAPs south of the Iraqi border right away.

During those first few months we flew a lot of mixed-force missions with the *USS Kennedy* and *Saratoga* air wings. That was a good warm-up for us. We were also holding down 24 hour CAPs over northern Saudi Arabia. Every once in a while the Iraqis would send a MiG-25 Foxbat or an F-1 (Mirage) charging south toward the border. They even ran some sophisticated tactics. They would send a couple of Foxbats down from Baghdad in the high-40s going as fast as that airplane would go, just raging at the border. Short of the border they would "beam" out. They never crossed the border. As soon as they turned to the beam, they would drop an F-1 out of the formation straight at the ground, and then he would run at the border, then turn north. There for a while it looked like they were trying out some fairly sophisticated tactics. Of course we were doing the same thing, running at the border and locking them up. One thing, though, we rarely saw them at night.

Our squadron commander, "Tonic" Thiel, wanted to keep the same four-ships together; therefore, we flew with the same four guys the entire time. As days passed we received the first three days of missions passed down to us, and we began planning for them. I was selected to be one of the four primary OCA mission commanders for the initial wave of attacks. Rick "Kluso" Tollini was tasked to lead the first OCA mission on the first night with his group, and I was handed the first day strike a few hours later. We had months to plan the missions. I planned the air-to-air mission with the 1st TFW Chief of Weapons, Capt Russ "Job" Handy. The overall mission commander from the Shaw F-16 wing (363rd TFW) was top notch, and we worked for months on the planning of this initial strike. My four-ship consisted of my wingman, Mark "Nips" Arriola, number 3 was Rhory "Hoser" Draeger, and his wingman was Tony "Kimo" Schiavi.

"My" mission was an OCA sweep for the first strike against Al Taquaddam Air Base, a large fighter base just west of Baghdad that was home to over 50 Iraqi fighters. I was the fighter-commander with 16 Eagles: eight from our squadron and eight from the 1st TFW. My second four-ship was "Kluso" Tollini with Larry "Cherry" Pitts on his wing, while his number three was Jon "JB" Kelk with Mark "Willie" Williams on his wing. I'm not sure of the names on the two 1st TFW four-ships. The strike package was made up of 40 F-16s. They were loaded-out with two 2,000 lb bombs on the first flights, then the last couple of four-ships had CBU (cluster bomb units). Al Taq had not been hit yet, and besides the numerous fighters, including Fulcrums and Foxbats, there was a chemical weapons storage facility that was targeted. There were four F-4G Wild Weasels and EF-111s providing SEAD (Suppression of Enemy Air Defenses) support.

Two things really helped lead to our successes as a squadron. First, "Kluso" really felt strongly that we should fly as paired four-ships from the very start, so from September on we flew with the same four guys—we CAP'd together, sat alert together, everything. We really got to know each other, and our tactics reflected this. "Kluso" is just a world class fighter pilot, and our successes as a unit are largely to his credit. Second, our senior leadership was

Mark "Nips" Arriola (left) and Chuck "Sly" Magill in front of an Eglin F-15C at Tabuk. *(via "Sly" Magill)*

great; they allowed the young warriors to lead the fight while they managed and ran interference for us. It's a real gut check for senior officers to turn the fight over to the younger, more current troops, but that's what our leadership did, and it showed their true faith in us to get the job done.

After a pretty much sleepless night we were eating breakfast as the guys came in from flying the first night missions, and I'll never forget the looks on their faces. They had all been shot at a bunch. They were tired, emotional, and pretty excited. I was envious, since they were now "seasoned" combat pilots, and had at least the first real combat mission under their belts, and even a couple of kills ("JB" and "Cheese"). I got a little Intel from them, but not much. I was pretty focused on my mission.

I started our briefing around 10 am, and besides our eight guys, the wing commander and a bunch of other folks were there. When Intel started briefing the enemy air defense picture—the heavily defended target area to include all the missile engagement zones—I looked over at my wingman, and his eyes were the size of silver dollars. I think I went through two bottles of water during that brief, my mouth was so dry. I'd never been this nervous before, and I got together with "Nips" after the brief and told him that I'd take care of him if he would just take care of me. I asked him if he was ready. He said absolutely, and we pressed out to our aircraft. As soon as I started that first engine, all the nerves left. I just focused on the mission. No time for nerves now; in fact, it's kind of funny, my wife Lisa was back home in labor with our first child. So I know all this is going on, but I have to channel it out and just focus on the mission.

After launching out of Tabuk we headed east to our tanker track. There was some tanker fall-out, and instead of two KC-135s for my eight-ship, I now only had one. I worked out an alternate plan with "Kluso," and we all ended up getting our gas and headed for the push point. We had named our push point "Student Gap," the same name as the push point on the Nellis AFB ranges used for Red Flag exercises. You might as well have a sense of humor about it all. Our plan was to push first, about 100 miles in front of the strike package. We would head due north straight up the middle of the country towards Baghdad to sweep for the strikers. From the target area we would then work west towards Al Assad Air Base, then south past H2/H3 airfields to cover those fighter bases and look for targets of opportunity. Basically, we were to fly a large, counterclockwise flow around the western half of Iraq.

Right on time the F-16 mission commander started the check in, and it went flight-by-flight in perfect cadence, just perfect. It was like a big Red Flag, but better than anything I had ever heard, because everyone was so serious. "Hoser's" radar had locked-up on him, but he got it working by the push time. So we flew north with eight Eagles in a wall in the mid- to high 30s. Immediately AWACS gives bogey-dope on two aircraft south of the target. We push over to a secure freq, and they let us know that two Fulcrums are on CAP about 15 miles south of the bullseye, which was the target. They also cleared us at that time to kill both bandits. So here we are, 150 miles south of the target, and we're already cleared to commit and kill.

As we push north we continue to get bogie-dope, and it appears the MiGs are in a north-south CAP at about 1,500 feet and very slow. My four-ship (CITGO) is on the left side of the wall, and "Kluso's" (PENZOIL) is on the right. It's an impressive sight to see eight Eagles in a wall blazing northeast on about a 030° heading. We can now see the bandits on our radars, and we sample them occasionally. CITGO is targeted on this group, and at about 60 miles "Kluso" starts asking if it's okay for him to take his four-ship north towards Al Assad to look at that fighter base. I tell him negative. I'm thinking that as we get closer, these two bandits will land at Al Taq, then Al Taq and Al Assad would launch the fleet at us, and I would end up 4 vs X(?). So I tell him no, and to stay with me, just in case. But by about 45 miles we haven't seen anyone else, and we definitely don't need eight Eagles to handle two Fulcrums, so I clear "Kluso" off to go to the northwest to check out Al Assad. I could see beyond the target area and clear the whole area, so I felt comfortable letting him go. He takes PENZOIL, and crosses high and behind me off on about a 300 degree heading.

It was important to monitor Al Assad, as it had over 70 fighters based there, and had not been hit the first night. Between these two airfields they had well over 100 fighters, and because they had actually flown some sorties on the first night we were all expecting them to "launch the fleet" at us, as this was the first day mission. They could have made it very interesting for us, even with eight Eagles.

About 40 miles to the merge, my radar warning (RWR) gear shows SA-2 and SA-3 SAMs targeting me. I call out a "mud spike," and most of my flight is still clean. I'm still searching visually for any missiles and don't see a thing. Then "Kimo" calls "Smoke in the air!" I call for combat 1 jettison (both wing tanks) and break down and right, still with no sight of the missiles. "Nips" Arriola was on my right and says, to this day, one of the coolest things he's ever seen were those eight tanks coming off in perfect unison while we broke away and down. I lose about 15,000 feet in the break and pick up a lot of speed. I'm now on about a 100 degree heading and look out to my right, and there's my wingman, in perfect combat spread. Number three did the same thing, but he went left and is now heading west. We had stumbled over an Iraqi ground unit of some size, and all they had to do to see us was look up, so they targeted us. I'm not sure how many missiles were shot, since I never saw them.

We defeated the SAMs, and I ask AWACS for bogie-dope, and they give us bearing-range-altitude (BRA) back to the bandits, which had not moved out of their CAP. My RWR shows the SAMs are behind us, so I call the flight back to a 030 degree heading. Until this point everything had been very antiseptic, just like a training mission...until that RWR audio went off like a fire alarm. That really got my attention. This wasn't a training mission, and they're trying to kill us! That's when the intensity really ramped up. I've got a lot of speed now, and the Eagle cockpit is loud like a freight train, the radios are going-off, the RWR is blaring, and we're only 30 miles from a merge with one of the best enemy fighters in the world. I look out to the right, and there's "Nips" still in perfect position. I look to my left and "Hoser" is line abreast, about five miles away with his wingman, so we're all going same-way, same-day. I call "Hoser" with "Group, 030, 1,500 feet." "Hoser" comes back with "Same," and just like that we're back in the fight. This flight integrity, after a disorienting SAM break, displayed the quality of the guys in my flight, and the importance of having flown together for the last six months.

As we close the range down through 30 miles we have ramped-down to about 15,000 to 20,000 feet. "Hoser" and I are sampling them, but not locking them up. We would roll the cursors over them and check their altitude, but we had agreed in the brief to hold our locks until we were ready to shoot, so as not to scare them off. As we get in to 22 miles the bandits turn cold, or north. I'm thinking this is it. They are going to land, launch the fleet at us, open up all the SAM sites and shred us—but they don't. I decide to try to run them down and call "Push it up, push it up!" We all go to full afterburner and accelerate out. In the back of my mind I'm thinking they might be "dragging" us into a trap, called a "drag-n-bag." In fact, I said that to "Hoser" on the radio about three times, "Hoser, drag-n-bag."

We have closed the range to about 16 miles when they start a right turn back into us. They were flying what we call "gomer echelon," where the wingman is slung well aft of lead, fluid from side to side. As the bandits roll-out hot they push it up from the 380 knots they had been doing to over 600 knots. At 14 miles "Hoser" takes his lock, but the wingman MiG had switched sides in the turn. "Hoser" isn't waiting around, he takes a single AIM-7 shot and calls "FOX 1!" He then checks to the right, over the top of me, and I can tell by the geometry that he had probably shot the guy on my side of the formation! So I take my cursors down the left side of the radar contact, get lucky, and get my lock on the other, or left-hand guy. If anyone ever says there is not a measure of luck in combat, I'm here to tell you, there's luck! The left bandit guy comes out locked on the radar, and I'm showing about 1,250 knots closure.

At about 12 miles I take an AIM-7 Sparrow shot. I'd shot a lot of 2.75 folding fin rockets in the Hornet, and sometimes the fins don't work, and they go off like bottle-rockets, going crazy. I'd also shot a lot of AIM-7s, but this one came off and went straight for the ground. I'm thinking, "that doesn't look right." I had checked

hard right after the first shot, so after a couple of seconds I pull back left, "center the dot,' and take a second FOX 1. This one goes straight out, and appears to be guiding perfectly. I had read a lot of Vietnam reports, and many guys had reported time compression during the stress of combat. Well, this is where I experience it firsthand. As this second missile came off, all the noise, the RWR, the jet, everything went silent. The missile appeared to be in slow motion. I could see the yellow and brown band, the slow roll as it slowly went out. Then at about 10 seconds time to go on the second shot, it was like someone turned all the volumes back up! WAY UP!

We were now in to about seven miles, and we start to get tally-hos on the bandits, tally-two Fulcrums. They are drifting off to the left, not pointing at us and not spiking us, so we are all clean. They were in that beautiful pale blue paint, just above a partly cloudy sky. I'm not concentrating on the targets at this time, I'm scanning behind them. If you fly the "Rodan" you learn pretty fast to keep searching for trailers or other bandits—because they can sure see you. We were at about 9,000 ft slant range, just about over the bandits, when our missiles got there. Number three's AIM-7 guided straight into the canopy of his MiG, and that's that. My first missile, the one that had gone straight down towards the ground, hits the right wing root of the MiG, and the jet starts to tuck under. Just then the second missile goes through the middle of the fuselage. The explosion wasn't as big as I would have expected, just more of a sparkle and a flash. I didn't get a great look at the whole event, as I was concentrating on searching for other bandits, but "Nips" counted down the missiles and saw the whole event.

I switched to AUTO GUNS, and we blew through the merge clearing for other bandits. I call back to AWACS "Splash two, splash two!" The strike package was just getting ready to push, and there was a brief collapse of comm discipline as someone replied, "Shit Hot!" That was pretty cool, but we were too busy to relax, doing our short range radar work and sanitizing the target area. This was all just like I learned at TOPGUN; don't hang around a fireball, clear the merge. Within seconds I notice that the ground is turning green, and I see a river go by. I'm way too low on fuel, way too close to the target, and still going north. We are doing 600 knots at about 12,000 feet, so I'm thinking, now what? I call for an in-place Immelman, now! I know I don't have enough gas to complete the flow, but I've got lots of knots, no altitude, and want to get everyone moving south. We need to get away from the target area and the Iraqi air defense system. Now all four of us are going straight up. Passing 26,000 feet going straight up I get locked-up by SAMs—we were right in the middle of the Baghdad MEZ. I'm on my back now in the mid-20s, and the RWR is lit up. I look out the canopy and can see the missiles coming, the boosters and smoke. So now I'm breaking again, I punch off my centerline fuel tank, and expend the rest of my chaff. These were SA-2s, 3s, and 6s, and I saw three of them, but there were probably more; it was hard to count them, since they were all stacked on top of each other. I hear everyone else call clean, and here I am doing the "funky chicken" over Baghdad! Just then I hear "Bitchin' Betty" say "Bingo Fuel," then "Fuel Low." I look in and see the fuel gauge go to zero. I think, "this can't be right." Maybe I got hit by something, so once we're

Four "Gorillas" of the 58th TFS pose with borrowed weapons while sitting alert. Left to right are; Mark Arriola, Scott Maw, Clark Butch, and Chuck Magill *(via "Sly" Magill)*

clear of the SAM zone I do a battle damage check. Everyone was clean, no damage, and they had about 7,000 lbs of fuel. I found out later that the fuel system had shorted out when I jettisoned that last tank. We found this to become common as the war went on.

As we are heading back, "Hoser" was giving me grief the whole time, saying, "Come on Sly, we got to do an air show." It is 400 miles back to home plate, and I keep saying, no, we just need to be professional about this, go out and do the next mission tonight. He is on me all the way back to Tabuk. Finally I agree, and I'm glad we did it. We come smokin' into the break at about 550 knots, drop off number two and four, and "Hoser" and I come back around. We had already called-in our expenditures, so the whole squadron knew what had happened. There had to be over 100 troops at the center field ramp, called "center stage." I drop down and line up on center stage in full AB at about 50 feet. Right over the top I pulled up and did an aileron roll at about 150 feet, and kept it going into a 270 degree roll into the pitch-up. "Hoser" did the same thing. I pulled so hard and banged the stick so hard to the left that the master caution light came on, and I'm thinking while I'm upside down, after this whole day, I'm gonna kill myself

in this stupid-ass air show. The wing commander didn't care for the show at all—in fact he wanted to ground us. We pulled into center stage, and the troops were absolutely going ballistic! Our Master Sgt asked if he could keep one of the missile umbilicals, since I had shot two. I kept the other. Everyone was hi-fivin,' and our ordnance folks and troopers were just jumping and celebrating. This result was the verification of over six months of their hard work coming to fruition, so it was just great to enjoy for a few minutes. There was no champagne or anything like that, just the debrief. Then we got ready to go back out again.

Later, at a TOPGUN briefing, I found out why the Fulcrums turned southwest and accelerated, but not into us. There was a Navy strike coming out of western Iraq, working with the west-sector AWACS, that flowed into the central airspace. The MiG-29s were attempting to run down the strikers. An F-14 RIO came up to me and said, "I saw your entire engagement." I said no way, but he went on to describe to me the whole event. Turns out the F-14s had the MiGs about nine miles behind them, and were about to turn back into them when they saw us go over the top shooting missiles. We never saw the Tomcats!

During the first two weeks of DESERT STORM "Sly" flew over 100 hours, and ended the war with over 250 combat hours in the Eagle. Captain Magill returned to the Corps in the reserves to fly the F/A-18, and retired as a Lieutenant Colonel. He continues to write and speak for both the USMC and USN Fighter Weapons Schools. He is currently the Chief Pilot for a major airline.

Captain Larry "Cherry" Pitts (USAF)

58th TFS "Gorillas," F-15C
Operation DESERT STORM
MiG-25 Kill
19 January 1991
Call-sign: CITGO 22

Capt Pitts entered active duty through Officers Training School in November 1982. After graduating pilot training class 84-02 at Williams AFB, Arizona, his initial assignment was as a FAIP in the T-38. "Cherry" was then assigned to the F-15, completing the Eagle RTU in the 555th TFTS "Triple Nickel," and then on to the 58th TFS for his first Eagle assignment. Prior to the engagement he had about 350 hours in the Eagle, and was a brand new two ship flight lead. The following account was created from an interview with "Cherry" for this publication.

I had been in the squadron about a year when DESERT SHIELD kicked-off. I had been the Life Support Officer, and had recently moved into the scheduling shop. When the squadron deployed I was on the squadron commander's wing, the second aircraft to land at Tabuk after flying 15.5 hours non-stop. After a couple of weeks, our five weapons officers got together and put paired four-ships together, and we then flew, sat alert—everything was done as a four-ship. This really bonded us together, and we knew what to expect from each other. My four-ship was "Kluso" Tollini with me on his wing, and "J.B." Kelk with "Willie" Williams on his wing. "Kluso" and "J.B." were both Weapons School Graduates, and they took turns leading as number 1 of 4 and number 3 of 4.

We saw numerous aircraft on radar over Iraq during DESERT SHIELD. We did see some high, fast MiG-25s, but they never crossed into Saudi as far as I know. We always set up for an intercept just in case they crossed south. "Roto" Till and I did engage two aircraft during DESERT SHIELD that got lost and crossed into

"Cherry" Pitts seen moments after landing at Tabuk, Saudi Arabia following the 15.5 hour non-stop flight from Florida. Larry and the 58th TFS would spend the next 8 months at Tabuk. *via Pitts.*

"Cherry" Pitt's F-15C 85-0099 seen later at Eglin sporting the kill marking of his MiG-25 kill. *Alec Fushi.*

"Cherry" Pitts outside the alert shack. During DESERT SHIELD, airborne CAP was maintained as well as always having a four-ship on alert. *Via Pitts.*

Sitting alert with Capt Larry "Cherry" Pitts (left) and Lt Mark "Nips" Arriola. *Tony Murphy.*

Saudi. I think they were Mirage F-1s. AWACS ran us on them and cleared us to fire. As soon as we had a sort and were in a WEZ, AWACS broke us off and ordered us not to fire. The F-1s realized their error, and had turned north back into Iraq.

"J.B." was the lead for the first night missions, so I was flying number four. "Kluso" and I ran on some guys, but only "J.B." got a MG-29 kill that night out of our four-ship. "Cheese" Graeter

"Cherry" on alert during SHIELD. Numbers one and two of the alert four ship were close enough to run to their aircraft (seen in background in the shelter), while numbers three and four had to drive to their respective aircraft if scrambled. *via Pitts.*

was leading the other four-ship, and he got two F-1s. We kept flying a very busy schedule for the next couple of days, and we were all getting tired. The 19th was day three of the war, and the missions just kept coming. It was "J.B.'s" turn to lead, and this was a pre-dawn launch for an escort mission. We were to cover a large strike going into western Iraq consisting of F-16s, F-111s, and the Weasels. Takeoff and the trip to the tanker were all uneventful. It was still dark as we refueled and waited for our push time to sweep in front of the strikers. AWACS then passed us word that the strike was weather canceled. As the sun came up, we could see a very low deck of clouds right down on the desert floor, almost like a thick ground fog. I was guessing that this deck went north to the target area, and that's why they scrubbed the strike. I was hoping that we would get to go back to Tabuk and get some sleep, but the authorities on the AWACS held us on the KC-10 for about four hours. We were kept there on some Intel that Saddam Hussein was trying to escape by aircraft, and if he tried it we would be there to intercept him. Maybe he weather canceled also, but for whatever reason nothing happened, and we were finally released to return to Tabuk. All I could think about was my rack and a combat nap! Our Ops officer met us and delivered more bad news. There were some SCUD hunters going into western Iraq, and they needed a four-ship to CAP for them. We were it.

This time "Kluso" (Rick Tollini, whom I had gone through OTS and UPT with) took the four-ship lead, with me as #2, "J.B." as #3, and "Willie" as #4. After a quick combat brief we launched and headed back to the tankers. The only action had been a Navy package on their way to a target west of Baghdad, which was now on their way out of Iraq on a southwest heading. They were heading back to the Red Sea; I had visited the *USS Saratoga* during SHIELD, and I wondered if that was where they were going. We were monitoring them, as was AWACS, which was doing a particularly good job this day. While we were finishing up on the tanker, AWACS told us there were bandits airborne north of the Navy strikers, and they were heading our way. There was no doubt from "Kluso's" radio call that these bandits were ours! We immediately started pressing northeast.

"Cherry" Pitts seen on the boom of a tanker over northern Saudi Arabia. *via Pitts.*

I was on the far right side of the formation, and we had two groups on the radar with about a 30 mile azimuth split, so my targeting responsibility was for the right, or eastern group. Before long, this group turns around and heads back towards Baghdad. This turned out to be the two MiG-29s that "Rico" and "Mole" engaged and killed. We had ramped down into the 20s, and the bandits (western group) were at about 10,000 or so, and going REAL fast. "Kluso" and "J.B." were putting their radars into this western group, and by 25 miles the bandits were maneuvering aggressively. I was splitting my time between the guys that were cold on the east side, which I still believed were my targeting responsibility, and the hot western group. I was starting to get nervous that this might be some sort of a "drag" tactic, setting a trap for us, so I wanted to shoot these guys quick. I made a few sample locks on the west group, but every time I did they would

Self portrait while patrolling over Iraq. *Pitts.*

maneuver hard and break the lock, so it was obvious they were aware of us, and probably had good radar warning gear.

We jettisoned our tanks, and I watched twelve externals tumble away. We started to focus in on the western group as they approached 30 miles. The bandits were now down around 3,000 feet and heading due south at us in a three to five mile lead-trail formation. "Kluso" was targeting the leader, and "J.B." was on the trailer. Just as "Kluso" was ready to shoot the bandits turned west, then further right to north. Now we're stuck in a tail chase outside of weapons parameters. Just then they both turned back to the right and came back south at us. Just as "Kluso" was ready to shoot again, the bandits beamed west and took it down on the deck. We lost our radar locks, and our SA for a bit here, but obviously at least one of the bandits had turned back hot, because I got a radar contact five miles off my nose, going left to right at 500 feet and 700 knots! I was at 10,000 feet, so I called "Engaged!" and split-S'd down towards the bandit. "Kluso" came back with "Press!," which set the roles as me as the shooter and "Kluso" supporting. The bandit was moving so fast that he flew off the right side of my radar scope, he had that much line-of-sight. "Bitching Betty" was screaming at me that I had over-Gd in the split-s (I pulled 12 Gs...), and I had lost the guy off the radar, so I'm not real happy right then.

That low cloud deck worked in my favor, as it helped me get a tally on him, and I was able to VID him as a MiG-25. He was heading east, but as I re-locked him with a boresight Auto Acq. mode he started a break turn to the right. Not that the turn radius of a Foxbat doing 700 knots is very impressive, but he tried. I had no trouble staying inside his circle, and as I ramped down I get to a 7 right aspect as he turns through west. This means I'm looking at the right side of his aircraft, and am just behind his wing-line at 9,000 feet slant range. He's at about 300 feet, and my radar showed he was doing 700 knots! I'm a couple of hundred feet above him with a good AIM-9 tone. I un-cage and shoot an AIM-9M with a good tone, and he put out a shitload of flares that drug it off. So I select AIM-7 with good parameters and get the "SHOOT" cue. I had never shot any of these missiles before, and as I shot that bad-boy there was a big "thunk," and it kind of held formation with me for what seemed like forever, then charged out there and goes right over his canopy. I'm sure this scared the hell out of him, but didn't work. The fuse must not have functioned. He continues his turn and rolls out heading north, now doing about 500 knots; he had lost a couple of hundred knots in his turn. Now I'm camped at his dead six at a range of 6,000 feet, co-speed.

I'm now wondering what it's going to take to knock this guy down! I select another AIM-9, un-cage and get a good tone, and I'm getting ready to fire when he puts out more flares and defeats the AIM-9 on the rail. So I re-caged, un-caged it again with a good tone, and fire it, but he puts out more flares and decoys it. I'm thinking there's no way I'm going to be able to close and gun this guy. So I select AIM-7 again, and I'm right in the heart of the envelope, 6,000 feet behind him, and it's going to catch him, since I'm co-speed. The second AIM-7 went right up his tail pipes and blew up the tail of his aircraft. His ejection seat comes out and I almost hit it, going right over the top of my canopy. I never saw him separate from the seat or a chute, but I wouldn't want to test an ejection seat at 300 feet! I don't see this, but "Kluso" fires an AIM-9 just after my second AIM-7. It went through the fireball right after the ejection. I didn't know this until the debrief. We ended up using five missiles on this guy!

As I pull off this guy after missing the ejection seat, I come off high and a little left. I immediately get a tally on an aircraft about five miles off my nose, to the north. I still had "Kluso" visual to my high left. I call this out to "Kluso," but I have no idea who it is. I've been at "max-rage" for a while, so I'm low on SA and fuel. As soon as I call that tally-ho, "Kluso" got an AUTO GUNS lock on him. "Kluso" had been hawking the fight in AUTO GUNS,

clearing for other guys like he was supposed to, but my SA was pretty low, except for the guy that just blew up. "Kluso" called "Locked," since he was not real comfortable with who this guy was. He gets on our inter-flight frequency and asked if anyone was in burner. I came back with an affirmative. "Kluso" then directed everyone to come out of afterburner. When this bogey doesn't, he knows it's a bad guy. He kills this MiG-25 and calls for everyone to come out south.

We were both hurting for gas, and the tankers were awesome, and came north to get us. While on the tanker, "Rico" and "Mole" showed up after killing the two MiG-29s we had seen as the eastern group. I was a little fuzzy on how "Rico" was claiming a kill while still having all his missiles, but it all came out later on the ground. We finally made it back to Tabuk for the flight debrief and a big cigar!

A couple of weeks later things had become pretty routine (boring), and the rigid four-ships had kind of broken down somewhat. "Kluso" was leading a four-ship roving CAP north of Baghdad, trying to stop the Iraqis from escaping to Iran. I was number 2, and on this day we had "E.T." Murphy, and as guest help from the Fighter Weapons School, Steve "Mongo" Robbins along with us. We were free-roaming all over Iraq, anywhere there weren't SAM rings. While we're up north of Baghdad we look down at this airfield, and all four of us see an IL-76 Candid sitting out on the ramp. We talk it over on the common freq confirming what we see, so "Kluso" calls it in to AWACS. He tells them that they have an IL-76 out in the open and the location, and suggests they send someone like an F-111 or A-10 to come up and take it out. We weren't thinking about strafing it ourselves, since "Cheese" and "Papa" had just gotten in big trouble for strafing a truck. Even Gen Horner had made it clear that the F-15Cs were not in the strafing business. We really weren't trained to do air-to-ground strafe; the FWIC grads had a little experience at it, but my training consisted of sitting in the hooch at Tabuk with some contraband whiskey while "Kluso" taught some techniques!

The very capable Roland missile seen at launch during a test firing. *U.S. Army.*

"Cherry" still in the cockpit of F-15C 85-0099 immediately after the MiG-25 engagement, photo by 099's crew chief. *via Pitts.*

"Cherry" poses for the standard "hero shot" back home at Eglin after the war. *33 TFW/PA via Pitts.*

The AWACS copied our call, and we went about our business and forgot about it. It was a ten hour mission, so we were up there all day. About three hours later "Kluso" calls back to the AWACS and asked if they had sent anybody up to take out the Candid. The answer we got was "ACE (command authority) wants you to confirm that it's a Candid." We're like, "Yeah, it's a Candid, take my word for it." AWACS came back with "ACE directs you to strafe that aircraft." We figure that's direction enough, even with the other previous guidance. "Kluso" decides to send in "E.T." and "Mongo" while we stay hi to cover. "Mongo" rolls in and hits the left wing root, and blows up the whole thing—people are running all over, it was a great shot. It was cool to watch, and they rejoin and all was well.

We hadn't flown another 40 seconds when we see two Cubs on another airfield. "Kluso" figures since we already had clearance to do the Candid, why not do the Cubs? So he decides now it's our turn, so "Kluso" and I each pick a Cub and do a visual sort on the radio, and in we go. I couldn't tell what happened, but "Kluso"

says he saw me get some hits on my Cub, but I didn't see it, as I was already pulling off. As we came off, thinking it was time to call this shit a day, we hear "E.T." and "Mongo" call in hot! This was never "Kluso's" intention, and by now the bad guys have their shit together, and the Roland missile systems are now up. The next thing we hear on the radio is "Mongo" calling a Roland spike and shot in the air. I'm looking back, and while I can't see "Mongo," I do see the Roland fire. "Mongo" is screaming Roland launch, and "Kluso" is screaming for everyone to get out south.

Once we're clear of the field "Kluso" does a check-in on the radio, and "Mongo" doesn't answer. I'm thinking, "Oh, shit, this is gonna suck." "Kluso" tries about three times, and there is still no answer. Finally, out of the blue "Mongo" comes up and says, "I'm here." When we got back on the ground "Mongo" looked beat up! We were all glad we survived, but we figure we are *really* gonna get chewed on for this. As it turned out, Gen Buster Glosson called "Mongo" personally and thought he was a hero! But we were also told not to do it again!

There has been some speculation that these two MiG-25s were possibly being flown by foreign advisors. When I asked "Cherry" about this possibility, his response was that, with the level of skill displayed both pre and post-merge, it leads him to believe that it could have been an "advisor." After completing his Eglin tour, "Cherry" attended Air Command and Staff College at Maxwell AFB, Alabama. Due to a severe back injury returning to ejection seat equipped aircraft was out of the question, so he stayed on as an instructor. Following this he transitioned to the E-3 Sentry AWACS aircraft, and served as both Operations Officer and Squadron Commander at Tinker AFB, Oklahoma. "Cherry" was selected for the National War College in residence, and served on the Joint Staff. He was promoted early to the ranks of Major, Lt Col, and full Colonel. Following his command tour at Officer Training School he retired as a Colonel, and is currently an International Captain on a Bombardier Global Express corporate jet in California.

Captain Rick "Kluso" Tollini (USAF)

58th TFS "Gorillas," F-15C
Operation DESERT STORM
MiG-25 Kill
19 January 1991
Call-sign: CITGO 21

Capt Rick Tollini served as the Chief of Weapons and Tactics for the 58th TFS. He is a graduate of the Fighter Weapons School F-15C Division, and was one of the designated mission commanders for the first wave of Operation DESERT STORM. As "Cherry" Pitts has covered much of the flight admin, "Kluso's" account will pick up at the start of the intercept, as he leads CITGO flight north on the commit against the two bandit groups. The following account is excerpted from the book F-15C Eagle Units In Combat *(© 2005 Osprey Publishing) with the kind permission of "Kluso" Tollini and the Author, Steve Davies.*

Tollini recalled that AWACS had erroneously identified both groups as MiG-29s, but he was more concerned with the fighters' intentions:

"It looked to me like they were doing some kind of a decoy tactic to get us to go after one while the other came in behind us. We got into a cut-off intercept on the first group from the southwest, pointing towards Baghdad, while they were headed due south from Al Assad or Al Taqaddum airfield, northwest of Baghdad. At 35 miles we locked them up, and they started heading east towards Baghdad. As we chased them, we saw the second group in a 30 mile lead-trail formation with the first group, flying in a north-

south orientation. That's what made it look like a decoy tactic to me."

Tollini continued to monitor the first group as it headed off to the northeast, then checked his flight to the north to go head on with the second group as it came south:

"Once we locked the second group up they also maneuvered—this time to the west—and I remember that, as they turned through west to the north, I thought we were going to have to chase them. Fairly quickly they did a 270-degree turn to the south, coming straight at us from 30 miles out in a three- or five-mile lead-trail

"Kluso's" F-15C 85-0101 seen later at Eglin in 1996, still with the "Gorillas." *Alec Fushi via Don Logan.*

58th TFS F-15C seen on alert at Tabuk later in the conflict. By this time the brand new AIM-120 AMRAAMs were being carried and can be seen here on the in-board pylon station above the external fuel tanks. While the 58th TFS was the first to fly the AMRAAM in combat, there were no shots taken using this missile during DESERT STORM. *Pitts.*

formation, down around 3,000 ft MSL (Mean Sea Level – about 2,000 ft Above Ground Level). My intention was to shoot a couple of AIM-7s and kill these guys BVR, so I locked the lead and 'J.B.' Kelk locked the trailer."

Author comments: Neither "Kluso" nor "J.B." got shots off prior to the merge due to timely and effective bandit maneuvers. Tollini's account will pick-up as "Cherry" Pitts is merging with the Bandit.

Tollini recalled the engagement from his own perspective:

"I had 'Willie' Williams searching high and 'Cherry' Pitts searching low after the second group of MiGs beamed us, and we lost them on radar. Fortunately, 'Cherry' was able to grab the trailer as he finished his beam to the east and then turned due south again, and I actually got the lead jet back on radar momentarily before both of them flew off of our scopes. 'Cherry's' guy started his right-hand turn underneath us, and my guy did a high-speed turn through the south, and I saw him leave the fight."

Tollini transitioned from lead to wingman when Pitts called "Engaged" on the first "Foxbat." He followed Pitts through the split-s maneuver that placed him behind the MiG-25:

"The MiG was in a right-hand turn, and we were at very close range when 'Cherry' camped behind him. I joined the fight in a left-hand turn from the southeast, and cut across the circle as the MiG continued its turn from the west towards the northeast. It was then that 'Cherry' started shooting off all of his missiles. He was not having any luck, so I radioed 'Two, come off,' about which he later said to me, 'Kluso, I don't remember you saying that.' My first shot got there a split-second later than his, and although I did not personally see the guy punch out, 'Cherry' said that my missile got there seconds after the seat came out of the aircraft."

With the troublesome "Foxbat" dealt with, Tollini began his own engagement:

"As 'Cherry' peeled off to the west I flew right behind his MiG, and watched it enter the undercast and impact the ground. We had already dropped our wing tanks, and we were all going really fast, so I pulled into a high-G right-hand turn through east to south. As I did that, I had an Auto Acq. mode slewed out to the south—I think more by accident than planning—and as I came around the corner to the south, the radar grabbed the other guy as he came back into the fight.

The instant I snagged him, 'Cherry' saw him visually and called him to me. Then it became an issue of ID again. When we merged the first time we had good ID, but having been spat out of

Following DESERT STORM, Iraq's surviving MiG-25s were used extensively to contest the no-fly zones. After Operation IRAQI FREEDOM in 2003, most of the survivors were discovered buried near Al Taqqadum Air Base, west of Baghdad. Here, a USAF team unearths a MiG-25 Foxbat. *USAF photo by MSgt T. Collins.*

Another view of the MiG-25 Foxbat after the sand and dirt was removed. Many MiG-25s, SU-25s, and a few MiG-29s were found buried in an effort to hide them from Coalition Forces. *USAF.*

the fight I didn't know who he was when he came back in again. I didn't know where 'J.B.' and 'Willie' had gone (they had actually departed the area to provide cover in case the original MiG-29 group attempted to pincer the flight), and I knew that there was a Navy package out there. This left me sitting barely a mile behind my target, looking at its tail, but unsure of what it was.

What I *could* see was the jet's two huge burner plumes, so I asked on the radio if anyone was in burner. Having received various responses, I called everyone to get out of burner—working on the basis that if my target was indeed one of us its pilot would comply. Well, he didn't, so I looked at him more closely, and saw that he had two missile pylons under each wing. Now I knew that it was not an F-15 or F-14. That was the moment I *knew* that my target was a 'Foxbat.' Then I started shooting.

I was in full burner, camped back there in pure pursuit. The pilot of this aircraft was not like the first MiG, in that he was not putting out any chaff or flares. Maybe he could not see me because I was camped in his 'deep six,' or maybe he'd run out of flares—I don't know. But he stayed in this high-G turn. My first AIM-7 was at low aspect, maybe 20 to 30 degrees off of the tail, and I hit the pickle button and waited, but I didn't see the missile flying out in front of me. We don't know for sure, but we think the rocket motor failed to light (the AIM-7 was less than reliable throughout the war, and Bitburg pilots in particular experienced a large number of malfunctions).

I thumbed forward on the throttle-mounted weapons select switch to select an AIM-9, at which point what looked like a single flare popped out of the aircraft—it was not very bright, and it could have even been the pilot punching out, but I think I would have seen more flames if he had indeed ejected.

In any case, I was not that confident that the AIM-9 would get there, having seen what happened to 'Cherry's' missiles, so as soon as I shot it I thumbed back to AIM-7 again. The AIM-9 flew

close to his burner cans—through the plume—but then sailed wide and missed. I then shot the second AIM-7."

In the temporal distortion that many pilots experienced at the time of their kills, Tollini watched the missile guide in a lag-pursuit mode for what seemed to him like minutes. It flew up from beneath the "Foxbat," and then punctured its belly, exploding milliseconds later:

"The explosion was huge, like the Death Star from the *Star Wars* film! The 'Foxbat' totally disintegrated, and I was amazed because that had not happened to 'Cherry's' MiG."

"Kluso" Tollini catching up on some news from home in "Cherry's" room. *Pitts.*

Author comments: With Kelk and Williams covering their egress, Tollini and Pitts quickly headed south for the tanker tracks. Too low on fuel, the tankers came north to rendezvous and refuel the flight. Tollini and Pitts had speculated prior to the war that they might end up fighting "advisors" as well as Iraqi pilots. Tollini offers this:

"Look at it this way. They were either the best or luckiest Iraqi pilots in the world, or they were not Iraqis at all. They should not have survived to the merge—our tactics, weapons, and training should have seen to that—but these guys used tactics both before the merge and at the merge that really impressed me. I often wonder."

Of the many members of the 58ᵗʰ TFS I have interviewed for this book, almost every man attributes a large share of the squadron's success directly to the work of "Kluso" Tollini. His aggressive, can-do attitude kept the 58ᵗʰ TFS going where the MiGs were. Rick retired from the Air Force and currently lives overseas.

Rick "Kluso" Tollini. *USAF.*

Captain Cesar "Rico" Rodriguez (USAF)

58th TFS "Gorillas," F-15C
Operation DESERT STORM
MiG-29 Kill
19 January 1991
Call-sign: CITGO 25

Capt Rodriguez's first kill marks one of the most aggressive fights encountered by any coalition pilot during DESERT STORM. "Mole" Underhill scored the first kill in this engagement, but since "Rico" has covered the "admin" portions of the flight his engagement is published first, out of chronological order. Col Rodriguez wrote the following account for this publication.

I would like to start by going over a little bit of the history of my squadron (58th Tactical Fighter Squadron), which I deployed with in support of Operation DESERT SHIELD, and then was subsequently employed in Operation DESERT STORM. The 58 TFS was commanded by Lt Col Bill Thiel, call sign "Tonic." We deployed in August 1991 from Eglin AFB, Florida, straight shot, all the way across the Atlantic to Tabuk Air Base, Saudi Arabia. Tabuk is located in the northwest sector of Saudi Arabia, near the Jordanian border. Although we deployed under the 58th TFS "Gorillas" flag, we were in reality a combined squadron. We had

eight additional pilots in all from the 59th TFS (the "Lions") and the 60th TFS (the "Crows"). We were all assigned to the 33rd Tactical Fighter Wing ("The Nomads") at Eglin AFB, Florida.

The big picture of the deployment, when it was all said and done, was that in about eight months of deployed flying we flew 3,140 sorties. That's significant, and I'll expand on that in a little bit. Of those 3,140 sorties, during the combat operations, which started on 17 January 1991, my squadron flew a total of 6,900 hours in 43 days. At the end of the entire deployment we had flown more than 15,000 hours, which equates to two years of

F-15C 85-0114 seen just after its return to Eglin AFB after DESERT STORM. *David F. Brown via Don Logan.*

60

the peacetime flying hour program as authorized by Tactical Air Command. The real bottom line is that our squadron attained 16 MiG kills, the highest of any squadron during the operation. Not only did we have the 16 kills, but we also had the first, second, and third kills of the war. The 58ᵗʰ flew more sorties and hours than any other F-15C squadron in theatre, and we also had more pilots with multiple kills—there were four of us. We were the first and the only squadron to carry AMRAAM during DESERT STORM, and that would be a whole story unto itself! We also had the only Marine Corps pilot to get a kill, Capt Chuck "Sly" Magill, on exchange duty with the 58ᵗʰ.

So when you sum all this up, from a "how did we get there" perspective, it all started back home under the tutelage of the previous Squadron Commander, "Paco" Giesler, who demanded and expected nothing less than a training program that would build warriors and hold people accountable to high standards. Squadron training and upgrades were rigorous, and busts were common, but that was okay. He understood these busts meant there was room for improvement, and it pushed the squadron to a higher standard. This all paid off when we deployed, and were able to excel in every mission area. That was one part of it, but this is a triad, and you can't do it with just solid training.

The next part, and the truly unsung heroes of the 58ᵗʰ TFS, were the dedicated and visionary maintenance team members that we had with us. I say dedicated because these folks gave it their all, day in and day out. When their jet was on the ground, they were working every aspect of it so that it was not only looking good, but flying good. Part of that maintenance team included the incredible weapons team, who were challenged to keep the aircraft loaded with weapons, chaff, and flares, and of course the disposable external fuel tanks. Those troops worked tirelessly to ensure that every missile that was loaded was ready to be employed against a hostile enemy. I say visionary, because these troops took the standard operating procedures from back home and adapted. They adapted to the harsh desert environment. They adapted to the 24/7 schedule, where there were many times you could drive down the flight line and there was not one aircraft on the ground; every jet was going to or returning from missions. They knew there was more tasking coming down, and they were going to have to generate aircraft and deliver, in style. They did. Never once did we hear any whining or complaining. What's more, during those 6,900 hours of combat operations, our maintainers produced a 98% Fully Mission Capable (FMC) rate. That is unheard of in peacetime, it is unheard of in combat, and they made it look easy.

The third pillar of the team that made this deployment a success was our tireless support team members. I say tireless, because there were no opportunities for crew rest for them. They came in and they worked, and worked, and worked until everything was done. From our security forces who maintained our perimeter in a very hostile environment, with less than adequate equipment, to our communications folks that worked miracles and got information to us. The services folks, from the minute they got there, were concerned about billeting everyone properly, they were concerned about the physical fitness aspects, and were even prepared to provide the mortuary affairs mission if necessary. They let nothing

stand in their way to provide for us. Transportation and supply, wow! Talk about a team that wouldn't take no for an answer. If the Wing or Squadron Commander said we need this or that, and it wasn't on our base, they went out and found it. This meant scouring the United States, and sometimes roadtrips over much of Saudi Arabia to get us what we needed. The personnel folks were awesome, because whenever there was a Red Cross message or an emergency phone call, or just keeping up with promotion boards, they never let a single person go unattended or un-responded to. The medics that came with us were just phenomenal. They were concerned about the health of everyone, not just those who were flying jets. They recognized that as we were flying these long missions, averaging 6-7 hours, two to three times a day, sleep deprivation and physical fitness were going to be an issue. Our medics, led by Capt "Doc" Kory Cornam, did an outstanding job keeping the whole team fit and ready to fight the fight.

As you look at what our wing, with 24 aircraft, was able to achieve during DESERT STORM, let it not go on deaf ears that the true unsung heroes are those maintainers and those support personnel that complimented our training programs from back home that made it look easy for all of us.

On 19 January 1991, I was the four-ship flight lead of the DCA mission, which was to protect all the assets, such as the AWACS, JSTARS, tankers, and the U-2 south of the Iraqi border. Well into our mission (2-3 hours), after we had already refueled several times, we were notified by AWACS that we needed to refocus our mission to look at several of the airfields in Iraq. We adjusted our CAPs to monitor H-2 and H-3 airfields in western Iraq, as well as Mudaysis, Al Asad, and Al Taqqadum air bases. These were the three main areas where we knew the Iraqis had fighters. As we adjusted our CAP we also got a re-frag on our mission, which required me to split up the four-ship. I sent three and four to the tanker first, so they would have enough gas to execute the new mission or make an intercept as necessary. I then took my wingman, Craig "Mole" Underhill, to the tanker. We topped-off with gas and awaited further guidance. While we completed refueling we monitored the AWACS strike frequency, and we heard several call-signs from our unit, as well as striker call-signs for F-16s and F-4G Wild Weasels. The new mission was a pop-up tasking to strike a newly discovered weapons storage area southwest of Baghdad. The plan was to put some 20-30 F-16s onto this target. They had a variety of targets to hit, and there would be a four-ship of F-15s out front to pre-strike sweep, and then "Mole" and I would be the post-strike sweep F-15s. We were loaded with four AIM-7s, four AIM-9s, three tanks, and a full compliment of chaff and flares.

As we proceeded northbound with the strike package, we decided our primary CAP location was going to be about 20 miles south of the target. The pre-strike sweep was going to run all the way to about 20 miles north of the target before turning back south, and they were a little low on gas, and also frag'ed for a secondary mission. So as we arrived on scene, and everything was looking good; the initial four-ship encountered a variety of targets. Hence, they never made it to the target area and, as a result, the area north of the target was completely unprotected. From our position we could see the entire strike package, both on radar and at times visually, as well as the area north of the target, so we felt pretty comfortable from where we were as we watched the strikers proceed to the target.

We received a call from AWACS, "CITGO 25, pop-up contacts, north 40 of the target area." As we turned back hot towards the target area, "Mole" and I were able to see all of the friendly contacts. Sure enough, about 60 miles from us we picked up two unidentified targets. We proceeded to line ourselves up and execute an intercept. We were up at 30,000 feet, and we proceeded northeast as we were watching the strikers attacking the target. The last strikers had yet to employ ordnance, but they had called in-bound from the IP, so we knew their timing was going to be perfect, and at some point here in front of us, radar-wise, the only things that should have been in front of us would be the two hostile contacts.

"Mole" and I accelerated past the Mach, and we started to execute the intercept on the two unknown contacts that were north of the target area. As we heard the final strike package call off target, and we picked them up visually as they proceeded southbound, we knew we had a clean target area. The tail end of the F-16 strike package is also calling "spiked," or that they are being locked onto by enemy fighters. At this point we're not sure what kind of aircraft they were, but they were about 35 miles in trail with the F-16s. The F-16s were not threatened, and they needed to continue southbound.

Once inside 25 miles we started to sort the targets in azimuth. We proceeded to lock them up, and the targets started to execute some maneuvers commonly known as beam maneuvers. Beaming reduces the closure rate, and also is an opportunity to break our locks from our radars, as the radar sometimes has a problem maintaining a track while the target is in the beam. It's also a maneuver that can be used to gain some energy.

At about 18 nm both of the targets executed a beam maneuver to the northwest. They held that beam maneuver for several seconds, and then, instead of coming back towards us, they proceeded to go towards the northeast, back towards their base of origin.

"Mole" and I had confirmed that all of our strikers were in fact southbound, and well away from the target area, and that these two targets were the only two in the area. They were quickly moving out of our ability to engage them, as we were in a tail-chase. They were about 12-14 miles off our nose, and they had taken it down pretty low; they had pushed it up just about as fast as a MiG-29 could run. We were not at our max speed, but we were well over the Mach; we didn't need to be at our max speed, and we had to think about conserving gas, and then potentially still exiting the fight, since now we were approaching the Baghdad area.

As we approached the Baghdad area, "Mole" and I both received indications that the SAMs from Baghdad were becoming active. They were starting to illuminate our RWR system, and we were about ready to get out of there when AWACS transmitted to us on Guard frequency, "CITGO, pop-up targets 330 for 13." 330 was the heading from me to the targets, and 13 was the range in miles to the targets, and I'm the most western aircraft in our formation. Out of instinct I threw my radar into AUTOGUNS and

slammed the throttles to full afterburner. I pulled 9-9.5g's in the turn to put 330 on my nose, and at the same time reached down and jettisoned my fuel tanks. Shortly thereafter "Mole" followed suit, so now we are in a staggered formation; I'm about 1.5 to two miles in lead of "Mole," and then my AUTOGUNS system locks onto the first contact.

The first contact is a short eight miles in front of me. He's at about 10,000 feet, and I'm at about 2,000 feet AGL. I lock onto this guy, and I start to go through the ID matrix to try to identify him, asking for AWACS and any other off-board systems to help us out. At this point that MiG-29 locks me up, and I get this indication on my RWR. I execute a defensive maneuver; I beam to the southwest and dispense a bunch of chaff to try to break his lock, and cause some problems for the MiG-29's radar, since I'm forcing a look-down scenario with ground clutter and I'm putting out chaff.

I pass on the information to "Mole" that there is a contact eight miles off my nose at 10,000 feet, and then "Mole" comes back that he sees the same thing on his radar. So I ask him to lock the leader, because that's who's locked onto me. As "Mole" executes his identification matrix AWACS declares, "Hostile, Hostile, Hostile!" At this point "Mole" employs a single AIM-7 radar missile against the lead MiG-29, and then executes a left check turn to stay in the same general flow with me.

When I hear "Mole" call "Fox 1" I look over my left shoulder. I'm low altitude, at about a thousand feet, traveling a little over 500 miles per hour. I see the missile come off of his airplane and pull hard to the right, so then I transition my look between the tails of my airplane and then to the right side of my airplane, and I pick up the missile right before it's about to burn out. The rocket motor of the missile burns out, and then it glides using its own momentum to track. From that point, from the last puff of smoke that I see, I then extrapolate north-northwest a little bit, and I'm finally able to see a silhouette of a MiG-29. Its nose was pointed about a half mile behind my aircraft and still holding a radar lock to me. This whole sequence of events happens in less than 10 seconds. Shortly thereafter the missile impacts the MiG-29 square on the nose, literally leaving nothing, and I mean nothing to the imagination other than a big fireball, followed by a large sparkler-like cloud as it all descended to the ground.

I called "Splash one, Splash one!" to AWACS, and to let "Mole" know that he had in fact achieved an aerial victory, and then we start to reform the formation. Shortly after I called splash one, the AWACS controller came back with, "Second bandit, three miles in trail." "Mole" and I are both at low altitude, about two and a half miles split, and he's basically at my dead six. I direct the formation to do a hard turn to the right (to north), and then both of us instinctively put our radars into the sectors that are our briefed responsibility, and we start looking for the second contact.

"Mole" gets the first lock on the new contact. He starts to run his ID matrix, and he determines that this contact is different than the ones before. So to err on the conservative side and not run the risk of a "frat," especially since at this point neither one of us is spiked by a hostile, we start to re-lock and re-accomplish the ID matrix, knowing full well that we may be forced into a VID intercept.

As the bandit was approaching we attempt to identify this aircraft from the front aspect, and at more than 1,000 miles of closure the silhouette and plan-form looked a lot like our western fighters, so before we lose an opportunity to maintain an offensive position, I direct the formation to bracket. This set up the VID intercept, which put me in position to run directly on the threat, to get as close as I can to him and try to identify this particular threat. At about a mile and a half, and well below him, I put the bandit on my nose, and I push it up to five stages of burner. As I pass just below his left wing by 50-100 feet I can clearly see the distinctive Iraqi paint scheme, his national markings, and that it is definitely a MiG-29. I call "Bandit, Bandit, Bandit."

Mole has positioned himself well above the fight at roughly 20,000 feet as I merged left-to-left and start a hi-g left turn to maneuver behind the MiG. I watch the MiG continue his left turn in a lazy, almost nonchalant, non-aware way. Perhaps he had seen a canopy glint to the north, where "Mole" had been about 30 seconds prior. As he is executing his turn, I'm able to maneuver from starting 180 degrees out to a position of advantage about 40 degrees off his tail at a range of about 4,000 feet. I finally get an indication that he sees me as he breaks into me, placing his lift vector slightly below me, and attempting to bring his nose around to the left to point at me. I have plenty of airspeed, so I let him complete his first defensive turn and deplete some energy while I float out to lag his turn and gain some more energy. I climb slightly to get above him somewhat. We continue through about one full circle, and by the time we are into our second 360 degrees I have managed to close to within about 3,000 feet. I still have a lock, and I'm bringing my nose to bear in an attempt to employ an AIM-7. I opt to go with the AIM-7 as we are at low altitude over the hot desert, and we had seen some problems with the heat-seeking AIM-9 in this environment. As I get my nose on the bandit he is at about 1,000 AGL, and I'm at about 2,000 AGL. The bandit then attempted to execute a split-S by unloading, rolling upside down, and pulling through the bottom. This maneuver normally takes about 3-4,000 feet of altitude to complete successfully, even with the MiG-29's small turn radius. I wasn't going to take any chances, so I rolled hard off of his tail and climbed it up into the vertical. I then rolled to look down and re-acquire a tally on the bandit. I then witness the bandit impact the ground. As he hit the desert floor he hadn't quite gotten perpendicular to the ground yet. I could clearly see his afterburners cooking, and his stabs were dug in. He hits the ground, and the wreckage continues to create a fireball for miles across the desert. I come off this position and am about to call for "Mole's" position when he comes up on the radio, "I'm at your right three, tactical low, let's get out of here!"

As we completed our mission, "Mole" and I realized that a lot had happened in a very short period of time. We had experienced our first combat, and we had started the engagement from a very

Capt Rodriguez pictured with his daughter upon returning to Eglin AFB, 1991. It is very unique that "Rico" got both of his kills in the same F-15C, 85-0114. *via Rodriguez.*

defensive position. The second group of MiG-29s had a complete advantage over us at the start of the fight. Through hard training and solid squadron standards between flight leads and wingmen, "Mole" and I were able to successfully complete this piece of the mission, with surprisingly little comm. We knew what each of us was doing, and we had our contract. When we deviated from the contract, we communicated it. We were also very concerned about the possibility of a frat, with the number of friendly aircraft in the vicinity. We also knew our primary job was to protect the strikers, and this was foremost in our minds.

We accomplished our first "real" combat battle damage check as we returned to Saudi airspace. We came home to a hero's welcome, as word had been passed back to Tabuk of our victories. "Mole" and I were not the only Gorillas to score this day, so our troops got to build up some more missiles, hang some new tanks, and best of all, hear first hand the accounts of the kills from each of us.

Capt Rodriguez has two more kills featured in this book: one more during DESERT STORM, and also the first kill of Operation ALLIED FORCE.

Captain Craig "Mole" Underhill (USAF)

58th TFS "Gorillas," F-15C
Operation DESERT STORM
MiG-23 Kill
19 January 1991
Call-sign: CITGO 26

Capt Underhill graduated Texas A&M in 1981, and was initially assigned as a Navigator on C-130s at Dyess AFB, Texas, for about four years. He was subsequently selected for pilot training, and was awarded an F-15C to Eglin AFB, arriving in August 1988. By the time of the August 1990 deployment to Tabuk, Craig was a two-ship flight lead with about 350 hours in the Eagle. As "Rico" Rodriguez has sufficiently covered the prelude to their engagement, Craig has agreed to pick it up at the push.

We were covering the egress of a strike package led by "Kluso" Tolini's four-ship. It was early in the morning—I think our Vul. Period was 0700-1100 to cover the HVAA CAP, and "Kluso" coordinated with "Rico" for our four-ship to help cover their egress. Our flight consisted of Cesar "Rico" Rodriguez as lead, with me as number two. Mike "Fish" Fisher was number three, with Pat "Pat-O" Moylan as number four.

While cycling our two-ship to the tanker, "Rico" and I were advised that "Kluso's" flight was getting tapped by MiG-29 Fulcrums, a couple of F-1s, and Foxbats (MiG-25s). So we dropped off the tanker and started heading north in a line-abreast formation, with me one mile on the east, or right side. While we are committing north, we observe some friendly contacts going down the left side of the scope that should not be there (more on

"Mole" Underhill back at Eglin AFB with his MiG-killing F-15C, tail number 85-0122, in 1991. *via Craig Underhill.*

this later), and then more contacts down the right that we identified as the egressing strike package. We also see a couple of unknown contacts behind the strikers following them out of the AOR. We are about 40 miles from these contacts when we lock them up and start working IDs on them. We get hostile indications—they are MiG 29s. At about 30 miles they turn back north and start heading towards Al Taqqadum Air Base.

About this time AWACS gave us a pop-up call, "Bandits bearing 330 for 13 miles." This puts them on our left, at about our seven to eight o'clock position. "Rico" immediately calls for "Combat 2," which includes jettisoning all three of our tanks, and for a break turn to the left. This in-place turn puts me at "Rico's" 7 to 8 o'clock, off-set to the south of him in 1.5 mile trail as we flew into this pop-up group. I had my radar in a 20 mile sweep mode, while "Rico" was in a short range auto-acquisition mode (AUTOGUNS). I get two contacts on our nose at 12 miles in a 3-5 mile echelon formation, with the trailer off-set to the north. I lock the leader and start to work an identification.

"Rico" had been having problems with his Radar Warning Receiver (RWR), and didn't have much faith in it. He could tell the contacts were hot-nosing us, but couldn't tell if he was targeted, so he decides to react defensively, turning 90 degrees to the left, kind of south-southwest. At about 8.5 miles I get a positive hostile and fire one AIM-7, which chugs away like a freight train. As the missile goes under my nose it starts to pull lead, and then proceeds to go right over the top of "Rico's" jet. That was an eye-opener! We always talk about "clear field of fire," but it's different when you see it.

We had been ramping down from the mid-20s throughout this engagement, so I was in the teens when I fired, and in his notch "Rico" was down to six to seven thousand feet. I check left to keep my target illuminated and to flow with "Rico," when I lose sight of "Rico" and go blind. I can't believe it; here we are 50 miles south of Al Asad, the only two friendlies in the area, and I'm blind! So I start to time share between watching my missile guide and looking for "Rico." I finally pick him up real low, at about the same time that I see my missile go pure on the bandit, so I'm pretty confident that it is guiding correctly, and start spending more time keeping sight of "Rico." Just then I hear "Rico" call "Splash one!," and I look back and see a brown cloud where the MiG used to be. At that sight I break lock with my radar and dive in the notch with "Rico." We were now flowing out to the southwest.

We were working to get our mutual support back together when AWACS called that the surviving bandit was five miles to our east. So we bend it back around, and while I delayed my turn a little, I still ended up slightly in front of "Rico." I got an immediate AUTOGUNS snag lock on a bandit at 10,000 feet in a right turn around the brown cloud that used to be his flight lead. I'm getting ready to shoot an AIM-7, when out of habit I ran another identification attempt and got a friendly indication. Being that this is about ten in the morning and we are looking up at the rising sun, all I could tell was that the aircraft had two tails. Seeing this, and with a friendly indication, I held off on shooting. As I closed to a gun weapons employment zone he entered an aggressive left turn, and was in a descending 135 degree bank slice. I tell "Rico" that he is going to have to VID this guy, since I was still getting the friendly indication.

As I come off the bandit and I'm flowing between his tails, I hear "Rico" call, "Engaged...Fulcrum" at the same time I see the same thing. I flowed out to the north to look for a re-entry opportunity and to clear the area for other bandits. As "Rico" slides in on the remaining Fulcrum, to the best of my recollection the MiG starts to tighten it up and stays extremely nose low. I see what I think are two wing tanks come off of the Fulcrum, and since "Rico" has the MiG so nose low I try to get a call off to "Rico" to watch out for the tanks. The fight is going downhill so fast that the tanks were already well above "Rico" by the time I get the call out. I don't think "Rico" ever saw them come off the MiG.

I'm now around to the north, starting to pitch back into the fight as the guy starts to roll and tuck one more time going from the northwest back towards the south. As he does that, I think "Rico" and I were thinking the same thing. With the maneuverability that the aircraft displayed at the Paris air show, we were thinking he was going to perform a split-S through the bottom and attempt to run. "Rico" lags off so as not to hit the ground, and I've locked the guy from the north. The MiG is pulling through about 80 degrees nose low when its nose impacts the desert floor. It was quite an explosion as this guy starts rolling across the desert.

Believe it or not, we end up in perfect tactical formation, just like you script in Air Combat Maneuvering (ACM) scenarios. I think we did one little check turn, and we're line abreast at 500 feet AGL, hauling the mail when my bingo bug goes off. This is a humorous side note—we had never reset our bingo fuel bugs from our HVAA area to now wandering several hundred miles into Iraq. So our bingo fuel is a *little low* for where we are now! To make a long story short, I decide I'm not going to step over the side for this, and I let "Rico" know that I don't have the gas to stay down low and fast. So we pop up to about 24,000 feet and start coordinating for a tanker. As we're headed south, I hear "Fish" and "Pat-O" pressing north against a couple of F-1s, and the Fulcrums that we originally committed against were also now coming south again.

We do pick up a tanker, the same one that "Kluso's" four-ship is on, even though we are not on the same frequency. But it was good to see all four of "Kluso's" Eagles, and to know that "Fish" and "Pat-O" were okay. Even after getting a good VID on the Fulcrum the friendly ID had shook me pretty bad, and I was pretty worried that we had waded into a couple of F-15s. Even though I was certain it was a Fulcrum by the time he hit the ground, it was still great to have full accountability on all the F-15s.

Another side note—I wasn't supposed to be on this mission. I had just finished my fifth or sixth sortie doing similar HVAA CAP

Craig Underhill's F-15C seen at Eglin AFB immediately after returning from Saudi. *David F. Brown via Don Logan.*

missions. I was supposed to have about twelve hours off, and then I was supposed to do a MiG sweep. As it was, I had landed at about 0030L, and had about four hours before doing this mission. I was bumped by our wing commander, who took my mission. So I got moved up to fly with "Rico," and I don't think I had ever flown an ACM mission with "Rico" before this in training. I know we had flown some two-ship BFM sorties, but to go out and fly this kind of mission with someone that you've never really trained with, and have it work out as well as it did proved that our training and standards in our Wing worked. Our roles and responsibilities were well understood, and our one "engaged-supporting" role swap worked like a peach. This was something I carried forward to other units...that standards are there for a reason. That way you can fly with anyone and it will work out.

The radar contacts we initially saw to our west as we committed north ended up being a Navy strike package that was being chased by the MiG-29s we were chasing. They contacted us after the war when they were upgrading from the A-7 to the F/A-18. Since they were just up the road in Pensacola, Florida, they invited our squadron up, and we had quite a party.

It was very rewarding to come up initial with "Rico" and do our victory rolls, while the flight I was supposed to be in was sitting number one for takeoff. So I guess I owe my wing commander my thanks for bumping me from that sortie so I could go out and do what I had trained to do for a couple of years. So that's my story of 19 January 1991. It was a pleasure to be flying with "Rico" that day!

Capt Underhill went on to serve twenty-three years in the USAF, retiring as a Lt Col in 2004. His career culminated at Nellis AFB, Nevada, where he served as the USAF Aggressor Squadron Commander, and the Deputy Commander for Red Flag.

Craig "Mole" Underhill with his Dedicated Crew Chief (DCC) back at Eglin in 1991. *via Craig Underhill.*

1st Lieutenant David "Abby" Sveden (USAF)

525th TFS "Bulldogs," F-15C
Operation DESERT STORM
Mirage F-1 Kill
19 January 1991
Call-sign: RAMBO 04

1Lt Sveden graduated from Union College, and received his commission through AFROTC in 1987. He had been at Bitburg on his first tour for nine months when this engagement took place. Dave had about 180 hours in the F-15, and was a wingman in the 525th TFS. Dave wrote the following account for this book.

Our squadron deployed to Incirlik Airbase, Turkey, in mid-December 1990, as a contingent of primarily European-based aircraft began to assemble that month. F-16s from Torrejon Airbase, Spain, were there for a pre-planned training deployment. They were joined by F-111Es based in England, F-16s and F-4Gs from Germany, and 10 aircraft from our Bitburg based 525th TFS "Bulldogs." Due to Turkey's host-nation rules, any more F-15s exceeded the maximum number of foreign fighters allowed into their country at one time. We were also not allowed to bring in AIM-7 Sparrow missiles, because the Turks viewed them as "offensive" weapons. The general consensus among the pilots was that Turkey would not allow offensive strikes to be conducted from its base. We dreaded the thought of deploying and getting our hopes up,

only to end up as spectators from what was a tantalizingly close vantage point.

Due to the planned deployment to Saudi Arabia of the 53rd TFS — another Bitburg based squadron — most of our training sorties were allocated to their pilots. The "Nifty Fifty," as we called them, came to our squadron through the fall and into December. They flew our jets and our sorties, since they were to deploy and we were not. As a result many of our pilots, including me, lost our "mission ready" status, and needed re-training before we could participate in combat operations. I arrived at Incirlik on New Year's Eve after returning from a stateside TDY (Temporary Duty). I spent the next two weeks completing a Mission Qualification Training syllabus to return to MR status as the 16 January deadline set by President Bush drew closer.

Lt Dave Sveden's F-15C 79-0021 seen at its home base of Soesterburg Air Base, Camp New Amsterdam, The Netherlands. This is the only 32nd TFS jet to score a kill during DESERT STORM. Only one 32nd TFS pilot scored a kill ("Muddy" Watrous) during DESERT STORM, but he was flying a Bitburg (BT) jet at the time. *Ed Groenendijk.*

The deadline finally arrived, and we still had no new information about the role we were to play in this conflict. As the war kicked off on the 17th I was assigned to sit alert, ready to launch in the event our base came under attack. No one was certain how neighboring Arab countries would react now that hostilities were under way. We borrowed some AIM-9s for the alert jets from the Torrejon F-16s. Unfortunately, we still lacked AIM-7s to properly arm our aircraft, and were going to be forced into a visual fight if launched to defend the base. I listened to news reports on a small radio my crew chief brought to our aircraft shelter. We spent most of the day there with little to do except wait. In the afternoon, one of the well known "Air Force One" 707 aircraft touched down, and the expected entourage met it as it parked. Secretary of State James Baker arrived for what ended up being about a three hour meeting with the Turkish Prime Minister. As the sun was setting Baker returned to his aircraft, and it quickly departed the fix. Whatever he said to the Prime Minister obviously was effective. About two hours later the first of 18 F-15Cs touched down loaded for bear, and preparations to launch our first strike quickly began.

Our mission on 19 January 1991 began with a tense session of mission planning, a briefing, and 1125Z takeoff to meet a 1300Z (1500L) Time On Target (TOT). We attempted a day mission the previous afternoon, but turned back at the border due to weather. The morning mission earlier on this day also canceled due to weather, leaving two of the three northernmost fighter bases intact. Unfortunately our target was Kirkuk airbase, which was 120 miles into Iraq, and required us to fly past these untargeted airbases. We were fairly concerned that enemy fighters from these bases would launch as we went past, and we'd become trapped at our "six," forcing us to fight our way out as we egressed. Apparently the flexibility required to re-target and honor this threat was not presented as an option at this early stage of the war.

Seven tankers and approximately 40 aircraft made up the package. The force consisted of 12 F-15Cs, 16 F-16Cs, F-4G/F-16 SAM suppression, EF-111 jamming platforms, and other support assets. Our four-ship lead was "Gunga" Dingee, who had just graduated from the Fighter Weapon School and PCS'd (Permanent Change of Station) to our squadron while we were deployed to Incirlik. Number two was "Von" Ludwig, a former A-10 pilot a couple of years into his first tour in the Eagle. Three was "Spyro" Prather, an instructor pilot approaching the end of his first three year tour in the F-15. I was four, a new wingman about nine months into my first flying assignment in the USAF. Our plan was a straightforward run at Kirkuk with a route chosen to avoid known SAM sites, and allow us to look at active fighter bases for reaction as we passed. We had two four-ship walls of F-15Cs pushing out 20 miles in front of the package. The additional four-ship remained in Turkish airspace to protect the HVAA. "RAMBO" was the lead four-ship callsign, with "Gunga" as air-to-air mission commander. "CONAN" was the second four-ship, made up of pilots from the 32nd TFG, based in the Netherlands. Pilots and aircraft from that unit were tasked to supplement our squadron. In fact, I had been assigned to fly one of their aircraft on this mission. Thanks to the established tactics used by the F-15 community, we were able to easily combine forces with these pilots. The four-ships were split by about six miles line abreast. Ten miles behind us the Wild Weasel aircraft were ready with their HARMs. The bulk of the package followed ten miles behind them, and consisted of F-16Cs carrying various ordnance loads designed for destruction of the airfield's assets and area denial.

We came off our tanker and climbed above the rest of the strike force. We hit our push point on time and crossed into Iraq. The large mountain range that visually depicts the border disappeared under our nose, and the relatively flat desert of northern Iraq lay before us. The sun was getting lower in the west, now at our two to three o'clock as we pushed south. Unfortunately, the contrail level at this time of year began at very low altitude, and extended well above 40,000 feet. We were forced to ingress below 25,000 feet to avoid highlighting ourselves. The weasels were reporting some sporadic SAM search radar activity, which was an obvious concern. A couple of minutes into our push, AWACS began to call out a single group of "Bandits" in a CAP just northeast of their

Dave's line-up card from his MiG-killing mission. These cards were filled out before every mission, and contain all the details required to execute the planned sortie. *Dave Sveden.*

base, Qavyarah West. Our route was drawing us to the southeast toward Kirkuk, and as we continued in that direction, this group of bandits was drifting to the right on our radar scope. At a range of about 40 nm from the bandits, "Gunga" called our four-ship to check right, and we began to split slightly from the rest of the package. As the bandits turned "hot" into us, we could see them on our radar. When they turned "cold," they would disappear.

We continued to close on the bandits as they orbited in their CAP. Finally, they either made the decision on their own or were told to commit on us. At the same time they made this fateful decision, "Gunga" committed us away from the strike package, and called for an additional check turn to the west. The bandits were on our nose, cold, and quickly popped up on our scope as they turned hot. I was designated as the guy to get the ID in our mission briefing, so I quickly took a lock and attempted to ID them in accordance with our ROE. Since AWACS already called them "Bandit," we only had to ensure they were not indicating friendly. As we closed inside of 25 miles, we jettisoned the two wing tanks we were carrying and continued the intercept.

Just inside of 20 miles, "Spyro" got on the radio and said, "RAMBO 3, has got a side-side breakout, on the nose for 20." "Gunga" came back with, "Same." Next was "RAMBO 3, sorted side at 7000 feet" and, "RAMBO 1 same, 9000." "Gunga," on the south side of our formation, locked the southern bandit, while "Spyro" took the northern. Based on the altitude of my lock, I realized I cross-locked the same aircraft as "Gunga."

This was not a big concern, as I wasn't expecting to shoot at this time. I was also reluctant to break my lock as we closed inside 15 miles. At this point, knowing that AWACS had a tendency to overuse the word "Bandit" in training, "Gunga" asked for a final "Bandit" declaration to clarify our ability to fire BVR. Technically they met our ROE to shoot, and I fully expected "Gunga" and "Spyro" to start letting loose with missiles at any moment. At 15 miles, head on, we were less than a minute from merging with the bandits, and seconds away from their first opportunity to shoot at us.

Because of the large check turns to the west at the start of the engagement, our formation became slightly skewed. "Spyro" and I were still line abreast, but were ahead and further north than one and two. As we now closed inside of 15 miles, the bandits began a turn to the north, away from "Gunga" and "Von," and directly at "Spyro" and me. We had the only available shots now. I didn't have this level of situational awareness at that moment. What I did know was I had an ID on a hot bandit on my nose approaching the point where he could shoot. I transmitted, "RAMBO – Fox" and sent my first live missile (an AIM-7) on its way. I looked south at "Spyro" to check his six and my formation, and saw the first of what would be three AIM-7s leave his aircraft. It did not guide, and he followed up with two additional shots. Since I still had some concerns about my bandit's ability to begin shooting back at me, I started a check maneuver to the north. This involved a hard turn away from the bandit while still keeping him illuminated with my radar. As I rolled and began to pull, I noticed my bandit started a hard turn to the north, taking his nose off me. As his nose continued past the point that he could not see me with his radar,

the threat he posed to me was negligible. I centered him in my HUD and got a tally-ho just inside ten miles, as his maneuver presented a planform view of his aircraft. I don't know if this was an actual attempt at an evasive beam maneuver, or possibly a turn directed by GCI. I continued to press the attack, and at about four miles, the bandit began to pitch back into me. I think he saw one or more of us at that time. As he came out of the beam, I launched a second AIM-7 before he could get his nose onto me, concerned my first shot had been defeated by his maneuvers. Three seconds after my second shot, my first missile arrived and detonated near the bandit's tail. His aircraft immediately went out of control and started tumbling end over end. "Splash!" "Gunga" transmitted, just as "Spyro's" bandit sledded into his second and third missiles, and that aircraft disappeared in a long, expansive fireball. "Two kills!" "Von" yelled.

Due to a fuel transfer malfunction in "Gunga's" jet he was getting low on gas. His fuel state required us to egress immediately, and he called, "All RAMBOs out north." Normally we would have flown past the fireballs toward the airfield the bandits took off from, now less than 15 miles to our southwest, looking for additional threats. I rolled to the right and turned my belly to the bandits, making a hard turn to north. As I rolled out, I looked west and saw my bandit inside of two miles, trailing flames and missing his tail, pointing straight down at the ground. I recognized the aircraft as a French built Mirage F-1. Since he no longer posed any threat I quickly began to look for new threats, especially to the southwest and the enemy airfield.

We egressed north toward the border. Once we crossed back into Turkish airspace we closed our formation. I was a little surprised to see "Spyro" was missing three AIM-7s. I only saw his first shot in the heat of the battle. We continued home toward the base. Once we were in radio range of Incirlik, we contacted squadron operations and told them they better put the champagne on ice. We were referring to an old bottle of Russian champagne that a departing pilot donated to our squadron bar years earlier. He put a label on it that read: "To be opened by the first Bulldog to kill a MiG." Of course we brought it along to Incirlik—just in case. Ops asked for tail numbers in an effort to identify the lucky Bulldogs. We passed the information along, and continued our return to the base. There were no victory rolls, but we hit initial at 500 knots and looked pretty good.

We had to hot-pit refuel the aircraft to turn them for the next mission. The first person I was able to talk to about the mission was the fueler on the headset. We talked briefly about the engagement and he congratulated me. We both seemed of the mind that this would be the first of many successful engagements. Little did we all know that the Iraqi's taste for air-to-air combat would quickly sour. With fueling complete I was able to taxi back to the aircraft shelters, where all available pilots in the squadron were waiting to congratulate us.

Almost before I was able to un-strap and gather my things, someone was painting a kill marking on the aircraft I flew. We were surrounded by well wishing pilots, and one came up to me and said goodnaturedly, "How dare you get a kill before me!" This scene was truly like something out of a movie. As I stepped around

"Abby" Sveden and "Spyro" Prather (holding bottle) at Sveden's jet moments after climbing from their cockpits. Note the "low-vis" 32nd TFS patch on the Soesterburg-based F-15C 79-021. *Dave Sveden.*

the side of my jet, "Spyro" quickly appeared with a big grin and a handshake. He had the champagne and shook it, popped the cork, and proceeded to douse my head. It wasn't very good to drink, but that really didn't matter much to either of us. We headed into the squadron to debrief and watch our tapes. Later that night we went to the O-Club and bought the bar.

I've told this story quite a few times. As an FTU instructor a few years later, I frequently had the privilege of passing on some firsthand combat experience to the next generation of MiG killers. One thing I always stressed about F-15 pilots in the USAF and our training was that just about any other Eagle driver put in my cockpit that day would have executed as well or better. I got one of the "right time – right place" chances available that day and made the best of it. The greatest thing about this mission and the ones that followed was the privilege to fly with true warriors. They are guys I easily trusted with my life, and knew would watch my back. They are fighter pilots in every sense of the word, and a new wingman couldn't have asked for better leaders. They made it look easy.

1Lt Sveden went on to fly two more tours in the F-15, and then joined an F-15 Air National Guard unit. Dave is a Major in the Air National Guard, and currently flies for a major airline.

F-15C 79-0021 seen at Soesterburg prior to DESERT STORM. Note the older style full-color 32nd Tactical Fighter Squadron "Wolfhounds" patch on the side of the intake. *Chris Blommendaal.*

Captain David "Spyro" Prather (USAF)

525th TFS "Bulldogs," F-15C
Operation DESERT STORM
Mirage F-1 Kill
19 January 1991
Call-sign: RAMBO 03

Capt Prather graduated the Air Force Academy, and was commissioned in 1986. He had been at Bitburg on his first tour for over two years when this engagement took place. "Spyro" had about 550 hours in the F-15, and was a four-ship flight lead in the 525th TFS. The following account was written by "Spyro" for this book.

For the record, I was number three in a four-ship of F-15Cs assigned to protect a large package of coalition strike fighters attacking targets in Northern Iraq on January 19, 1991. Our call sign was "RAMBO 1-4," and we were one of three F-15 four-ships on that mission. We were part of the world famous 525th TFS "Bulldogs" from Bitburg, Germany. The rest of our package consisted of USAF F-16s, F-4s, EF-111s, and RF-4s. We were directly assisted by dedicated AWACS, KC-135, EC-135, and EC-130 aircraft.

Our flight lead, Steve "Gunga" Dingee, was also the overall air-to-air mission commander that afternoon, which allowed us to place ourselves in the area most likely to see enemy air action.

We were right. Several minutes after crossing the Turkish-Iraqi border, AWACS called out a bogey two-ship approximately 60 miles southwest of our position. As our sister four-ship led most of our package southeast towards Kirkuk, our flight flew towards Qayyarah West and the bogeys, with several Wild Weasel F-4s/F-16s in trail.

RAMBO 1 ("Gunga") was an outstanding combat leader, who inspired confidence in everyone playing a part in the air-to-air portion of the mission. He calmly directed our four-ship to commit to intercepting the bogeys, and to jettison our external tanks. I really wanted to watch all the tanks falling, but was too preoccupied with the task at hand to roll upside down momentarily to look.

F-15C 79-0069 seen in May 1986. *Don Logan collection.*

RAMBO flight, left to right: "Abby" Sveden, "Spyro" Prather, "Von" Ludwig, and "Gunga" Dingee. *via Prather.*

The presentation on my radar looked like thousands of practice intercepts before. The cadence on the radios between AWACS, RAMBO 1, and myself was also very much like training, and almost seemed routine. What wasn't routine was the uneasy feeling of approaching SAM rings, and the amount of time I spent watching the ground beneath our formation some 25,000' below, worriedly anticipating SAM launches at any second.

Looking behind us sometimes revealed the smoke of friendly F-4s, and looking to my left I noticed I was creeping forward of my leader a mile and a half away. As we checked our wall formation to the southwest, my wingman and I were slightly ahead of RAMBO 1 and 2. RAMBO 2 was Larry "Von" Ludwig, on the far left of the wall. RAMBO 4 was David "Abby" Sveden, to my right. The intercept geometry was crucial to the resulting weapons envelopes and bandit maneuvers that would allow shots only from "Abby" and me. Unlucky for RAMBO 1 and 2.

There was also minor confusion concerning the long-range confirmation of the targets as "hostile." That was a very important ingredient to employing weapons before the Iraqis could lock and shoot back. With radars sorted to different targets, it became apparent that the F-1s had been committed to intercept us. We were now closing at Mach one to within 20 miles of their home base, and I wondered whether the enemy SAMs would remain quiet with their own aircraft operating nearby.

Just outside of 10 miles from the F-1s I shot an AIM-7 Sparrow, still beyond visual range. We had accelerated and descended to 15,000 feet, while the F-1s remained below 7,000 feet. My missile didn't guide. I shot a training missile in the Gulf of Mexico a year earlier, and I knew it should be leading the target like a football throw. As it sailed away from the target, I recalled the highly-complicated electronic sequence required in a successful AIM-7 shot, and remembered the difficulty I had getting my radar to work earlier in the mission. This was not going well.

Everything still looked good on the radar, so I quickly shot another missile. Good missile! The AIM-7 is large, with a lot of initial smoke. Watching multiple Sparrows flying from a wall of Eagles towards two bad guys was an impressive sight I'll never forget. Now I felt a very strong desire to make sure the HUD camera was filming this, because no one would ever believe it otherwise! I also shot a third missile about 7 miles out, as it was normal to send two "good ones" for an acceptable probability of kill for a forward hemisphere face-shot. As I shot the third missile, I noticed a spec in the target designator box in the HUD. The range was too great to identify the Mirage F-1, but I could see it turning to my right. It turned almost 80 degrees, but the missiles corrected. I momentarily felt a little like a spectator, waiting an eternity for the missile to time-out. I saw the second bandit, in formation with my bandit, and saw "Abby" shoot an AIM-7 as his bandit maneuvered to pull its nose back towards our formation.

Then, flash! Although a fairly bright, overcast afternoon, the fireballs were bright! I didn't like the attention the fireballs might bring to the engagement from other possible Iraqis nearby. With my HUD pointed at the bandits, "Abby's" target came apart first in an elongated explosion. Two to three seconds later my second missile detonated in a round fireball, quickly magnified by the explosion of my third missile. Wow!

"Gunga" made a "Splash two" call to AWACS, and we turned over the fireballs to head back north. We didn't have enough gas to stick around much longer, and leaving the SAM rings flying towards Turkey seemed like a great idea. When we rejoined in close formation on a tanker in Turkey, I was stunned to see that all the missiles were still hanging on RAMBO 1 and 2's aircraft. "Abby" was missing two. We were all missing all our external tanks. We quickly sorted out the basic facts over the secure radio. Only then was it obvious that RAMBO 1 and 2 didn't get a shot. I knew they'd be disappointed on the ground.

The scene at Incirlik upon landing was also memorable. Word had traveled fast around the base prior to our return. It was the second full day of air-to-air combat since Vietnam ended. We only knew of a handful of other kills so far. Our squadron maintenance folks couldn't wait to see the lucky aircraft missing ordnance, and

Iraqi Mirage F-1EQ in a clean configuration. The Mirage F-1EQ was reported to be a favorite among Iraqi pilots due to its western-style cockpit controls and excellent handling. *USAF.*

were excited to paint the kills on the airplanes. Some squadron pilots met us at the airplanes. They were happy for us, but obviously all waiting for their chance to do the same thing the next day. We opened a special bottle of Russian champagne. Many years before someone had labeled it, "To the First Bulldog to Kill a MiG," and placed it in the Bulldog bar in Germany. All of us dreamed of opening it someday, but doubted whether anyone would ever get the chance. We did.

Air-to-air combat has always had a significant amount of luck influencing outcomes. We were certainly in the right place at the right time, and the Iraqi F-1s were not. There are so many fighter pilots who would have loved to have had our opportunity! There were some significant Bulldogs who were forced to leave the squadron before we went to war. Their mark on the unit was greatly felt, even if they weren't there flying with us. We didn't forget to raise our glass to those old "Bulldogs," including "Spalding," "Snooter," "Treeman," "Glue," "Grit," "Dzeus," "Ricki," "Cutt," "Fang," "Hose," "T-Bag," "Wrut-Row," "Bloomer," "Sniz," and Apex (the bulldog).

Capt Prather went on to fly two more tours in the F-15C, and also flew the F-16 as an Aggressor for five years at Nellis AFB, Nevada. "Spyro" is a Lieutenant Colonel in the Air Force Reserve, and currently flies for a major airline.

With my Dedicated Crew Chief, SSgt Liburd. *via Prather.*

Captain Anthony "Kimo" Schiavi (USAF)

58th TFS "Gorillas," F-15C
Operation DESERT STORM
MiG-23 Kill
26 January 1991
Call-sign: CITGO 26

Capt Tony Schiavi graduated UPT at Laughlin AFB, Texas, in 1988. Upon completing F-15C training at Tyndall AFB, Florida, he was directly assigned to the 58th TFS of the 33rd Tactical Fighter Wing, Eglin AFB, Florida. "Kimo" had been in the squadron for two years, and had flown 10 DESERT STORM missions prior to this engagement. The article on which this is based was published in the title Gulf Air War Debrief, *and is reproduced by permission of Aerospace Publishing Limited, 2006. © Aerospace Publishing Limited and © "Kimo" Schiavi. "Kimo" has edited this account for this publication.*

The mission we were on was protection—a "high value airborne asset" (HVAA) combat air patrol, which we called a HVAACAP (in this case protecting an E-3B/C Sentry AWACS aircraft). By this time in the war, we were doing so well in the air-to-air portion that we had a lot of flexibility. This was unlike earlier when, if you were tied to the HVAA, you were doing only HVAACAP. If you were doing a sweep, you did only that. Things were more stringent because the threat was much higher.

We had an eastern AWACS, a central AWACS, and a western AWACS, and they all just covered their own ground. "COUGAR" and "BUCKEYE" were the call signs for the western and central AWACS.

But at this point we're into the war about nine days, and we're doing pretty well. Maybe you're on a HVAACAP mission, but they'll call up and say, "Hey, there's a strike package of x number of F-111s, how would you like to do a pre-strike sweep for them?" Or a CAP between a threat area and a target airfield? So you could go up on a routine HVAA mission and have something good happen.

We'd been up on CAP for about an hour and a half. We'd just gone down to the tanker to get our first air refueling. We were 80 to 90 miles southeast of H2 and H3 airfields, near the Jordanian border. We were a four-ship on the tanker. My two-ship was the second to fuel up. As we were coming off the tanker, AWACS

"Kimo" Schiavi in front of his MiG-killing F-15C, 85-0104, at Tabuk, Saudi Arabia, after his kill. This configuration was standard for almost all F-15C sorties flown during DESERT STORM. *via Schiavi.*

called and said, "Hey, we've got bandits taking off from H2, a whole group of them, heading northeast." At that point in time CHEVRON 26, our flight lead, Captain Rhory Draeger, asked for permission to commit on them. AWACS said, "Go get 'em."

We started to commit northeast to get an intercept vector on these guys, a cut-off vector. We had our other two-ship head south. In the F-15, firepower is awesome. When you get four F-15s running in a wall toward somebody, there's no way you're not going to come out victorious. So our game plan at all times, when we can do it, is to keep the four-ship together, to use that firepower. They were a little bit lower on gas, just because they'd been on CAP while we were down at the tanker. They were instructed to come with us, as long as they could, as long as they had the gas, and we'd go in as a four-ship against these guys.

These guys (Iraqis) take off from H2 in a big gaggle. We're coming at them. They're heading northeast, and we're trying to cut them off. They were not heading for Iran, which was too far from H2, but were just moving, the way they were doing all the time.

About 100 miles away from them, we're going as fast as we can with three bags of gas. Initially I'm thinking, "There's no way we're going to catch these guys. They're 100 miles away, and with our vector we're slowly starting to cut them off, but it's going to take a long time and a lot of gas." We close it to about 80 miles, and we're probably just about at the point where we need to turn back, getting too far up there, into an area where they have ground threats. So right at this point, just as we're saying, "We're not going to be able to get these guys," four more take off right behind them from H2 — and we're IN THERE — we're in a perfect geometry for these new guys.

Do they know about us? My conjecture is, the first group of Iraqis called back and said, "We're gone, we're out of here. Now you can launch the next bunch." Or, maybe the first group is saying, "Here's our chance to drag four Eagles and sandbag the sons of bitches." That was one of the things we had to think about as we started this turn into this intercept: what happens if these guys, the first group, do a 180 (180 degree turn, so that we're caught between two groups of bogies). They could get us in a pincers. And we were obviously thinking about it. Captain Draeger was thinking about it.

Of course, AWACS can see quite a ways, so we'll have warning if they try to box us in. So we don't know if they're aware of us — but always think worst case.

AWACS eventually loses the first group because they're so far away. At this time, we still don't know what type of aircraft are in either group, although in fact they're MiG-23 Floggers. So that's something else you have to think about — what airplane am I going up against? And you have think worst case. You don't know. But of course when you're intercepting and chasing the guy by the tail you're not worried quite as much, because he's not going to shoot you while he's flying away from you.

So we're running our intercept against the second group of MiG-23s to take off from H2. They're at low altitude. They're below 1,000 ft. With our radar, as awesome as it is, at 80 miles we're painting these guys, and we can see them at low altitude.

For reasons unknown, one of these guys suddenly turns around, goes back, and lands. Maybe an aircraft problem.

Now we're 40 miles, and with this guy going back, we don't know if they're running some new tactic on us or what they're doing. But the other three continue, and we're watching them on the scope. They're coming on our radar scope in the kind of Soviet-type formation, what we call a "Vic" formation, that we've talked about all the time.

It's so funny. Here, war is happening. And it's just like training. There're three blips on our screen. They're in the standard "Vic" formation.

We're coming in about 30 miles from the merge. We punch our wing tanks off, but keep the centerline tank on; okay, so now we have better maneuverability if we get in an engagement. If they decide to engage us and our missiles don't work or whatever, we'll be able to turn more tightly without those tanks.

We're descending through the mid-twenties doing about Mach 1.1 or 1.2. The weather was overcast. We couldn't see the ground. We're also thinking, "We may never see these guys." We can shoot at them, obviously, but once the missiles go through the clouds, at best we'll see a glow.

The critical decision as you get within 20 miles is, "Okay, who's going to target whom?"

That's Captain Draeger's job as Number One to decide. So he does that. His phiolosophy is "...hey, I'm going to take the map-reader first, and that's usually the guy out front; if you kill the guy that's leading the thing, everybody else will go, 'Oh, sh!t, what do we do now?'" So he targets the leader, or the map-reader, as he calls him.

He targets me as Number Two on the northwestern trailer. Draeger and I are One and Two. Now there's only one (Iraqi) left, so he says, "Okay, Three and Four, both of you take the southernmost guy."

We acknowledge. I say, "CHEVRON 2, sorted. 270. 25 miles." It's just like William Tell. If they were closer together, it might be necessary to refer to them by using a BRA call — but that's not necessary.

The other two pilots were Captain Cesar "Rico" Rodriguez as Number Three — he's the guy who got the maneuver kill earlier, the Iraqi who flew into the ground — and Captain Bruce Till was the last guy.

So we're coming in, and the other thing we're looking at is, are we spiked or not spiked (locked up by the MiGs)? That's our other indication of whether they know we're there, our RWR scope. At this point, there's no indication — but you can never be sure your system is working accurately.

So the flight lead has called the targeting plan, and now all we have to do is lock the guy we're supposed to lock, and shoot. Like I said, we got an early "bandit, bandit" call on these guys at about 35 or 40 miles, so we know these guys are bad, which takes a lot of the guesswork out.

We take our shots. Captain Draeger shoots first. We're now well inside 20 miles. He shoots. His missile comes off. I see it (guiding). I shoot next, just a couple of seconds after him. Because

Bruce and "Rico" are offset from us they have to wait a little longer before they get in range, so it's probably several more seconds before you hear "Rico" fire.

As the missiles start flying off, we pick up the first tally-hos about 10 miles from the merge. We can see the Floggers running across the desert, fast. A lot of times you can see the missile, and you can keep a tally-ho on that missile.

I mentioned the weather before. At about 10 or 12 miles there's a sucker hole that just opens up. So we go diving through. So now we're in a visual environment, versus shooting through the clouds. For some reason it's just opened up, which is perfect for us.

Captain Draeger's missile hits his man, hits him right in the back—the old Flogger running across the ground, there—and he's flying so low you can see the dust kick up around it. He calls "splash." Then he looks again. The airplane flies right through the fireball and comes out the other side. It hit him, but didn't just knock him out of the sky. He's burning, but not down. Captain Draeger goes to a heater (prepares to fire a Sidewinder heat-seeking missile), to put some heat on this big fire. But before he can do this the fire reaches the wing root, and the plane suddenly explodes in a huge fireball. I'm so busy watching this, watching this guy blow up—so amazed by the damage the warhead did, that I've almost forgotten my own missile.

Captain Draeger comes off the target and he says, "Let's come off north." First thing you do when you start blowing guys up is, you think about getting the hell out of there, fast. Once people see fireballs that gets their attentions, and you don't want to be around.

Right about then my missile hits my guy. I call a second "splash." There's another big fireball. After the first guy blows up, the other two guys do a hard, right-hand turn, right into us. Whether they picked up a late visual on us, and saw us, and were coming down through the clouds or what, I don't know—but what they were doing was too late, and my missile hit him.

With my trusty Dedicated Crew Chief in front of F-15C 85-0104 after the kill. *via Schiavi.*

As for what the MiG-23s looked like, they were camo'd, and they were two-and-a-half to three miles in front of us when they actually blew up, so we saw them pretty well. Number Four's missiles were maybe two seconds late, so Number Three (Captain Rodriguez) got the kill.

There was a road right underneath them. I think they were navigating following the road. The first guy blows up, and the other two blow up on the other side of the road—three fireballs right in a row. My guy blows up, zoom, and a moment later I hear "Rico" call the third "splash."

So as we come off, our big concern now is our Bingo fuel. We still have our centerline tank, but as we start to egress Captain Draeger and I punch off our centerline tanks so that we can get some speed up and get away from any ground threats (we're fairly low in here), and now our big concern is to get back. Post

Myself with "L.A." Brooks in front of our hootch. "LA" was in many of my flights, and would also go on to graduate the F-15C Fighter Weapons School. *via Schiavi.*

engagement, low on gas, our next big concern was getting some additional fuel to make it back to base. As was often the case during the war, a refueling tanker came north across the border to meet us, which enabled us to get much needed fuel without having to fly an inordinate distance to one of the fragged refueling tracks. Once we got our gas it was time to make the long trek back to base. First, though, we had to deal with number four's hung missile, which he jettisoned prior to landing.

We call AWACS and tell them that we see three fireballs on the ground.

AWACS says, "Say type," and that's when we say, "Floggers." We didn't use any code word. We just said, "Floggers."

The arrival show had become standard by this time—fly the tactical overhead, low approach, and then pull up for an aileron roll pitch up to pattern altitude, and then a full stop landing. Seemed like everyone was out on the flight line as we taxied in, and you could see that they were excited, but probably the most excited folks were the crew chiefs and weapons troops as I pulled into the chocks, because if it were not for the professional job they all did to ready the jet and weapons well, who knows how it might have turned out. Anyway, when I got out of the jet and the weapons guy handed me the umbilical for each of the AIM-7s that I fired, I gave one back to him as a sign of thanks. I don't know where he might be today, but I hope he still has it.

Colonel Schiavi went on to graduate the USAF Fighter Weapons School F-15C Division, and is now the Vice Wing Commander of an Air National Guard F-15 unit. He has over 2,500 hours in the Eagle.

Captain Rhory "Hoser" Draeger (USAF)

58th TFS "Gorillas," F-15C
Operation DESERT STORM
MiG-23 Kill
26 January 1991
Call-sign: CITGO 25

Capt Draeger scored his first kill of DESERT STORM by downing a MiG-29 on the first day of the conflict. He also downed this MiG-23 on 26 January. As Captain Draeger is deceased, details of the second kill can be found within the accounts of his wingmen's kills. Below are additional comments by his wingman, Tony Schiavi.

When we deployed to DESERT SHIELD in August 1990 I didn't really know who Rhory "Hoser" Draeger was, although the same was not true about his reputation as a fighter pilot and Eagle Weapons Officer. So when the paired four-ships were announced early in DESERT SHIELD, I was both looking forward to being on his wing (I deployed as a wingman), but also a little apprehensive. When it came to flying Eagles there was "no slack" in "Hoser's" world. As is sometimes the case, with rumors and not knowing what is fact and what is a tall tale, I specifically remember a story that "Hoser" had cancelled the push of his eight-ship at a Red Flag exercise because every time they turned in the marshall the formation was not perfectly line abreast, and someone was always blind. So he took the flight and flew practice CAP turns in Elgin/

Caliente MOA for the whole Vul time. So you can see where the apprehension might have come into play.

Of course, it didn't take long for me to experience the "no slack Hoser." I am sure that "Sly" and "Nips" will remember this; we were flying back to base after a DESERT SHIELD sortie, and "Hoser" took us down to low altitude to practice our four-ship low altitude formation and SAM reactions. Well, I guess I was not in the perfect formation that he demanded, and he finally said, "Two, if you don't get into line abreast you're going to climb it up and go home." To say the least I was pissed, and didn't talk to him for two days, but I got over it, and it was his way of making you better; and I will tell you today, I fly perfect line abreast formation if I am on the wing, and demand the same when I am leading. He was one

Capt Rhory "Hoser" Draeger seen just after DESERT STORM back at Eglin AFB, Florida, on the ladder of F-15C 85-0119, in which he got his first kill, a MiG-29 Fulcrum. It is interesting to note that at this point, the USAFE-style kill marking of the Iraqi flag is seen, with the date of the kill and type of aircraft on the flag. These markings later were changed to green stars in the States. *USAF via Robert F. Dorr.*

F-15C 85-108 was used by Capt Draeger to down a MiG-23 Flogger on 26 January 1991. Tail number 108 is seen on display the following year at Birmingham, Alabama. *Gary Chambers.*

of the main reasons I fought so hard to go to the Fighter Weapons School, even as a crusty young major.

I was upgraded to flight lead during DESERT SHIELD, and with nothing better to do than fly and prepare to kick Iraq's ass it was quite the program. "Hoser" quickly took me under his wing, and he really had a large impact on how I employed the Eagle, as did guys like "Cheese," "JB," "Kluso," and "Sly." We spent a lot of time together during the eight months we were deployed, and got to know each other well. He was a private type of person until you got to know him, and if he liked you he would do anything for

you. He loved to play golf and be in the outdoors with his wife and dog, and although the Air Force was important to him, there were other things that drove him, like his family. So I was surprised when he got out, but then again, not really. I was glad that he at least stayed in the Guard, and he had a great impact on the Guard community, as well. It was a shock to all of us who knew him when he was killed and taken away too early. Accidents happen, we all know that, but his was one that shouldn't have happened—I think of him often, and am thankful that I knew, learned from, and got to kill MiGs with one of the best Eagle pilots there was, is, or will be.

F-15C 85-108 at Eglin AFB sporting "Hoser" Draeger's MiG-23 Flogger kill marking. *Ben Knowles via Don Logan.*

Captain Cesar "Rico" Rodriguez (USAF)

58th TFS "Gorillas," F-15C
Operation DESERT STORM
MiG-23 Kill
26 January 1991
Call-sign: CITGO 27

This engagement marked Capt Rodriguez's second DESERT STORM kill, making him one of four Gorillas to score twice. The following account is taken from a taped interview with Col Rodriguez.

On this particular day many things proved different. Foremost was the weather, which precluded most of the strikers from taking off and going north into Iraq. Of the few aircraft over Iraq, almost all were DCA air-to-air assets roaming the country. This provided the Intelligence, Surveillance, and Reconnaissance (ISR) assets a chance to get closer to Iraq and learn more of the enemy we were fighting.

Our formation was a four-ship, and I was flying the number three position. Number one was Capt Rhory Draeger, who at this point also had one MiG kill. His wingman was Capt Tony "Kimo" Schiavi. My wingman this day was Bruce "Roto" Till. "Mole"

was holding down the squadron supervisor position, so I flew with Bruce.

We were proceeding north towards Baghdad when we got the initial call that something was airborne just west of Baghdad, and AWACS thought it might be a fighter. Our formation was in a 2 + 2, with my element three to five miles behind the lead element. We headed north to see what we could find. After running on several bad contacts that might have been high speed cars, we ended up about 30 miles southwest of Baghdad, and Rhory was just getting ready to turn the whole formation south to continue on with the roaming CAP.

It was pure luck that "Rico" Rodriguez scored both of his DESERT STORM kills in F-15C 85-0014, which is seen here at Seymour Johnson AFB, NC, in the late 90s. *Don Logan.*

AWACS informed us of aircraft activity near H2 and H3 airfields, in the far west of Iraq. As we had plenty of fuel it was no problem for us to investigate this situation. Rhory re-aligned the formation into a wall heading southwest. On the far right was "Kimo," then to the left was Rhory, myself, and then "Roto" on the south side of formation. We stayed up in the high 30s to save gas, and to stay above the cloud deck below us. At about 80 miles AWACS informs us that there are aircraft taking off, and as we approach 70 miles we also got radar contact. Thanks to some fantastic support from AWACS we were informed that these were MiG-23s before we even had a chance to lock the contacts. At one point there was some confusion as to whether there were three MiG-23s or four, but we were just waiting for the range to decrease so we could break-out and sort the individual contacts. As we proceeded west-southwest, we noticed that, based on our maps, these contacts appeared to be following a major highway northeast towards Baghdad. Our post-flight speculation was that once these aircraft landed, they would refuel and attempt to run to Iran. This turned out to be the first day of the desertion of the Iraqi Air Force. The clouds were still pretty thick, so we didn't think that we were going to get to see our missiles do their job, but at about 40 miles the clouds started to break, and we could see all the way to the ground. We felt more comfortable, as we could now VID the threats if required.

Rhory collapsed the formation so that we could get through a hole in the clouds in our decent. Once underneath, at about 15,000 feet he spread the formation back out into the wall, and that's when the enemy formation became clear. The MiG-23s were in a "Vic" formation, with the leader on the point, and the two wingmen space aft on a 45 degree line on each side. There was a two mile space between the leader and the other two as they navigated along the highway.

As we sorted the formation, the targeting plan was for Rhory to target the leader, "Kimo" would target the northern arm, and "Roto" and I would target the southern arm. As we started to get into weapons employment range, I started to hear shots being taken. Rhory shot first at the leader, and his missile appeared to hit the fuselage, or perhaps even go down the intake. Either way, it did not detonate. The missile trashed the entire engine, and as that pilot felt the impact, he started an easy left turn to the north. In the turn the entire MiG-23 aircraft became engulfed in flames, as the missile damage became pretty evident.

The two wingmen checked away from their leader, making a right turn to the southeast. This was directly at us, and it shortened the distance for the missiles that we already had in the air towards them. "Kimo" had a missile on the north guy, and "Roto" and I both had a missile on the southern. "Roto" shot 1.2 seconds after I employed my AIM-7 missile. Shortly thereafter, at about seven miles away I observed "Kimo's" missile impact his MiG and disintegrate it as my missile-to-MiG merge occurred. The destruction was so complete that 1.2 seconds later, when "Roto's" missile arrived, there was not enough airplane left for it to fuse against. His missile continued on across the desert floor for some time before it tumbled.

In a matter of just a few seconds there was a large smear of fire on the north side of the road where "Kimo's" MiG remains had impacted, and there was a matching fire smear to the south where my MiG had hit. Rhory was still pursuing his MiG, and had an un-caged AIM-9 ready to employ when his MiG finally exploded. None of the MiG pilots managed to eject.

What was interesting about this mission was that Rhory and I as the element leads both had MiG kills "under our belt," and our wingmen were wondering why we were so calm throughout this engagement. The prior experience helped us stay calm, and our wingmen perceived this, and it helped them execute very well in their first engagement. Another unsung hero of this engagement was a KC-10. When we first realized there were going to be MiG-23s involved, and this could turn into a high speed event, we asked AWACS to get a tanker heading north right away. While coming north to some tanker crews might have meant going up to the border and stopping, this KC-10 crew knew we needed the gas, and without hesitation crossed into Iraq to join with us. As my element came off the kill I snapped south, and there, only 40 miles south of us, was the KC-10 heading north towards us, deep in Iraq.

"Cherry" Pitts (left) and "Rico" Rodriguez sitting alert at Tabuk.
a Pitts.

"E.T." Murphy (two kills) on a combat mission over Iraq in "Rico" Rodriguez's F-15C 85-0114. This photo was taken at the very end of the conflict, when the AIM-120s became available, and are visible above the drop tank in this rare photo by "E.T.'s" wingman, Capt Pat Moylan. *Pat "Pat-O" Moylan via "E.T."* *Murphy.*

I informed Rhory of this, and he cleared us to rejoin the tanker, and he and "Kimo" would follow shortly. As the tanker approached 20 miles I directed him to start his turn to the south, and this resulted in "Roto" and I rejoining straight to the boom, and we were taking gas over Iraq.

This mission truly encapsulated the capabilities of not only the Eagle, but showed the value of the AWACS and the tankers all working as a team to complete the mission as a total success.

"Rico's" next kill is covered later in the book during Operation ALLIED FORCE.

Captain Jay "OP" Denney (USAF)

53rd TFS "Tigers," F-15C
Operation DESERT STORM
2 X MiG-23 Kills
27 January 1991
Call-sign: OPEC 01

Jay Denney graduated Auburn, and got his commission via ROTC. After graduating UPT at Reese AFB, Texas, Jay was assigned to the F-15C and the 58th TFS at Eglin AFB, FL. After graduating from the Fighter Weapons School F-15C Division, "OP" was assigned to the 36th TFW, 53rd TFS at Bitburg Air Base, Germany. Prior to the deployment, "OP" was a Weapons and Tactics Officer for the 36th TFW. "OP" penned his account for this publication.

I was deployed on 20 December 1990 with the 53rd TFS "NATO Tigers" as "Guest Help" from USAFE to the 9th AF/CENTAF AOR with the 4th TFW (P) at Prince Sultan Air Base (PSAB), Saudi Arabia. The 4th was commanded by Col Hal Hornburg, and the 53rd TFS was commanded by Lt Col Randy "Bigs" Bigum. We deployed 40 pilots with a combination of 53 TFS and 22 TFS membership, known as the "Sporty Forty." Numbers were restricted by CENTAF due to food/water/housing constraints. We had 24 F-15Cs, and a combined maintenance package of the top-of-the-line maintainers and support from Bitburg. There seemed to be plenty of tents, MREs (Meals-Ready-to-Eat), and sand at PSAB.

I had flown eight missions since the kickoff on 17 January 1991. These were mostly defensive counter-air CAP missions, but some were offensive counter-air Sweeps. We had also flown two escort missions to Al Taqqadum, west of Baghdad. Our comfort level was growing, as we had all gotten in the groove of mission planning, coordinating via field Secure KY-68 phones with various units deployed all over the Middle East. We were overcoming the problems of late air tasking orders (ATOs), which were still being hand delivered, one copy per base (we had five squadrons) by C-21. Prior to Day One we had done some training missions (Large Force), and studied our two days of the plan intently. Day Three planning order was one piece of paper that said "repeat Day Two."

So now we're 10 days into DESERT STORM. The 1st Tactical Fighter Wing from Langley has one kill, and Eglin has around 10+,

F-15C 84-0025, seen at an airshow in Belgium after the 53rd FS moved to Spangdalhem, Germany. Note the two MiG kill markings under the canopy, and the change from Bitburg's "BT" to Spang's "SP" on the tail. *Michael Baldock.*

While not high quality, this never-before published incredible shot is of "OP" Denney in F-15C tail 84-0025 immediately after the engagement, while still in the CAP over Iraq. Note the missing right-aft AIM-7, and also the missing wing tanks and right-outboard AIM-9. *Jeff Brown via J. Denney.*

three alone the day before (26 January 1991). I had just talked to Capt "Cheese" Graeter from the 58th TFS, my previous squadron, to congratulate him and his guys on kicking ass in the west.

On 27 January we found out that there was now a plan called the "Langley Kill Box." A 50x100 mile container south of Baghdad would be manned by 1st TFW jets in hopes of building their kill numbers (these details are the result of Captain's executing and discussing plans directed from on high by the "1st TFW mafia" led by Gen Buster Glosson, Col McBroom, and others in Riyadh). My four-ship was tasked to provide High Value Asset protection (HVAA) CAP south of the border for Tankers/AWACS. Based on the lack of a threat to date, and the fact that we would be south of some Tanker tracks, we felt a more efficient use of our aircraft would be to sit on the ramp at Al Kharj (PSAB) and call "Hot North, Cold South" on the radios, versus actually burning fuel flying.

We briefed on the road from the tents to breakfast. During ground ops we lost number two (Geraldo Delillo) and number three ("Jiffy" Jeff Brown) for maintenance issues that were resolved shortly (we only had one MND (Maintenance Non-Deliver) for the entire tour in Saudi, a collapsed nose gear). While they worked their problems, I took my number four ("Coma" Powell) and

OPEC 01. Back row left to right: "Coma" Powell and Geraldo Delillo. Front row left to right: "Jiffy" Jeff Brown and Jay "OP" Denney. *via J. Denney.*

departed. We went to the Orange tanker track, got our gas, checked in with BULLDOG (Central AWACS) and, lo and behold, they pushed us right into the "Kill Container." I had to authenticate and confirm, since our assigned CAP was south of where we got our gas—maybe this won't be a bad day after all!

We pushed north, and capped just 60 miles south of Baghdad. We hadn't been in the CAP for more than 30 minutes when we got snapped on bogeys southeast of Salman Pak East Airfield (SE corner of Baghdad). We were about 50 miles in trail with the bandits northbound. We passed over an SA-3 SAM site with some hesitation and continued north. We closed to 40 miles in trail as we were abeam Baghdad's east side, and we were now as far north as any Saudi-assigned Eagles had been. We were not closing despite our best efforts, and BULLDOG called us off the intercept. We flew south to Al Assad Air Base and capped near the airfield we thought they had launched from for another 30 minutes. We got a call that my second two-ship was inbound, so we departed for the tanker, thinking we'd seen the highlight of our day.

After getting our gas, we returned on station and did a high-five swap with the other element as they departed for the tanker track. Right away BULLDOG again snaps us to bogeys, "Bullseye 'Pepsi' (Salman Pak East) 130/80 (130 degrees for 80 miles)." We did not have digital bullseye in our software at that time, so with a little good ol' "pie in the sky," we took off eastbound hunting. We were in the 32-34 block, checked 90 degrees to the right to East, and stroked Min AB to hit the Mach. I started in an 80 mile scope, wingman on my north (left side), sun high to the south, bogeys north-northwest bound. I hammer down for the ID, no friendlies. They were low in the 5000' regime, and we were getting "hits" only, as they were almost in a perfect beam to us due to geometry (not their SA). We closed on the group. At approximately 20 miles the bogeys had turned to the northeast. By this point we had locked on, ensured no friendly indications, and AWACS had declared them hostile. We armed hot and, with the bandits cold, I directed my flight to break lock. I re-sanitized the low block, and with great discipline "Coma" reset his radar coverage and sanitized high.

Unbeknownst to us at the time, Intelligence had picked up Iraqi GCI telling this flight that they had Eagles in pursuit. With the Iraqi GCI subsequently jammed and no RWR spikes from us, they again turned north and pitched back towards Baghdad. We were now supersonic, ramping out of the 30s; clear of the SAM zones, and closing as we made a lead pursuit turn. We had two contacts, in azimuth (side-side), echelon southeast. My flight was northbound, with "Coma" on my western (left) side, slung slightly aft and high about 2.5 miles out. We targeted in azimuth; I was six miles in trail of the closest contact, and "Coma" was about eight to nine miles in trail of his group.

Based on the radar software at the time, with our 250+ knots of closure, our weapons indicated we were in range for AIM-7 shots. "Coma" called "I've got R2." I said standby, as I was closing for an RTR shot. I fired first from an altitude of 16,000' at my target, which was at about 300.' "Coma" fired immediately after. We could see the shadows of the bandits better than the aircraft as they descended to 100 feet. I watched my AIM-7 steam towards the MiG; there was a fireball as the missile passed the MiG-23 at a 90-degree angle (straight down) from above. I called "Splash One" while checking "Coma's" six, and watching his first missile trail northward—it just never made it. About that time I selected AUTOGUNS, and noticed I was still locked to the first bandit. He had flown out of the fireball, and was in a gentle left hand turn about two miles in front of me, so I un-caged an AIM-9 and fired. This time I watched as the aircraft erupted like a Molotov cocktail across the flat desert terrain.

By now "Coma" had rolled and pulled his nose down towards the bandits, re-locked, and fired two more AIM-7s. As he locked he called "Tally two," as he had a two-ship that was in welded wing/fingertip—a MiG-23 and a Mirage F-1. I scanned from his group to the northeast and picked up a fourth bandit about four miles at right one o'clock. "Coma's" first missile hit his first bandit, and the MiG again exploded and cartwheeled across the desert floor about 4,000' to my left side as I passed it. I saw the chute of that pilot at about 200' above his aircraft fireball.

53rd TFS flight line at PSAB, known as Texas Stadium. The 53rd TFS accounted for 11 kills during DESERT STORM. 1Lt Bob "Gigs" Hehemann.

I then saw the fourth bandit turning west, bringing his nose toward "Coma." "Coma's" second bandit then exploded, as he was hit by the second AIM-7. "Coma" was at about 7,000' altitude, and two miles abeam me on my left side. I was at 300' feet and 500 knots rolling in on the last MiG. I could not get a boresight lock, so I un-caged an AIM-9M and got a perfect screaming tone. I fired a no-lock shot from 8,000' aft. I wanted to gun the MiG, but he was too low and not turning hard enough to give me a shot. As soon as I fired he reversed his turn back to the right, and the missile appeared to go right up his tailpipe. I had called for "Coma" to break right when it looked like the MiG "might" have been turning on him; he was now directly over top of us, and I was 4,000 feet aft of the MiG and climbing as he exploded. We were closing in towards Salman Pak East, an airfield with a large array of SA-2 SAMs. It seemed like the moment the last MiG went down, our RWR erupted with SA-2 spikes. We continued a hard right turn to the southeast, stroked our afterburners, jettisoned our wing fuel tanks (empty), and started climbing out towards the south.

At this point the radios erupted, as everyone wanted to know the status. It got much quieter after I stated, "OPEC, Splash four!" We continued southbound, and amazingly the tanker controller had vectored a tanker north, and the tanker Heroes had pushed it up and were 50 miles north of the border as we rejoined on them and topped off our gas. After a quick weapons inventory, we returned to our CAP for another hour and a half, hoping we would get a chance for some more action that day.

When we returned to Al Kharj, we were in the middle of a sandstorm with almost zero visibility. No one would have seen us do a victory roll down initial, and we didn't have enough gas to divert, so the scariest part of the day was just getting the jets

"Gigs." Famous picture I took of "Opie" Denney (left) and our sound man (AKA Mr. Microphone), Capt Mike "Jethro" Miller, on our way back from a little R&R up in Riyadh. I put our guitars over their shoulders and took a few photos. "Jethro" almost got bit—probably should have. It's all good. *1Lt Bob "Gigs" Hehemann*

down. The storm cleared up pretty quickly, and we were reloaded with fuel tanks, topped off the gas at the hot-pits, then taxied into "Texas Stadium" to be met by the real warriors: all of the crew chiefs, weapons, specialists, support, and ops from Bitburg who were out on the ramp. It is a true testament that "Coma" and I just happened to be in the right place at the right time, but the daily execution by the entire maintenance and operations teams, as well as the AWACs, Tankers, Intelligence, and other support assets in perfect coordination (or great flexibility) made it happen.

Capt Denney went on to fly a total of 48 combat missions during DESERT STORM for a total of 388 combat hours. "OP" just wrapped up a stellar career, going on to command the 60th Fighter Squadron, the 33rd Operations Group, and retired as the Vice Commander of the 1st Fighter Wing. He currently flies for a major airline.

Captain Ben "Coma" Powell (USAF)

53rd TFS "Tigers," F-15C
Operation DESERT STORM
MiG-23 / F-1EQ Kills
27 January 1991
Call-sign: OPEC 02

Capt Powell graduated the Air Force Academy in 1984, and after graduating UPT at Columbus AFB, Mississippi, Ben was assigned as a T-38 FAIP for over four years. He was then selected for F-15C training at Luke AFB, Arizona, in the 426th TFTS. "Coma's" first Eagle assignment was to Bitburg AB, Germany. He had been in the 53rd TFS for about seven months, and had roughly 200 hours in the Eagle prior to his deployment to Saudi Arabia for Operation DESERT SHIELD. This account is drawn from an interview with Lt Col Powell.

I deployed with my squadron on 20 December 1991 to Al Kharj Air Base, also known as Prince Sultan Air Base (PSAB). Our usual paired four-ship consisted of our leader, Jay "OP" Denney, number two "Geraldo" Delillo, number three "Jiffy" Jeff Brown, and myself as number four. Besides our MiG killing sortie, a couple of sorties stand out in my memory. They had installed "Eagle Eye" on our jets, which was really just a hunting rifle scope strapped to the side of the HUD. I thought this was the silliest thing I'd ever heard of, but I learned I could unscrew these scopes and use them to look at things on the ground. I could use it like a telescope, and on one particular day I found an Iraqi truck park.

There must have been a thousand trucks, so I called it in to the AWACS. They asked us to keep our eyes on it, which we did. They sent some A-10s to attack the trucks while we watched. My first contribution to the war effort!

Another sortie that was unique was on 21 January. An F-14 had been shot down, and they were trying to figure out where they went down. So after our regular mission was over they asked us to top-off at the tanker and go back in to try to figure out where they were. The pilot was missing, and searching for him was kind of dicey. There was a low cloud deck, around 3,000 feet, which forced us down below that deck to look for him. We looked for a

F-15C 84-0027 used by "Coma" Powell on his double kill. *Paul Hart Collection via Don Logan.*

"Coma" Powell in F-15C 84-0027 on "OP's" wing after the engagement, while still in the CAP over Iraq. Note the missing wing tanks and missiles—just an incredible shot! *Jeff Brown via J. Denney.*

couple of hours, with everyone below shooting at us, but we never found him. But that sortie sure sticks in my mind, and even though we never found that guy, maybe we helped by finding out where he *wasn't*, so it made it easier for someone else to find him. (*Authors note: Lts Devon Jones (pilot) and Larry Slade (RIO) crewed an F-14A+ of VF-103 from the* USS Saratoga *when they were shot down over western Iraq. Lt Slade was captured, but Lt Jones was rescued and returned to the "Sara."*)

The day of our kill was the same day of the Super Bowl that Whitney Houston sang the National Anthem for. After the flight fall-out on the ramp "OP" and I went as a two-ship, with the intent to get the four-ship back together and re-sort to our normal positions. This never ended up occurring due to how our rotations to the tanker worked out. We had started out in a more southern station doing HVAA CAP, but about halfway through our six hour CAP we had been pushed north to a new CAP about 100 miles south of Baghdad. We were operating under the control of the center AWACS, call sign CHOCTAW. The initial radio call from CHOCTAW was one I'll never forget, "OPEC—CHOCTAW, kill bandit, 090, 100 (miles), west-bound." So we left the CAP knowing what our mission was going to be.

As we pressed east I was on the left, or northern side of the formation in the mid-30s, around 35,000 feet. We got our initial radar contact somewhere inside of sixty miles, and at around forty miles we took some sample locks with the radar. When we spiked them they turned and ran. So we broke our locks so that they would lose their spikes, and sure enough, they turned back into us. This time neither "OP" nor I locked them until they were inside twenty miles. We were both thinking the same thing, because we had

trained so hard together. As we locked them again they attempted to turn and run, but they didn't pick a good heading; instead of turning to put us dead on the stern, they left us about forty degrees of cut-off.

Now the bandits are going northwest, and we are going almost due north to cut them off. They have descended from about 15,000 feet down to very low altitude, and we are seeing them as a two-group picture, in lead-trail. We stay in the 30s so that we can go as fast as full afterburner will take us, since we don't want these guys to outrun us. The two groups are now in an echelon formation,

"OP" Denney (left) and "Coma" Powell "debriefing" in front of "OP's" jet after the kills. *via Denney.*

Besides the MiG-23 Flogger, "Coma" Powell also killed a Mirage F-1EQ identical to this Iraqi Mirage. *USAF.*

but we still sort in lead-trail. "OP" calls "Sorted, leader," but I still only see one contact. It takes my radar a few more sweeps to see both groups and call, "Sorted, trailers." They were so low that when I take my lock, the radar shows the bandit altitude as a negative number.

We both take stern AIM-7 shots, and I watch my missile track as long as I can. It was looking good until the motor burned out and I lost sight of it. But both shots missed, and I have a suspicion that it had something to do with the extreme difference in our altitude. I wasn't crazy about getting any lower, since we were getting closer to all the SAMs and triple-A, but I also didn't want to shoot again with a big altitude difference. I roll over and do half a split-S, and as I pull the bandits into the HUD and get the TD box on them I see their formation. They are right down on the deck, maybe 100 feet. I see "OP's" group to my right, and about three miles off my nose I see my group. "OP's" group was about a mile and a half at my right two o'clock, and as I finish my split-S and start to level off about two miles behind my group, I can now see that there are two aircraft there. At the same time I see the fourth aircraft at my right one o'clock for about three miles.

"OP" had come down at the same time, and had arrived behind his guys first due to the formation of the bandits. He shoots his first guy, a MiG-23, with an AIM-9. I've gotten down to about 3,000 feet, and I can see two jets in my TD box. They are at about 100 feet, and so close together they look like they are in fingertip formation. I can also see that the one on the right is a MiG-23 and the one on the left is a Mirage F-1. Since I had already shot one AIM-7 and it didn't get the job done, my game plan now is to "quick pickle," or rapidly shoot two AIM-7s. I figure one of these guys is going to blow up, and I'll shoot the remaining bandit with an AIM-9. I had over 250 knots of over-take, so I wasn't worried about getting into an AIM-9 WEZ.

Something I had heard was that when you get to your first real fight and your adrenalin starts pumping, you're going to get nervous and forget everything except the very basic things. I actually found that at this time, it was just the opposite. For me time just seemed to slow down, and every little tidbit that I had ever learned came flooding back into the ol' cranium. Since my plan was to shoot two

AIM-7s, I remember that the second missile will come off the aft station, and since I still had my external wing tanks, I had to load the jet with at least three to four Gs so that the missile will miss the tank. I put some G on the jet and fired twice. I watched the missiles track, and it appeared to me that the first AIM-7 drove right up the tail pipe of the F-1. He just disintegrated in a huge fireball. The second AIM-7 drove right up on the left wingtip of the Flogger. The missile fused, and then I saw secondary explosions on the fuselage of the MiG-23, at which point he nosed over and flew into the ground. There was no ejection attempt from either aircraft.

At this point I see the last Flogger off to my two o'clock, so I pull hard to point at him. Since I was already in an AIM-9 WEZ on him all I would have to do is un-cage and shoot. I was thinking this was going to be a really good day for the home team! But as I pulled him into the HUD, I realized that I couldn't shoot him for a couple of reasons. First, "OP" had driven right up behind him, and if I shot, I might hit "OP." And I also knew that if I shot this guy off his nose, "OP" was going to be really pissed! So I watched "OP" hose this guy with an AIM-9 from maybe 1,500 feet back, and that pilot ejected right away. I'm watching him in his chute about 6,000 feet off my nose, and I knew this was too good not to do something with. While I knew I couldn't shoot him, what I did was to fly as close to him as I could, in full afterburner in a high-G turn around him. When he got back to his bar that night, I didn't want there to be any doubt about what got him!

We were definitely inside the Baghdad MEZ, and up to this point they hadn't shot any SAMs at us, probably because they didn't want to hit their own guys. Now we're getting spiked, and it's time to get out of here fast. We jettisoned our now-empty wing tanks and climbed out heading south. After a trip to the tanker we finished our CAP period. We RTB'd as a four-ship, but I stayed in the number two position. When we get back to base we are on weather hold, and we almost had to divert. But the sandstorm cleared, and we were just able to get in doing straight-ins. We had it set up so if you had jettisoned or expended ordnance, we would taxi through the tank farm for new tanks. Then it's through the missile area for new missiles, and eventually we get back to our parking spots. Even after all this there are still a lot of folks out there to meet us, and it was a great moment.

Following his return to Germany in May 1991, Capt Powell remained at Bitburg until the base closed in 1994. After following the 53rd FS to Spangdalem AB, Germany, for three years, he subsequently served at Tyndall AFB in the Eagle FTU as an IP. He served on the North American Aerospace Defence Command (NORAD) staff for three years, as well as the Joint Operations staff at Kefelvic AB, Iceland. "Coma" recently retired as a Lt Col while serving as the Inspector General for the 33rd Fighter Wing, Eglin AFB, Florida.

Left to right: "Coma" Powell, "Gigs" Hehemann, and "Vegas" Dietz at Bitburg after the war. *via 1Lt Bob "Gigs" Hehemann.*

Capt Don "Muddy" Watrous (USAF)

32nd TFS "Wolfhounds," F-15C
Operation DESERT STORM
MiG-23 Kill
28 January 1991
Call-sign: BITE 04

Capt Watrous' kill marked the only air-to-air kill in the history of the "Wolfhounds" (32nd Tactical Fighter Squadron). "Muddy" graduated from Rensselaer Polytechnic Institute (RPI) in 1982, and after commissioning and completing graduate school he completed UPT at Laughlin AFB, Texas, in 1984. He was retained as a FAIP, serving there until the middle of 1988, when he was selected for F-15C training at Tyndall AFB, Florida. "Muddy" had been at Soesterburg AB, The Netherlands, for just over a year prior to this deployment. He had about 250 hours in the F-15 (only about 65 hours as a two-ship flight lead) when he got his kill. The following account is taken from a personal interview with Col Watrous.

I was part of the 32nd TFS "Wolfhounds" at Soesterburg when Operation DESERT SHIELD kicked off. Shortly thereafter, the United States sold 24 F-15s to the Saudi government to plus-up their defense. Unfortunately, twelve of those aircraft came from our squadron! We were the only fighter squadron in the 32nd Tactical Fighter Group, so the impact of losing twelve of our aircraft was huge, especially while maintaining the same pilot manning we had with 24 Eagles. So, with too many pilots, half the jets, and a ZULU alert commitment, both the quality and quantity of flying went downhill in a hurry. This turned out to be significant when our squadron commander tried to get us involved in the American

build-up—just like any other fighter squadron, we wanted to be a part of the game. However, the basic message we got back was "Thanks, but no thanks – your proficiency sucks." So we spent the next few months watching the situation develop on CNN with no indication that we were ever going to get to be involved.

After months of the build-up there were indications that things were heating up, and there was a chance we *might* get to participate. A small group of pilots in the squadron were singled out as possible players, and they were given the majority of the few available sorties to ensure their proficiency was where it belonged. The rest of the squadron sat alert, worked the duty desk, and bitched about

F-15C 79-0022 seen prior to DESERT STORM, assigned to 22 TFS, Bitburg, Germany. 22 TFS and 32 TFS pilots flew a combination of Bitburg and Soesterberg jets during their DESERT STORM deployment as the air-to-air component of the 7440th Composite Wing at Incirlik AB, Turkey. *Lieuwe Hofstra.*

Capt Watrous' usual paired four ship: " Blade" Dooley (#2), "Merc" Morris (lead), "Baghwan" Baughan (#3), and "Muddy" Watrous (#4). *via Watrous.*

not flying. However, this ended by mid-December, when we were told again that, due to our lack of aircraft and recent proficiency, our squadron would not be playing. So, unless you were needed for alert over the holidays, most of the pilots left for Christmas.

It was just after New Year's when we got word that things were really going to happen soon, and there was a plan to open a second front in the north—and we (32nd TFS) were going to be a part of it! The plan called for us to deploy a small contingent of jets, pilots, and maintainers to Incirlik AB, Turkey. Although we did not know the timing of DESERT STORM, we were expected to leave on 17 January and self-deploy all the way, as there was no tanker support available. Family members were not to be told where, why, or for how long we would be gone. We packed our bags, came to work on the 17th, and sat all day waiting for diplomatic clearance to overfly France, but it never came. Feeling frustrated, our commander told us all to go home at the end of the crew duty day and try again tomorrow. It was odd to return home after saying goodbye, but we managed fine until the next morning, when we woke up to news coverage of the start of the war. We still had to keep quiet about the purpose of our deployment, but our wives definitely had it figured out! With bombs lighting up the TV screens, France agreed to let us overfly their country.

As I recall, we departed for Sigonella with six primary jets and two spares. As we entered French airspace, a formation of Mirage jets joined on us and "escorted" us until we were clear to the south. After everyone successfully refueled at Sig the spares turned back, and the rest of us continued to Incirlik.

We landed at "the Lik" on the evening of the 18th, and joined forces with the Bitburg boys, who were already there. Some of our pilots flew that night, and some of us went on the day schedule. We considered ourselves fortunate to have missed all the extended DESERT SHIELD build-up but still get to show up for the shootin' war. Similarly, after the air war was over we were able to self-deploy home, bypassing the tanker/transport delays, and reuniting with our family and friends within a week. We had a good war.

Although we were part of a composite squadron with the 525th

TFS from Bitburg, I flew almost exclusively as part of a dedicated four-ship of Wolfhounds led by "Merc" Morris, our weapons officer. Number two was "Blade" Dooley, and number three was "Bagwan" Baughan. I was number four. We flew the day schedule for two weeks, and then switched to nights, flying two days on and one day off. Our missions were a mix of OCA, DCA, CAP, and two-ship alert.

My kill came on the morning of 28 January during a barrier CAP mission. We had learned the Iraqis were flying their airplanes to Iran to escape destruction, so we were instructed to establish a 24/7 barrier along the Iran/Iraq border to stop them. The Incirlik fighters were responsible for much of the border area north of Baghdad, with the Saudi-based guys covering the rest. We would launch four Eagles and a tanker, refuel over eastern Turkey, proceed south to the border region, and maintain a roving BARCAP for about two hours. We would then return to the tanker to refuel, and repeat the cycle to cover about a six-hour window before being relieved by the next four-ship of Eagles.

The first period on the 28th was covered by a Bitburg four-ship, starting around midnight. When we relieved them early that morning they reported several radar contacts, but nothing significant, and no engagements. We saw the same sorts of things during our first shift in the AOR—a few contacts, but nothing that met commit criteria. As we approached Joker fuel, we headed north to refuel.

Our normal air refueling order was numbers one through four. Numbers one through three were finished and on the wing of the tanker, and I was on the boom when the AWACS controller interrupted our air refueling frequency to tell us we had bandits airborne. They committed us on "Bandits, 170 for 60, estimate medium, tracking 060, 600 knots." I came off the boom with almost a full fuel load as the rest of the flight was turning south. I caught up to them to complete our "wall of Eagles," with me in the east, three and lead in the center, and number two in the west.

As we pressed south, I was able to break-out all four bandits— I had a phenomenal radar that day. The bandits were in a container (*or box*) formation heading east, and we sorted by azimuth. Based on our formation, lead and two sorted the trailers, while "Bagwan"

Ready to go, left to right: "Merc" Morris, "Blade" Dooley, "Baghwan" Baughan, and "Muddy" Watrous. *via Watrous.*

and I sorted the leaders. As we closed on them, the trailers turned south and ran, while the leaders continued east. As the bandit formation spread out in azimuth, so did we. I was leaning as far east as I could to still maintain formation.

Unfortunately, in contrast to the excellent radar I had, "Bagwan's" radar was not up to par; I think it actually died during that commit! He was trying to maintain SA on the world without the benefit of his radar, while trying to keep sight of lead, and still lean east with me. As I approached my visual limit with "Bagwan" with my bandit almost gimbaled, I called "stripped east." He responded with "press, engage if able." With relief from my visual contract with three, I leaned further east for more cutoff, but was already aft of the beam.

The bandits were still heading east at low altitude as I approached shot range from their left, seven to eight o'clock. With them in a line abreast formation I locked the nearest, or north, bandit. I was at 25,000 feet, and the bandits were at 3,000 feet. As far as I knew there were no other aircraft in the area, and I was in the right place at the right time with a great radar. Although AWACS had declared them to be "bandits," I asked for (and must have received!) confirmation before taking my first shot. Once inside shot range I fired an AIM-7, waited five seconds, and shot another one. While I had never shot a missile before, everything

was indicating normal in the jet—just like in the sim! Although I felt the missiles leave the airplane I did not see a rocket plume. Without ever having experienced a live missile shot, I concluded the missiles must be pulling lead in the vertical, below my line of sight.

I continued my pursuit while timing-out the missiles. They looked good by all cockpit indications until the countdown got to zero and both bandits were still on my radar. So there I was, with no visual, no tally, no joy on either of my missiles, and two hostile jets low off my nose. I was now heading almost due east in a stagnated tail chase. With little to no overtake in full afterburner and no cutoff, I decided to use the vertical to close in for another shot. I nosed over and punched off my tanks, all three of which were still pretty full from the recent refueling. Simultaneous jettison of all that weight at supersonic speed resulted in a pretty big jolt, but also provided almost instantaneous overtake.

When I closed enough to provide a high P_k (Probability of Kill) shot, I locked the southern bandit and shot for the third time. I felt the same thump and still saw nothing. After another few seconds I shot my last AIM-7. This time, the familiar thump was followed by a white missile track extending out in front of me. I followed the smoke vector visually to where it was pointing and got a tally on two aircraft, very low and very fast. I estimate that they were about

On the boom following the successful engagement, refueling from a KC-135. Note the slightly shortened left wing. *via Watrous.*

MiG-killing F-15C 79-022 of the 22nd Tactical Fighter Squadron, the 'Big 22
Don Logan collection.

200 feet off the deck. The one missile I saw tracked to the right wing root of the southern target and appeared to fuse on contact. The bandit's right wing blew off, and the jet started to roll right. It was roughly inverted when it impacted the ground in a very long fireball. I did not see a chute.

I then locked up the other bandit and had a really good tone on my AIM-9, but was outside max range for the missile. Although I had minimal closure when I shot my last AIM-7 and was going about as fast as the Eagle would go, the remaining bandit had pushed it up, and was now pulling away from me at over 100 knots of negative Vc. I held my shot, and asked AWACS how close I was to Iranian airspace. I knew I was relatively close when this started and was burning up a lot of real estate. With no answer, no overtake, very little vertical, no cutoff, and "Bitching Betty" telling me I was below Joker, I broke off the attack and headed north.

As I came off I called "Blind" to number three. He came back with "Blind" also, which surprised me. As I was looking around for "Bagwan" and/or other bandits, I noticed movement out of the corner of my eye. It turned out to be a piece of wire flapping in the airstream outboard of my left wing. As it tuned out, it was the wire that used to go to the position light on the left wingtip. Apparently, when I jettisoned my tanks at that speed, the jolt caused about two feet of the left wingtip to depart with them. Maintenance later told me that delamination of the wingtip caused it to break off under the load of the jolt. There was no evidence that the tanks hit the jet, and the mighty Eagle was flying just fine.

"Muddy" seen a few years later in F-15C 79-022 with kill marking displayed.
via Watrous.

But I really couldn't concern myself with that at the moment I had been in full afterburner for quite a while, and was getting pretty low on gas. "Bagwan" and I managed to get rejoined, and learned that our tanker was heading back to base; we were not due back to the refueling track for over an hour, and a relief tanker was enroute, but still quite a ways out. Everybody worked together, and our original tanker turned around to help me. Thanks guys!

"Bagwan" and I made it safely to the tanker. While I was on the boom, the boomer (boom operator) asked me if I knew that my left wingtip was missing, and asked if he could take a picture. I said sure, as long as you send me a copy! I didn't really think he would, but a few months later I got a package in the mail with a picture of me on the boom, with snow in the background, and part of my wing missing. I never knew his name, but wish I did. He was a great boomer, and a good photographer, too.

Lead and number two stayed in the area to complete the mission while "Bagwan" and I RTB'd; the bandits they chased south got away by landing near Baghdad. While we were enroute to Incirlik we called in our weapons status, so everyone knew I was out of AIM-7s and came out to meet us when we landed. There was quite a crowd when I parked.

After the debrief I was given a bottle of champagne, but was told I couldn't drink it until I could prove I had a kill. Because I was alone when it happened and the explosion was below the field of view of my HUD, I had no evidence to back up my story. However, after three days of looking at that bottle, the Intel guys were able to produce conclusive evidence to confirm my claim and positively identify the bandit as a MiG-23 Flogger. They also indicated that the second bandit I was chasing crashed shortly after penetrating Iranian airspace, possibly due to fuel starvation. I sure did enjoy that bottle of cheap champagne!

Capt Watrous went on to fly a total of 21 combat sorties during Operation DESERT STORM. Following his Eagle tour at Soesterberg he was selected to attend Test Pilot School (TPS), and has spent the rest of his career flying a variety of aircraft in the test world. He is currently a full Colonel, and Commander of a Test Group.

Captain David "Logger" Rose (USAF)

58th TFS "Gorillas," F-15C
Operation DESERT STORM
MiG-23 Kill
29 January 1991
Call-sign: CITGO 3

Dave Rose graduated Texas A&M out of "The Corp" in 1984, and went to UPT at Williams AFB, Arizona. After finishing F-15C training at Tyndall, he reported for his first operational tour with the 53rd TFS at Bitburg. Two years later, in January 1988 he transferred to the 60th TFS at Eglin AFB, Florida. "Logger" was selected to lead the contingent of seven pilots from the "Fighting Crows" that were guest help to the 58th TFS for the deployment to Operation DESERT SHIELD. Lt Col Rose penned this account for this book.

I was at my ten-year high school reunion in Corpus Christie, Texas, the weekend that Saddam invaded Kuwait. When I got back on Sunday my Squadron Commander called me, and asked if I would like to deploy in support of an extended overseas operation, and I of course said, "Yes Sir!" There were seven of us from the "Crows" going to augment the 58th, and I was fortunate enough to be the mission commander for this group.

I flew in the deployment which, after 15.5 hours and a lot of "piddle-packs," arrived at Tabuk. We land, and it's a very big base, but very bare-based, and out in the middle of nowhere. We are hosted by the Saudi F-5 squadron, and we go to their Ops building, which is a very nice, big building. We ended up sharing their building as their guests. Out back, they had put on a big ol' welcome dinner for us, with long carpets and big platters of rice

and goat. It was awesome. So we sat outside on the carpets and had a "goat-grab." The best thing was once we were bedded-down, the American exchange F-5 pilot that was there took us downtown to the USEMETUM. While we were not in combat we were able to go downtown, off-base, and go to the USEMETUM, where they had tennis courts and satellite TV. But the BEST thing was to be able to go by the Dairy Queen. They had Blizzards® at the Dairy Queen in Tabuk, Saudi Arabia. So it was awesome! They stopped us from going off base a few months after we got there, but while it lasted it was pretty cool.

Once the war kicked off, we were flying roughly once a day, sometimes twice. Being the guest-help, we were mostly flying the night DCA missions, but we weren't complaining—at least we were in the fight. We had a formed four-ship that were all "Crows,"

Triple MiG-killer F-15C 85-0102 seen at Eglin AFB in 1993. *Ben Knowles via Don Logan.*

so we had trained together, and we knew how to employ together. "Copper Tone" Gallahger was my formed wingman. "Fish" Fisher was my number three, and "Pat-O" Moylan was number four. We flew about eleven or twelve sorties prior to 29 January in this formation; in fact, the MiG kill mission was the first mission that we switched, and "Fish" led and I flew as three. We stayed formed as a four-ship like this until right up to the end of the war. Our standard DCA missions up to this point had been six hour VUL times, with an hour out and an hour back, eight hours total. Basically, the alert missions were also going to do the same thing.

29 January turned out to be the first day of the "Cindy" CAP. This was a BARCAP northeast of Baghdad. The day prior, the Iraqi Air Force had started to fly their aircraft to Iran. So everybody was, like, what the heck? We've got to go stop them from doing this. So we were frag'd to go up there and man this CAP, which was named the "Cindy" CAP, and was located well north and east of Baghdad. We basically had two choices to get up there: we could either shoot the gap on the west side of Baghdad between Al Taq and Al Assad, then get north of Balad AB and press east over to the CAP. Or, we could hug the Iranian order on the east side of Baghdad, way to the east. We could barely squeeze between the SAMs of Baghdad and the Iranian border, and then slide up to the CAP. We had no idea what they were doing, or why they were going to Iran, but we were going to man the CAP and stop them.

The first VUL period that day was the 0600 to 1200L; "Kluso" Tollini and his four-ship were the guys covering that first VUL. "Kluso" has some guest-help from the Weapons School, Steve "Mongo" Robins, in his flight, and they cover the first six hours of the Cindy CAP without incident. We had not been up north of Baghdad yet, so it was pretty interesting to get to go up there and check out a new area of the country. There is a huge lake just northwest of Baghdad, and there was a ton of smoke coming off the refineries and targets that were still on fire. The weather was also different on this day (the 29th), as there was a broken overcast at about 18-20,000 feet. It was either go high and stay above it or go below, and we decided to go below. This way we could see any SAMs as they came up, and also, that far north, AWACS couldn't see much, and even less down low.

This was also the first day that the tankers had agreed to refuel us over Iraq. They had a track down by Al Juf, over southwest Iraq, which was great, as it kept us closer to the fight. So we got our gas and pressed north to shoot the gap between Al Assad and Al Taq. On our way in we contacted "Kluso" on their aux frequency, and they said that there had not been much in the way of ground, or SAM, activity and no air activity. They had found some heavy aircraft on the ground that they wanted to point out to us. One was an IL-76 Candid transport that they had found parked out on a very austere field probably about 100 miles north of Baghdad. They had called it out to AWACS, and AWACS authorized them to strafe it. So they got to go down and strafe it; they got all four guys across and they hit the thing, which was impressive, since these are 'C' model guys, and not exactly tactical experts at strafing. Since they had surprised them, there was very little AAA coming back up at them. Then they found a Cub, which is like a C-130, on a field near Balad, which is just north of Baghdad. They get permission to

strafe this one also, and in they go. Number four, "Mongo," rolls in, and this time they shoot a ROLAND missile at him, and he's calling the SAM-break and everything. Then they do a flight check and "Mongo" doesn't check in, but the second time he does check in. So that got their attention, and they relayed to us not to get too close to those two aircraft, since they were now aware there are folks out here trying to hit them.

We get established in the CAP for our noon to six VUL time, and almost immediately we send a two-ship back to the tanker to top-off, cycling two-ships this way to keep at least a two-ship in the CAP at all times. This was a little different, as the Frag had us going north to Turkey to get gas, ie, the guys out of Incirlik. We had never done this, and had not coordinated with the Incirlik guys up to this point. So "Fish" and "Pat-O" go off to the north to get gas, and we're listening to them in the aux. Naturally, the command and control up there in the north have no idea who they are or that they are coming. The weather was not good, so they're looking for a tanker in the weather and working the authorization, but eventually they worked it out and got their gas. After this we decide we're not going to go north again for gas, so "C-tone" and I head back down to our tankers in the south. We get our gas from the tanker over southwestern Iraq and press back up to the CAP. Not long after this "Fish" and "Pat-O" also leave for the southern tanker.

We were doing a roving BARCAP right up against the Iranian border, which is incredible, as far as the terrain and such is concerned. The terrain was rolling hills, and had an elevation of about 3,000 feet MSL. It was pretty barren, and you could definitely see the border where, during the years of their conflict, they had built barricades, trenches, and emplacements all along the border. That was interesting to look, at as we were CAPing, basically east-west. About this time "Coppertone" gets a contact on a low, fast mover about fifty miles northwest of us. He calls this out and I search up there myself, as we had just rolled-out heading west. I get the contact about forty-five degrees right on the scope and I lock him up. He is down low, and doing about 720 knots right on the deck at about 300 feet, and clearly he's goin' east. I call it out to AWACS, which doesn't see the contact, but does pass that there are friendlies in the area. So that was a good call. Now we know we've got to do an intercept, so I turn the flight basically due north to take him far left on our scopes for geometry, to cut him off. As we continued to search, we did get some indications of friendlies around there, so we determined it would be best to do a visual ID (VID). We didn't want to shoot BVR with friendlies in the vicinity and risk a "blue-on-blue." This meant our intercept would need to put us behind the contact so we could visually confirm that they were hostile types before engaging them. So we pushed it up, and we were at about 16,000 feet because of the overcast, doing about 650 knots. We're still carrying our three externals plus all eight missiles. "Fish" and "Pat-O" are off the tanker and coming north, but they're about 100-150 miles behind us, but are with us on the aux radio.

At about fifteen miles I lock the leading edge of the contact and call for us to jettison our two wing tanks, which we had burned empty by this point. I could discern no formation, so I just locked

Soviet MiG-23 Fogger-J seen with the wings full forward, carrying the standard load of two radar guided AA-7s on the wings, and two heat seeking AA-8s nboard. The Iraqi MiGs may have been carrying the older AA-2s in place of the AA-8s, as was common in export versions. *USN.*

he contact. I rolled in from about 15,000 feet down to about 8,000 feet two and a half miles behind a brown-on-brown Flogger. This MiG-23 had his wings all the back at 72 degrees; the Flogger was a swing-wing Soviet built fighter that has three positions for the wings, and he has his all the way back. This guy is right on he deck—like 100 feet—and doing 720 knots. It's a very small, skinny silhouette. The ROE up there was pretty simple, since if t's not an Eagle, we could shoot it. So once I confirmed it was a Flogger, and definitely not an F-15, I was cleared to engage.

I had an AIM-9 tone on the bandit, but I chose to shoot an AIM-7 radar guided missile, just because it's a bigger warhead. This was the first time I had shot an AIM-7, and I felt the "thunk" as it came off, and I saw the smoke trail. It has over a ten second burn time on the motor, so it was very easy to follow the missile as it guided towards the target. It detonated right on the back spine of the Flogger at mid-fuselage. The enemy fighter immediately hit the ground, and then there was a big fireball. I call "CITGO, splash one Flogger, come off right." "Coppertone" comes back with, "CITGO 4, snaplock, nose three." He had gotten another contact on a second bandit. So I came back to the east, which had me slung-out in echelon at about 5,000 feet. "Coppertone" has this guy locked-up about 3.5 miles in front of me, and I lock-up this second Flogger also. By this time we're getting into the foothills, and the bandit is having to climb up over those, so he's a little easier to see.

"Coppertone" is in a WEZ so he shoots an AIM-7 at this second Flogger. As I look over and see him shoot, I see another F-15 about 3,000 feet line-abreast of my wingman. So I'm thinking who the heck is this guy, because I know our other two-ship is over 100 miles away? This other Eagle also shoots an AIM-7 at this bandit. "Coppertone's" missile detonates to the right of the bandit, but he keeps flying. The other Eagle's missile impacted the dirt prior to getting to the target. So this Flogger is still flying, and I choose to

climb up a little for a better WEZ, and I also take a shot at this guy. I wait and wait, but there is no fireball. We're getting really close to the border, and the fuel was getting such that it was time to retire back to the tanker. They had already come off the target, and I was waiting to see the time-out of the missile. The bandit is having to climb now, since the hills are turning into mountains, and there is no fireball, so I had no idea what had happened to my missile. But after three shots, this was one lucky enemy fighter!

We climbed up and went southwest, back to the tanker track. I had requested that the tankers come north, since the engagement had cost us a lot of fuel. It was about four pm, actually 4:15, and all we could see in front of us were the contrails of all the Eagle CAPs across the country, so the tankers had no problem coming north. We got on the tanker and got a top-off, and went back, since we had another hour and a half of our VUL time to finish. This time we checked in with the northern AWACS out of Incirlik and requested the information on these other Eagles that we had encountered. It turned out that they were out of Incirlik, and frag'd to man a similar BARCAP on the Iranian border, but farther north up the border. We had no coordination in this, and fortunately everyone's IFFs were set correctly, so we were able to ID each other as good guys.

After completing our six hour VUL, we pressed for the tanker and then for home, which was another hour after refueling. It was pretty significant that a full moon was rising right after the sun had set. We get back to Tabuk, and the tradition was that if you had a victory you did an aileron roll coming up initial. But the sun had just set, so we weren't supposed to come up initial; we're supposed to do straight-ins because it was night. I ended up having the other guys go in, then I did a low approach and an aileron roll. I pulled closed and came back around and landed, and the Wing Commander met me at the jet, and I thought I was in deep kimchi, because of the "pattern work." It turns out that he was there to congratulate me for being in the right place at the right time.

So in short, my wingman "Coppertone" actually did the outstanding work of finding the enemy. We were fortunate enough to get in an intercept position to keep up with these guys doing 720 knots by using the geometry and getting behind them to VID, so we didn't shoot our friends. This way we were able to stop at least one of them from getting to Iran. I don't know what happened to the other guy, but we were in the right place at the right time. I found out later that the Floggers were based at Kirkuk, and had launched from there. The northern AWACS had detected this, and had vectored the Incirlik-based Eagles onto them. The wingman had flown a "hotter" intercept, and got himself into a WEZ; neither of them knew we were there until my missile blew up the first MiG. So we didn't know about them, but our correct IFFs kept a "blue-on-blue" from occurring. Our coordination got much better in the following days.

I attribute our success as a unit to many things. We had some of the best Weapons Officers, and the time to learn from them in the months leading up to the war. Guys like "Cheese," "John Boy," "Kluso," and "Hoser"; it was just outstanding to learn from these guys and others, and then have the chance to step up. Our maintenance troops were unbelievable; I don't think I ever ground-aborted an aircraft, not once in six weeks of war. They just worked their butts off. To have jets that worked, and weapons that worked, that's what made it happen.

Capt Rose flew a total of 35 combat sorties for 235 hours of combat during DESERT STORM. "Logger" graduated from the F-15C Division of the USAF Fighter Weapons School, and then went back to USAFE to the 32nd FS in early 1992. After closing the "Wolfhounds" at Soesterburg, he spent the next 13 years doing Eagle and Raptor testing at Nellis with the 422 TES. "Logger" "bedded-down" the initial Raptor test program at Nellis, and was the first Air Combat Command F-22 pilot. Lt Col Rose is currently working Raptor tactical integration programs and operations at Nellis AFB, Nevada.

Capt Dave "Logger" Rose (left) and Capt Tony "E.T." Murphy with F-15C 85-0102, in which "Logger" got one kill, and "E.T." got two kills. 33rd TFW Commander Col Rick Parson's name, and kill star, are on the jet, but he got his kill in another F-15C. *via Tony Murphy.*

Captain Greg "Dutch" Masters (USAF)

525th TFS "Bulldogs," F-15C
Operation DESERT STORM
IL-76 Kill
2 February 1991
Call-sign: RIFLE 01

Capt Masters joined the USAF in 1978 (spending the first four years attending the USAF Academy, commissioning in 1982), and had well over 1,000 hours in the Eagle prior to his Bitburg tour. The following account is drawn directly from notes that Capt Masters kept during DESERT STORM, and has been edited by "Dutch" for this book.

Few people realized the plan for Turkey, and specifically for the "Bulldogs" of the 525 TFS. We had sent ten F-15s and most of the squadron down to Incirlik AB, Turkey, as a routine "Weapons Training Deployment" (WTD). Also at Incirlik were a number of F-16s and F-111E fighter-bombers. Since that time we were prepared to send an additional 14 Eagles, but were on hold for diplomatic clearance. I was packed and ready to leave on the sixteenth (of January). Early on the morning of the seventeenth, I got a call that U.S.-led forces had attacked Baghdad three hours earlier, and to grab my bags and come in. At eight o'clock that morning we blasted off fully loaded with eight air-to-air missiles and a fully loaded gun. It was a 2 1/2 hour flight to Navy Sigonella,

on the island of Sicily, where we landed in a thunderstorm, shut down one engine to "hot-pit" refuel, and took off again without getting out of the airplane for another 2 1/2 hour flight to Incirlik.

When I got in the squadron operations building our Ops Officer told me I was leading a four-ship in the morning, and the mass brief was in twelve hours. I hurried to break out the Air Tasking Order (ATO, or "Frag"), and put together my part of the mission. Once that was done, we didn't have time to eat before meeting in my Ops Officer's room at 7:00 pm to discuss the overall game plan. My new roommate and I went back to the room for some peanut butter and jelly. By the time I finished my mission planning and got to bed it was 10:00 pm. We got up at three (3:00 am)

"Dutch's" F-15C 79-0064, seen in the standard "four by four by three by gun" configuration on the line at Incirlik. *Don Logan.*

and headed into the mass brief, where the dozens of F-16 strikers, F-16 and F-4G "Wild Weasel," KC-135, and EF-111 crews were gathered.

Afterward, we were briefing our 12-ship of F-15s when we got word the mission was delayed; we needed the extra time. Then our morning mission was postponed until the next day, which was *very* disappointing for me, and probably for all of us. Instead, my wingman and I were sent out to sit alert. We were scrambled that afternoon, and were airborne in less than five minutes to protect AWACS. We landed after dark, and prepared for an early morning mission. Saturday morning we launched the fleet, hammered targets in northern Iraq, and returned without losing any of the strikers or jammers we were protecting. That was a three hour mission. I finally got back to the room for a short nap before being night battle commander. The battle commander runs the squadron (coordinates launch and recovery, takes calls from higher command) in the commander's absence (he was flying). This was my routine for the first couple of weeks of DESERT STORM.

On 2 February I was air-to-air mission commander, and had eight F-15s and four F-16s at my disposal to protect a large F-16 strike force attacking an airfield south of Kirkuk, as well as other high value airborne assets (HVAAs) north of the border, and to cut off Iraqi aircraft attempting to escape into Iran. I was RIFLE 01, and my number two was Capt Rich Fullerton. The second element was lead by Capt "HM" Hepperlin, and Capt Mike Rockel was his wingman. My four-ship was flying barrier-CAP (BARCAP) east of Kirkuk and west of the Iranian border prior to the strike package pushing across the Turkey/Iraq border, when my number four got a radar contact at 4,000 feet. We chased him down as he headed west toward Kirkuk. His route was obscured by clouds and below our radar coverage until this point where we found him. We were five miles behind him and closing fast by the time I ascertained he was not a friendly and shot my first AIM-7 Sparrow (a radar guided missile). I jettisoned my external wing tanks and prepared to

follow up with a second shot, but the first missile guided perfectly. Because he was below a cloud deck we didn't see the explosion, and the kill is not (yet) confirmed. However, my number four's radar and mine both went "MEM" (Memory, or lost the target) when the missile timed out, and after we turned around and came back we couldn't find him, so we are fairly sure we got him. Efforts are being made to confirm the kill.

Afterwards, I was asked by Steve Davies, author of *F-15C Eagle Units In Combat* (Osprey Publications), "How did you feel about A) your achievement and B) the human aspect of the kill?" I thought that was a good question. At the time of the kill, I was really too busy to think much about it. My four-ship was getting dangerously close to the SAM defences around Kirkuk, so I was more interested in keeping my wingmen out of trouble than celebrating a victory or confirming the kill.

It was a long mission, so by the time I got back on the ground I had almost forgotten about the engagement. (I know that's hard to believe, but I was pretty tired.) However, the maintenance troops saw the missing AIM-7 and were ready to paint an Iraqi flag on the side of my jet. I hated to rain on their parade, but since the impact occurred below the clouds, we couldn't confirm the kill at the time.

I really wasn't faced with any deep feelings of remorse or overwhelming jubilation. I was doing my job, just like the men that undoubtedly died in the aircraft I shot down. I held no animosity toward the Iraqi soldiers and airmen trying to shoot me down, as I understood they were fighting for their country, just like I was. However, I would have no compunction about doing it again. Saddam Hussein was a threat to the entire free world, and his annexation of Kuwait and moves toward Saudi Arabia showed he was willing to use his enormous military and almost limitless wealth from oil to take whatever lands and peoples he wanted. Comparisons between Hussein and Hitler are strikingly similar. Just like Hitler, Hussein was no stranger to exterminating individuals or large groups of people that he didn't like. Perhaps if we had stopped the Germans and Japanese early when they first started annexing neighbouring territories and countries we could have avoided the world war that cost so many lives. The press and political pundits are crying for evidence of weapons of mass destruction to justify our final rout of Hussein's regime. I would think that his actions in the past, to include use of chemical and biological weapons against people within his own borders, would be reason enough to finish what we started, particularly in light of his failure to abide by the terms of his surrender.

All that said, yes, I was happy when they confirmed the kill. As an air-to-air fighter pilot, this is a mark of success. However, a more important mark, in my opinion, is that I never lost a wingman, nor any of the aircraft I was assigned to protect as air-to-air mission commander. That's an accomplishment achieved by everyone on my team, not just me as an individual. My kill, I'm forced to admit, was more a case of being at the right place at the right time—something that any one of my fellow F-15 pilots could have accomplished in my shoes. To be honest, part of me would have liked to have had more of a challenge from the Iraqi Air Force, but then we might have lost more people, so overall I'm

Left to right: Capt Rich Fullerton, Capt "Dutch" Masters, Capt "HM" Hepperlin, and Capt Mike Rockel at Incirlik after the engagement. *via "Dutch" Masters.*

A cartoon by "Dutch"; lots of spare time spent sitting alert proves that boredom and fighter pilots can be a dangerous and/or funny mix. *"Dutch" Masters.*

glad it went the way it did. I had two friends (Air Force Academy classmates) shot down in this war, one of whom didn't survive, and the other was a POW. They are among the true heroes of this war.

The kill was confirmed a month after the war as an Iraqi IL-76 Candid. The media later commented that it was possible that the aircraft was flying the Iraqi Air Marshal back from Iran, where he had been coordinating the disposition of Iraq's fighters that were fleeing into Iran. This story checks with other details, including the timing of the Air Marshal's death. This story was never confirmed in the Western media.

Capt Masters went on to graduate from the USAF Fighter Weapons Instructor Course and stand up the 366th Wing at Mountain Home, AFB, Idaho. The "Gunfighters" were the USAF's first modern composite wing (multiple aircraft types in a single war-fighting unit), modelled after the composite wing assembled at Incirlik for Operation PROVEN FORCE in support of DESERT STORM. "Dutch" retired from active duty in 2002 as a Lieutenant Colonel.

Captain Thomas "Vegas" Dietz (USAF)

53rd TFS "Tigers," F-15C
Operation DESERT STORM
2 x MiG-21 Kill
6 February 1991
Call-sign: ZEREX 53

Capt Dietz graduated the Air Force Academy, and completed UPT at Laughlin AFB, Texas. After completing F-15 training he was assigned to Eglin AFB, Florida, and then back to Luke AFB, Arizona, as an Instructor Pilot. After graduating the F-15C Fighter Weapons School he was assigned to the 53rd TFS at Bitburg Air Base, Germany. He had approximately 1,500 Eagle hours, and was the 53rd TFS's Weapons and Tactics Officer when the squadron deployed to Al Kharj, Saudi Arabia, for Operations DESERT SHIELD and STORM. "Vegas" penned his account for this publication.

By February 6, 1991, my wingman (1st Lt Bob "Gigs" Hehemann) and I were seasoned combat veterans (at least in our own minds). We had flown together every day for the past two months, and we could almost finish each other's jokes. That was our squadron commander's plan; the same team every day to ensure the best communication possible.

By now our missions were dominated by intense boredom. The typical mission lasted 8.5 hours with three aerial refuelings (the highlight of the flight, I might add). At least "Gigs" and I were on the "day team"; our squadron mates on the night team clearly had the more difficult task, and were less likely to see MiGs (Soviet built fighter aircraft) in the air. Thankfully, the Sony WalkMan® had been invented.

"Vegas" Dietz's F-15C 79-078 seen after DESERT STORM, sporting its two kill markings and a full combat load. *Don Logan collection.*

Debrief: A Complete History of U.S. Aerial Engagements, 1981 to the Present

"Gigs": "Rockin' with Ordnance" was our band's (Preset Freqs) promo video we were going to send to MTV (never sent it). Left to right: Me (Gigs), Major Scott "Mace" Mason on the bass, Capt Jay "Opie" Denney drums, SSgt "Skinman" Skinner (lead singer and crew chief), and Major "Gumby" West keyboards. *via 1 Lt Bob "Gigs" Hehemann.*

It was mid-morning, and "Gigs" and I were tasked to control the skies along the Iraq/Iran border east of Baghdad. Our mission was twofold: protect friendly aircraft operating in the area from Iraqi jets, and prevent the enemy from flying aircraft to Iran (Saddam's latest attempt to protect his assets).

AWACS rudely interrupted my excellent karaoke version of 38 Special's "Hold on Loosely" to point out the fact that several Iraqi MiGs were airborne about 60 miles northwest of our position and heading due east. It was the last "point out" they would provide due to the low altitude of the enemy, but it was critical, as our radars were not covering that airspace. We would not have found them on our own.

"Gigs" and I turned north, and pushed the throttles up to cut them off before the Iranian border. Descending out of 30,000 feet, our F-15C Eagles accelerated with ease, and quickly we were over Mach (speed of sound). We popped through a deck of clouds about 25 miles from the enemy, and the visibility below was excellent. "Gigs" was at my right three o'clock, about a mile and a half away in perfect position, as always. You'd never know he was the most inexperienced wingman in the squadron (played a pretty good lead guitar in the squadron band, as well).

As much as I hate to admit it, I remember being scared to death. Not that we wouldn't win this battle, but that we might screw something up. The F-15C success rate to date was near 100%, and most importantly, there were no friendly fire incidents. My main concern was that our sister squadron from Bitburg (the 525 TFS "Bulldogs") was patrolling the northern half of Iraq from a base in Turkey, and we were near the dividing line of our areas of responsibility. We had to be sure our targets were Iraqi.

After sanitizing the area around the targets with our radars I locked on to the lead group, and "Gigs" targeted the trail group. With clearance to fire from AWACS, I launched a radar guided missile at approximately eight miles from the lead MiG. Nothing

happened; the missile fell off my jet and the rocket motor didn't fire.

I looked over at "Gigs" to see a missile fire off his jet and guide perfectly. In a moment of selfishness I remember being pissed. The thought of cheering "Gigs" on while he carved up this group of MiGs like Eddie Rickenbacker against a bunch of Fokkers was more than I could handle. I quickly fired a second missile. The sight of it roaring past my canopy in route to the MiG, now five miles in front of me, was pure satisfaction.

Looking forward the MiGs were easy to spot. Flying very low (100 feet above the ground), the movement of their shadows across the desert terrain provided a sharp contrast. Unfortunately my radar drifted off the target, and my missile missed its mark. The MiGs were in close formation (about 100 feet apart), and I rolled in 1.5 miles behind them, launching one heat seeking missile at each fighter.

It seemed like an eternity (actually about 10 seconds) as the missiles traveled to their targets. The proximity fuses detonated as advertised, but the targets seemed unaffected, as they continued on course. It became obvious the Iraqi pilots were unaware of our presence. As I prepared to launch two more missiles I saw flames erupt from both MiGs. In seconds they began a shallow bank to the left and impacted the desert floor in a ball of fire. Regrettably, there were no parachutes. Such is a fact of war.

Proud of my success, I was snapped back to reality by thoughts of my wingman. Frankly, I hadn't checked on him for probably 30 seconds; quite a foul in the air-to-air combat business. As I turned my head to the left, anticipating that "Gigs" should have crossed over me as I rolled in on the two MiGs, I spotted another enemy fighter at my left 10 o'clock. To my dismay he was in perfect position to shoot his gun at me. As I prepared to defend myself I realized its tail section was missing, as was its canopy and pilot. Flames were pouring out of the fuselage. "Gigs" had covered my six perfectly.

Right after landing following the engagement, "Gigs" Hehemann (left) and "Vegas" Dietz "high-five," while both civilian and USAF media film the event. *via 1 Lt Bob "Gigs" Hehemann.*

I found my wingman at my left 9 o'clock, and another fireball in the desert floor at his left, 11 o'clock. Quite a day for any fighter pilot, let alone a lieutenant with just over six months of experience to his credit. Confident the skies were clear of any more enemy aircraft, we plugged in the burners and left the scene of the carnage as fast as we arrived.

"Gigs" and I patrolled the skies for another hour and a half before being relieved by two squadron mates. Unbeknownst to us, word of the squadron's latest four victories had spread like wildfire at our deployed base. The sea of teammates on the ramp for our arrival will be forever etched in my mind. It was a priceless reminder of the magnitude of airmen it takes to control the skies.

My fondest memory is of an exchange with a young airman after climbing out of the jet. He brashly informed me that were it not for his repair of the radar the night before, I never would have scored those kills. He was justifiably proud, and exactly right. I was equally proud to be in a unit where someone so young realized how important he was to the unit's success. Probably the biggest misnomer regarding air-to-air combat is the thought that it is a one-on-one competition.

Finally, it's important to put this encounter in perspective. Compared to our training this engagement was simple. Furthermore, "Gigs" and I were merely in the right place at the right time. I'm confident that any other American trained fighter pilot would have achieved the same result. The only explanation I can think of for "Gigs" and I achieving these victories is that we were better looking than the other guys in our squadron. Oh well.

Capt Dietz would go on to score another kill the following March.

1ˢᵗ Lt Robert "Gigs" Hehemann (USAF)

53ʳᵈ TFS "Tigers," F-15C
Operation DESERT STORM
2 x Su-25 Kill
6 February 1991
Call-sign: ZEREX 54

Lt Hehemann graduated from the University of Cincinnati in 1987 Cum Laude with a BS in Mechanical Engineering. He went on to graduate from UPT at Reese AFB, Texas, Class 89-06, having won just about every award there is to win, including an assignment to the F-15C. "Gigs" reported to Bitburg Air Base, Germany, and by the time of the DESERT SHIELD deployment, he had less than 200 hours in the Eagle. "Gigs" penned this account for this publication.

Lt Gen Robert Oaks, the USAFE Commander, stood in the front of our main briefing room in the hardened ops of the 53ʳᵈ TFS and began to speak. I'll never forget that he made an effort to come and visit every last one of us before we left for Saudi, and I'll never forget his words, "Good morning. I'm Bob Oaks, and I know exactly what each one of you is thinking right now...." Immediately I chuckled to myself, "Sure you do. There is no way you know what I'm thinking right now, General, I'm a 1 Lt on my way to combat, and you're a Three Star getting ready to retire!" Then, as if he was reading my mind, the tall Vietnam combat vet stood there in his flight suit and told me exactly what I was thinking:

"You're asking yourself what you need to change during your training sorties over the next two weeks to prepare for REAL combat. Now that you know you're on your way into combat, you want to train the way you plan to fight. I'm here to tell you not to change anything, because you're doing it right—you HAVE BEEN training the way we fight. You go out there and fly the jet the way you've been trained to fly it, and I'll see every last one of you back here when it's all over."

I repeated his words to myself in my cockpit many, many times over the following weeks and months.

"Gig's" F-15C 84-019 seen after DESERT STORM in full combat load. *Don Logan collection.*

The "elephant walk" and launch from Bitburg Air Base, Germany, that bitter winter morning of 22 December 1990 was memorable—snowing sideways, 200 foot overcast, and less than one mile visibility (below our peacetime takeoff minimums). We taxied 28 fully loaded F-15Cs from the TabV shelters and lined 'em up out on the alert ramp and down the parallel taxiway—28 times four AIM-7 Sparrows, four AIM-9 Mikes, 940 rounds of 20mm HEI, and three 4000 pound external bags. It was an awesome sight to behold. The plan was to "taxi 28 and launch 26 to get 24." As number four in the Squadron Commander's four-ship, I had a front row seat in the arming area, and launched with the first eight-ship group for Al Kharj, Saudi Arabia. I was on "Vegas'" wing for the six and a half hour trip down, and I was as stoked and nervous as I've ever been. When all five stages lit and I was hurtling down the runway into the whiteout above it hit me: Holy shit, we're going to combat.

"Hey "Gigs," don't worry about it—by the time we fly a combat mission, you'll have it down." Spoken in a way only he could say it, the way he had done it so many times before, and would do so many more times over the coming months and years, "Vegas" put me at ease, and let me know he believed in me. He was talking about my poor performance on the tanker during our six+ hour journey to Saudi. Like every word that Vegas ever spoke, it was true: it was indeed ugly. We got gas so often in the coming days leading up to the war, however, as he predicted, by the time it counted I could do it with my eyes closed.

It is this incredible patience and ability to say the right thing at the right time to get the best effort and results from your student or wingman that separates the best instructors from the rest. Captain Tom "Vegas" Dietz was, without doubt, the best instructor I'd ever flown with, and it's a good thing "Bigs" put me on his wing, because I had a lot to learn. A tireless FWIC Graduate hungry to save all average fighter pilots from themselves and build the best fighter squadron in the Air Force, "Vegas" spent countless hours planning, analyzing, and coordinating every mission we flew. As number three and four in Lt Col Randy "Bigs" Bigum's four-ship, we had been flying together for about a month prior to the deployment, and would continue to do so throughout the war. I drew an incredible straw being paired with "Vegas" for the war, and once again found myself in the right place, with the right people, at the right time: Lt Col Randy "Bigs" Bigum, 53rd TFS Commander; Capt Lynn "Boo Boo" Broome; and "Vegas." Beyond his tremendous skills as a fighter pilot and instructor, "Vegas" was an absolute riot to hang out with. When he's too old to fly jets, he'll certainly be able to find work on stage.

The big thing that sticks out in my mind about flying all those missions in Iraq was the night of 16 January 1991, and finding out that we were really going to war. It was set to kick-off at 0300L on the morning of the 17th with a strike of F-117s and a huge night sweep of 24 Eagles across Iraq. There was an eight-ship from our squadron led by "Killer" Miller, with an eight-ship from Eglin in the west, and eight more from Langley in the east. Our four-ship was on the day schedule, so we spent most of that first night as the SCUD missile warnings went off in a fox hole. Our biggest concern was that all eight of our Eagle brethren made it home safely, and

we found out in the morning that they did. I heard some pretty harrowing stories from some of the F-16 guys at the breakfast table. Once in the squadron, I remember the Intel briefing from our Intel Officer that it was expected that the Iraqis would get as many as 50 MiGs airborne out of Tallil and Jalibah Air Bases on the first morning during our sweep. Our four-ship was escorting about 18 F-16s doing the bombing, with Wild Weasels and an EF-111 for stand-off jamming. I was doing the math, and since we had 32 missiles in our flight, if they put up 50 MiGs we were going to have our hands full!

The entire mission was planned and briefed comm-out. I'll never forget that first drive north; it was definitely time to pucker up a little of the seat cushion. But as we pushed north, I was thinking about what Gen Oaks had said about flying the airplane the way we were trained, and we would all come home. So I was working hard to maintain my contract as the most eastern guy in our wall of Eagles, and run the radar to the best of my ability. I saw some friendly indications on the far right of my scope, and they turned out to be four Eagles coming out of Iraq. I could see three of the four as we passed, and I could tell the guy closest to me still had his tanks and all eight missiles. To my left were our three Eagles, and that made me think that the Iraqis had about as much to be afraid of as I did. It kind of gave me some confidence. We pushed on in, but no MiGs launched, so we set up our reset CAP. The Vipers dropped their bombs and egressed, and we followed the package out. It all went like clockwork, and as the missions went on my confidence grew, because you'd been there, "been to the mountain."

We fell into a very regimented routine of eat, sleep, and fly. As time went on Saddam changed his strategy, and tried to hunker down and hide his air force. But as the bunker-busting bombs had been designed his forces were starting to dwindle, as his jets were getting destroyed in their shelters. He again changed his strategy to "let's run east and hide my air force in Iran." We had divided Iraq into three lanes, and the responsibility for the far east part of Iraq along the Iranian border fell to the 1st TFW, and their two squadrons based at Daharan. As the story goes, Gen Buster Glosson called the 1st TFW and asked them to set up Barrier CAPs (BARCAP) east of Baghdad to stop these MiGs from escaping. They wanted the MiGs destroyed so they would not come back later. As the story goes, the 1st TFW declined this tasking due to the SAM coverage and limited on-station times available that far into Iraq. The next thing we know Buster Glosson is calling our wing, the 4th TFW Provisional, to see if we were interested. The Wing Commander deferred to our Commander, Lt Col Bigum, who said, "Yeah, that sounds like fun, we'll do that." Of our 11 kills in the 53rd TFS, eight of them came from BARCAP patrols in eastern Iraq. On 27 January "OP" Denney and "Coma" Powell got their four kills. They had a great mission, and came back and talked about it, so we knew there might be some action up there.

These missions required a lot of planning and leg work by "Vegas" and Lt Col Bigum, as well as everyone who flew them. The BARCAP area was sandwiched between the SAM rings of Baghdad, which was still heavily defended with SA-2s and SA-6s, and the Iranian border. It was an hour and fifteen minutes to get to the tanker, twenty minutes in the tanker track, and another 35 minutes to get to the CAP, weaving around the SAM rings. At 34,000 feet and 290 knots that only left us about 25 minutes on station. We flew these as six-ships, since it was necessary to constantly shuttle two-ships back to the tankers. These turned into eight hour missions. It was also a challenge to cover the low block with the radar, as we were high, slow, and very close to Baghdad, which forced some extreme look-down angles to cover the search volume. AWACS was also not always very helpful in this CAP, as they had to stay so far south out of the SAM threat.

On 6 February, at about nine in the morning, "Vegas" and I were on our second shuttle in the CAP when AWACS called out two unknown contacts 60 miles north of our location heading east at low altitude. "Vegas" checked us about 45 degrees right to a northwest heading, and we picked these guys up on our radars. AWACS almost immediately lost them down in the weeds, but we were able to maintain radar contact on them. "Vegas" and I stroked it up, and started down on a beam intercept, since we were starting up so high. The ROE dictated that we ascertain that they were both positive hostile with a lack of friendly indications, as well as clear field of fire. We continued to work on the ID while we ramped-down through a cloud deck that forced me to collapse to a close route formation until we popped out of the bottoms at about 20,000 feet. I slid back out to tactical on the right, or east side, as we were now heading about 340 degrees. I had been sanitizing the high block when "Vegas" told me to bring my radar down and get a sort. On the radar we saw a lead-trail presentation with two groups, but we had no idea of how many aircraft were in each group. "Vegas" targeted me into the far, or trail group. At about 18 miles I brought my ACQ symbol in from the back and took a lock, but I wasn't sure of the sort, so I called "Locked."

After "Vegas" and I solved the sort problem and ID'd them, he shot first into the lead group with an AIM-7 at just over 10 miles. I brought my nose down to go pure, and point at these guys and take my first AIM-7 shot. I was at 10,000 feet, and took a shot just outside of 10 miles into the trail group showing a 12R aspect. (In other words, I was looking at the front, right quarter of his aircraft.) My group was in the weeds, and had accelerated from 340 knots to 380 knots, so while we were not getting spiked, they seemed to be aware that they were targeted. "Vegas" crossed under my nose in a right hand turn through north as he was converting behind his east-bound group. I saw my missile track into the ground just long of the dot in the TD box, so it may have fused on the ground or just been a bad missile. I still had a shoot cue, and the target was still in the TD box, so I took a second AIM-7 shot. I was almost 6,000 feet directly above him, pointed down in my conversion, and as the missile came off my jet the TD box drifted off the target, so I knew the radar had broken lock. So there's no chance the AIM-7 was going to guide, and that shot was trashed.

At that point I disregarded the radar and thumbed-back to an AIM-9. As I squared the corned above and behind that guy I was about two miles behind with a lot of closure. I didn't bother with the radar, I just bore-sighted the AIM-9 on the MiG and got a great heat growl. I un-caged the missile and let her rip. Just as I fired this missile, I saw a second aircraft at my right one o'clock. Everyone was now running east; "Vegas" was on the group farther to the south out at my right two o'clock, and the bandits were at about 100-300 feet, and we were just above them at 400-500 feet. As I saw the second MiG, I ripped my nose to the right to point at him, bore-sighted another AIM-9, un-caged, and shot. This missile also appeared to guide, doing that wavy, Sidewinder thing.

I then saw a third target to the right, so again I pointed and set up to shoot, but as I got ready to come down on the hammer, that guy exploded. This was one of "Vegas'" kills, so I then put my attention back on the first MiG I had shot at out at my left 10-11 o'clock. He had just hit the ground, and the best way I can describe it is like seeing a lit cigarette being drug along the concrete, with all the burning embers coming off, and long fire across the ground. That was pretty impressive. So I pointed at the second guy I had targeted, and I was closing inside of a mile when I saw the missile fly up and impact the tail of his aircraft. The aircraft was blown in half behind the wing line, and the nose pitched violently, flat-plating up and right. I could immediately VID the aircraft as a SU-25 Frogfoot, fully equipped with pylons and missiles. The tail was on fire, and I was closing rapidly on the nose section, so I had to bring it right, where his nose was also pointing. Looking right I saw "Vegas" close aboard, about 2,000 feet to my right, and it looked like the Frogfoot could turn on the gun at us. Turned out he was no threat, and we never saw a chute. He impacted the sand, and both of "Vegas'" MiG-21s are splashed, so he called for burners and a quick climb to get out of the low altitude environment. I flowed back out into tactical formation line abreast, and we got spiked by an SA-6 SAM site to the south, but we avoided him and proceeded back toward the CAP point. The whole engagement, from the first shot to my last, was only 15 seconds. You've never felt an adrenaline rush like that, with missiles flying and jets blowing up!

As we climbed back up AWACS reported another group 30 miles behind us going same-way, same-day. We had each fired two AIM-7s and two AIM-9s, so that was half our load-out. I remember thinking, "I sure hope "Vegas" calls for a 180-right, because I want to go back and do that again." But wiser, cooler heads prevailed,

This photo of myself (left) and "Vegas" was taken the following morning (7 February 1991), after the flags had been painted on the jets. *via 1Lt Bob "Gigs" Hehemann.*

"Gigs'" F-15C with the double-kill markings, seen at RAF Fairford in 1991. *Ed Groenstein.*

and "Vegas" opted to take us back to get more gas and our wits together, then cover the rest of the patrol. That is what we did, and the rest of the patrol was uneventful. When we got back to Al Kharj AWACS had already passed the word, so it was like a scene out of the movie TOPGUN. There were camera crews there from CNN and the Air Force, and we even gave some interviews right there on the ramp. It was a great opportunity to thank all of our great maintenance and weapons crews that worked so hard to make these kills possible. This video made it back to the States pretty quick, and my sister saw the video and said, "I'm pretty sure that's my little brother!" My 15 minutes of fame!

Lt Hehemann would go on to get one more kill in March 1991.

Lt Stuart "Meat" Broce (USN)
CMDR Ron "Bongo" McElraft (USN)

VF-1 "Wolfpack," F-14A
Operation DESERT STORM
Mil-8 Kill
6 February 1991
Call-sign: WICHITA 103

Stuart Broce entered the Navy via the Merchant Marine Reserve (California Maritime Academy), graduating in 1986. He went through primary flight training at Whiting Field, Florida, and jet training at Meridian, Mississippi. He was selected for F-14s, and went through the RAG at NAS Miramar. This was "Meat's" first tour in the Tomcat, and he had roughly 200 hours in type at the start of the cruise. The following account was written by Stuart for this publication.

Rear Admiral "Zap" Zlatopper was the junior of the three carrier battle group commanders stationed in the Arabian Gulf in early February 1991. With the Operation DESERT STORM air campaign being waged around the clock, Admiral Zlatopper's relative lack of seniority earned his battle group, based around the aircraft carrier *USS Ranger*, the 8 pm to 4 am shift. What that meant to the F-14 Tomcat aircrews of the VF-1 "Wolfpack" and VF-2 "Bounty Hunters" based on the *Ranger* was, of course, a lot of night flying, which isn't much fun off a boat, especially during a war.

During DESERT STORM CAG 2, the air group aboard *USS Ranger*, was an "all Grumman (aircraft corporation)" air wing, composed mainly of F-14 Tomcat fighters, A-6 Intruder bombers,

EA-6B Prowler jammers, and E-2 Hawkeye radar control aircraft. At the time the F-14 served strictly as an air-to-air fighter, and had not yet picked up the air-to-ground role that it grew to dominate later in the decade. As such, the F-14 picked up the duties of patrolling the skies over the Arabian Gulf for enemy aircraft—and even then got vectored away from the only pair of enemy aircraft that dared poke their noses into the Gulf so that Saudi pilots could down them and, ostensibly, become more vested, visible members of the allied coalition.

Other than a handful of hairy night forays over occupied Kuwait and southern Iraq to attack enemy ground positions, we didn't spend much time over land. Even those strikes rarely went more than a hundred miles or so inland, and never in the daylight.

"Meat" and "Bongo's" F-14A, Bu Number 162603, seen later in March 1992 at NAS Miramar. *Jeff Puzzullo.*

Forward view of the *USS Ranger* (CV-61) making way. *USN.*

So, there I was, one of the few pilots available with the crew rest (in the Navy, at the time, three hours of uninterrupted sleep) behind me to soak up one of the very few good deal day missions the *Ranger's* air wing stumbled into. The mission was planned to be a two-hour flight to provide air protection for a "high value asset," a *Ranger* EA-6B Prowler on a jamming mission in support of a daylight air strike in occupied Kuwait. It promised to be a nice break from the endless night formation flying in crappy weather that had become the norm since we pulled into the Gulf on 15 January, the day prior to the start of the war. I kept a journal:

January 21: Last night I flew from 10 pm to 2 am, again. Night flying isn't much fun without getting shot at, but last night, flying at our assigned CAP (combat air patrol) altitude, we were fired upon by someone on an oil platform just visible through the clouds. I'm glad they use tracers: you can see where they're aiming. In the post-flight debrief, my flight lead said he saw tracers pass between my left wing and horizontal stabilizer—no mention during the flight, though.

Heading back to the ship at a reasonable altitude, and south of the bad weather, I was looking at the lighted cities along the eastern coastline of Saudi Arabia twenty-five miles away. It was a gorgeous sight. The stars were out in force in the desert air. Every flight, so far, I'd seen at least half a dozen shooting stars, so when I saw what appeared to be a meteorite disintegrating over the nearest city to me, I told my RIO to look. Just after he looked the meteorite went below the horizon, hit the ground, and exploded in a bright, white flash. Another followed seconds later—"Scud" missiles from Iraq. Many miles to the north, artillery opened fire in apparent retaliation thirty seconds later. Welcome to war. It all just became a bit more real to me in my air conditioned bubble.

Back overhead the ship, the ship's controllers were trying to kill us. We had just enough gas to get back at our scheduled

recovery time and comfortably shoot an approach or two. An hour later, after getting a little gas from a tanker, I made it aboard on my first pass, luckily. If I had shown up with that little fuel three weeks ago, I would have had to talk to CAG. Last night I had more gas than most out there. No one said anything. My lead, probably still thinking about getting shot at and watching the missile attack, got aboard on his sixth landing attempt. He had to hit the tanker again some time during the ordeal. I guess that's what we make the medium bucks for.

We tried to keep crews paired as much as possible, but my usual RIO (Radar Intercept Officer in the back seat), Steve "Spike" Riker, was off on a two-week stint in Saudi Arabia as guest help in some planning cell, so the VF-1 Commanding Officer at the time, Ron "Bongo" McElraft, was scheduled to be my RIO for the flight. The flight lead for this day mission was LCDR Bill "Whiskey"

Self-portrait of "Meat" Broce over the Indian Ocean just prior to DESERT STORM. *Broce.*

Bond, a great stick, and the only flight lead in the squadron that I trusted—a nice break from my RIO-turned-pilot regular flight lead, who generally sucked, and couldn't understand why a nugget (brand new pilot) couldn't fly in perfect formation at night, *inside* a thunderstorm. The strike brief and fighter element briefs, expedited by three weeks of combat experience, were made more interesting by the promise of actually seeing the ground, and returning to the ship in daylight for a welcome change. We actually had to spend a little extra time briefing day recovery procedures.

Almost every fighter launch during the war included one spare aircraft and crew in case one of the mission jets had mechanical problems before the launch. Our spare crew was pilot Scott "Ash" Malynn and RIO Dan "Zimby" Zimberoff. "Ash" was the third most "junior" pilot in the squadron, in terms of fleet Tomcat experience, with only a year and a half in the squadron. I was the junior pilot, with about six months under my belt, and only three weeks of actual on-station experience, all but one day of that during the war. I had missed all of the squadron workups, and my total fighter experience prior to the war had been a few sessions of getting beat up by senior squadron flight leads in practice dogfights, lots of night traps, and a training Sparrow missile launch against a TALD (Tactical Air-Launched Decoy) over the Indian Ocean on the way to the Gulf.

Startup in the hazy sunlight on the flight deck was uneventful. The waters of the Arabian Gulf were typically calm, and that day was no exception. Due to positioning on the deck, my jet was the first Tomcat to get broken-down, or have the tie-down chains removed prior to taxi. As I taxied to the catapult, I looked over toward "Ash" and "Zimby's" jet and noted one of the yellow shirted flight deck directors motioning to the ground crew to launch the spare jet. As I found out later, "Whiskey's" jet was parked from the prior mission in such a way that when he taxied out behind me, one of his tires bumped up against one of the curbs on the flight deck that were supposed to prevent things from rolling off the edge, and prevented forward motion. Instead of assembling men and equipment to rectify the situation, the decision was made to launch the spare.

Ten minutes later "Ash" and I joined up on the way to the rendezvous point. After a series of confused hand signals trying to figure out who had the lead at that point (the contingency wasn't covered in the brief) I took the lead on the squadron radio frequency. I figured that, though I was the junior pilot, I had the skipper in the back seat. No one protested, I think because everyone knew that "Bongo" could be somewhat of a micromanager. We continued north over the gulf at our assigned rendezvous altitude.

"Bongo" didn't talk much in the jet, but a couple of minutes later, as we performed our weapons checks, he told me that our radar system was hopelessly inoperative. As the Tomcat RIOs handle all but dogfight radio communications, "Bongo" was our voice on the radio—we didn't fess to anyone but our wingman. It didn't change the fact that we would continue—we already had our spare aircraft along with us, it was only an escort mission, and there were other non-radar ways we could launch our eight missiles (four AIM-9 Sidewinders and four AIM 7 Sparrows) and 700 high-explosive 20mm bullets. The radar sure would help, though.

As soon as our weapons checks were complete, and ten minutes prior to the rendezvous point, our controller broke the quiet on the radio and told our flight to switch to a new frequency for "alternate tasking." We switched the radios and checked in.

I never figured out who it was that we switched to, but they told us to proceed to an Air Force KC-135 tanker at the far north end of the Gulf, top off, proceed to a new CAP (Combat Air Patrol) station, and look for enemy air activity there. As the controller read off the coordinates, something didn't seem right. With the autopilot on, I dug out all the area navigation charts I carried that had never been unfolded. The highly unusual change in tasking and the urgency in the new controller's voice indicated, to me at least, that something was up.

The skipper acknowledged our orders. I looked in the rearview mirrors and saw the back of the charts he was unfolding as well, to find our new station. We soon realized that none of our charts went far enough north. Not by a long shot. I figured the CAP station was about halfway between the Gulf and Baghdad, but I had nothing in the cockpit to back that up with. At the time, the best navigation

An excellent view of another VF-1 "Wolfpack" F-14A, side number 113, seen at NAS Fallon, Nevada, in 1988. *USN photo by Michael Grove.*

information in the F-14A, by *far*, came from an early, commercial handheld GPS unit with a crappy user interface: five buttons and a two-line LCD alphanumeric display. Still, I was pretty fired up for the new tasking. Besides, I thought, we had eight missiles, two huge motors, and total unpredictability (absence of a plan) on our side.

After topping off at the tanker we pressed on, skirting known SAM sites in Kuwait and on into southern Iraq. As we continued north the weather got worse, and before long we were dodging thunderstorms at 25,000 feet. As we flew past Basra—a city of over a million in southern Iraq, and the last area we had chart coverage for—I noticed gray puffs of smoke appearing around "Ash" and "Zimby's" jet, a mile to the left. Apparently some of the Iraqi heavy anti-aircraft artillery was making it up to our altitude. So much for our unpredictability. I increased our jinking—probably too much, as "Zimby" later told me that his radar was having troubles keeping up with the maneuvering. No such problem in our jet.

A few minutes later, I remember thinking that we were already farther north than anyone in the battle group had gone. Then I realized that we were well beyond the reach of a quick rescue—if we shelled out from then on, combat evasion would ensue. I purposely never thought much about being captured.

Realizing that we were up where the USAF F-15s were getting all the kills during the war, I mentally reviewed the weapons options for the jet; it didn't take long. I had the capability of launching both the Sidewinders and Sparrows, but only by pointing the Tomcat directly at the intended target, and even then, launching them only in degraded launch modes—*highly* degraded in the case of the radar guided Sparrow.

Soon we were out of radio range of our E-2 Hawkeye controllers back in the Gulf and under Air Force AWACS control. The skies grew darker, and cloud coverage increased to the point that glimpses of the desert and marshes below became infrequent.

About twenty minutes later we reported that we were on station, and turned toward our best guess at Baghdad's direction to start flying a racetrack pattern in hopes that "Zimby," perhaps the most technically proficient RIO in the squadron at the time, could get a good picture on his radar. "Zimby" remained quiet, which meant he wasn't seeing anything. I moved the weapon select switch on the stick from "OFF" to "AIM-7," figuring that the Sparrow had, marginally, the best range of our limited shot options. Meanwhile, I scanned the ground through the clouds in an attempt to mark our position, and detect any telltale signs of a missile launch. There was a small settlement, a river, and a few lakes in the area. I was also looking for any artillery, heavy equipment, revetments, or any other military activity.

After about ten minutes on station, our controller broke the (until then) radio silence with, "Wolfpack, engage bandit, vector 210-36, angels low, nose on!" Translation: "Hey! Turn to a heading of 210°. Attempt to destroy the enemy aircraft 36 miles in that direction. He's low and heading toward you!" No word on what type of aircraft it was.

On the radio, I immediately passed the tactical lead for the intercept to "Ash" and "Zimby," as their functioning radar dictated. We lit the afterburners and turned to maintain wingman position.

Without a radar all of our intercept training, including radar sorting contracts and section (two-ship) tactics, were out the window: we were along for the ride as two extra pairs of eyes, and probably in "Ash" and "Zimby's" thoughts, simply a 20mm gun platform.

At some point after the initial turn to intercept I asked "Bongo" to verify something we all heard, but had trouble assimilating: the use of the word "bandit." I think the call was, "Understand we're cleared to fire?" The immediate reply was something like, "Affirmative! Cleared hot, weapons free!" spoken by a new, very senior-sounding, and almost angry voice from the AWACS.

I selected the master arm switch to "on" for the first time in a non-training environment and said, "Recorder on!" over the intercom, thinking somebody was about to die, and I wanted it recorded on our onboard HUD camera/voice recorder, and either debriefed back at the boat, or pulled from the wreckage and reviewed. There was no response from the back seat.

As we accelerated and spread out the calls came fast. Every ten seconds or so the AWACS controller updated us with bearing and range calls. The bearing remained constant, indicating that the bandit was headed directly at, or away from us, but the miles ticked off very rapidly, indicating the former. At ten miles from the contact, with no word from "Ash" and "Zimby" about a radar contact, we were screaming downhill, weaving through the cloud layers at the speed of sound. In the excitement, I think "Ash" forgot to pull his throttles back out of afterburner. I repeated "Recorder on!" Again, no response from "Bongo."

I leveled off at 3,000 feet. With "Ash" well below me, and over a mile to my right, the controller said "Merged plot!," meaning that one of our Tomcats was occupying the same spot as the enemy aircraft on his radar screen. I went into hyper-scan, splitting my time between looking around "Ash's" jet and ours, jinking, and flipping the jet from side to side, looking for any sign of aircraft, or the dreaded smoke trail of an enemy missile.

After four or five frantic seconds the skipper said, "Come left! Helicopter!" I looked left and glimpsed the helicopter back behind us, flying in the opposite direction two miles away, at about five hundred feet. I slammed the jet into a 7g turn and held it for about 270°. During the turn, in addition to getting the Tomcat's direction changed in near record time, I also grayed myself out to where I couldn't see anything smaller than a mountain range. I had to strain to get my vision back quickly when the g's let off.

After a few seconds thinking I'd blown it, I visually picked up the camouflaged helicopter about two miles in front of us, heading toward a small village, now flying at about fifty feet above the ground, and going pretty fast (for a helicopter). The main rotor was tipped noticeably forward, and I remember thinking, "So *that's* what 'full tilt' means." The helicopter's fuselage was football shaped, and familiar from our endless aircraft recognition training on the boat during transit from the states. It was a Soviet-built Mi-8 "Hip" armed transport, and though I couldn't name it at the time, I knew none of the allied coalition forces had them in theater.

It wasn't a conscious thought, but I knew right away that a Sparrow shot wouldn't work in that situation. I switched to AIM-9 and set up for an immediate boresight Sidewinder tail shot, but hesitated as I brought the nose to bear when I saw the village just beyond the helicopter. I pulled off at about a thousand feet without even trying to get a tone (over the intercom, from the missile's seeker head indicating it "saw" a heat source), not as a noble, conscious attempt to minimize civilian casualties, but more as an instant visceral aversion to firing a missile toward homes.

Instead, I pitched up and to the left with the thought of gaining a little bit of altitude and lateral separation, then reversing for high-aspect attack from above, and about a mile off the helicopter's left side. I knew the maneuver would buy time for the target to get beyond the town. It also helped me bleed off a couple of hundred knots, down to an airspeed of about 350 knots. At an apex of about 3,500 feet, I rolled to about 135° angle of bank and pulled the nose around to put the seeker head position indicator centered on my HUD onto the helicopter's exhaust.

When I rolled wings level and started downhill, the next six or seven seconds seemed pretty busy. The seeker head didn't sing to me like I was hoping it would. I moved the nose of the jet around slightly to find a hotter spot—knowing that the missile seeker didn't always line up with the crosshairs on the HUD. As I did this "Bongo" said, "'Meat,' what the hell are you doing?" Though his situational awareness and timing weren't good, the message was understandable, since we were accelerating toward the ground from an already low altitude, and I didn't have time to explain my plan and get his opinion. So I ignored him and kept fishing for a tone, realizing that I wouldn't get one looking down over the desert during the day. What I did notice, however, was that there was a slight change in the background growl when the seeker head passed over the helicopter's exhaust, so I attempted to cage the missile to the target with a button on the left throttle.

After my third attempt to get a lock-on, and running out of room and altitude, I let the nose drift a little behind the target on a hunch that there was enough of a heat signature for a lock, despite the lack of a tone. The HUD's seeker head position indicator stayed superimposed on the helicopter as it drifted slightly from center. In a fraction of a second I thought, "Well, that's about as good as it'll get today, and I've got three more...*and* a bunch of bullets." So I pulled the trigger.

As I started the firing sequence, "Bongo" reiterated his concern, "PULL UP! WHAT THE HELL ARE YOU...." He stopped as the missile roared off its rail and rocketed *loudly* past the canopy to his left. "Oh!"

The noise and flame surprised me, too, as it drowned out the sound of the wind and the engines briefly. Besides, it was the first, and last, Sidewinder I ever launched. Immediately off the rail, the 'winder did what it was supposed to do; it aggressively pulled lead on its high-line-of-sight-rate target. I was certain that it had gone stupid and was racing for a sand dune miles in front of the helicopter, so I thought about possibly getting a gun shot in the four-tenths of a second remaining before I had to pull up.

Right about then, out of the corner of my eye, I saw the Sidewinder's flame turn *hard* toward the target. As I started to pull, I turned my head and watched the missile cover the last few hundred yards and fly *into* the helicopter's left exhaust port. The helicopter instantly turned into a bright yellow fireball a couple

of hundred feet in diameter, with pieces flying out radially in all directions. I pulled hard to avoid the big pieces and flames.

With a slight climb started, and assured we would miss the wreckage (barely), I dipped a wing and watched the fireball collapse into what looked like an Olympic-pool sized mass of dense orange flame slamming into the ground, kicking up massive amounts of dirt and rocks. The flames gave way to thick black smoke, and out in front of the whole mess of fire and parts, I saw a single rotor blade flipping through the air in apparent slow motion. The whole sequence took maybe four seconds and, eerily, was absolutely silent, other than our normal jet noises.

I lit the blowers and headed straight up to get away from what I was sure would be hundreds of pissed off Iraqis with shoulder launched missiles. I told "Ash" to meet us on top of the weather, and "Bongo" gave AWACS a call as he searched his kneeboard cards for the correct code words: "Uh, splash one, uhhhh...helicopter!"

We rejoined silently. I took the lead again with visual signals, and we coordinated with the AWACS for a trip back down to the Arabian Gulf to refuel. We were met in line at the KC-135 by two jets from our squadron on another mission. The flight lead of that flight, Ed "Opus" Gassie, pulled up close to my left side. As I looked over at him, he looked back and forth between my empty missile rail and me several times, then raised his visor and gave me a "What the f**k?" shrug before backing off.

"Ash" and I topped off, then returned, as ordered, to the same CAP station for another stint. The trip north seemed longer the second time. I was sure we were going to get another call since, up to that point in my career, *every* overland CAP station I'd set resulted in a kill within fifteen minutes, but the second call never came. After about an hour we got the signal to proceed to a refueling station southeast of our position, near the Saudi border west of Kuwait. We drained the last "give" fuel from a KC-10 there just as a flight of four F-15 Eagles pulled up, then we headed back to the CAP station for another half an hour.

Night fell as we departed the CAP station to return to the Gulf. On the way out of Iraq, at AWACS request, we descended back through the weather to perform battle damage assessment on a very recently attacked strategic target. We stayed close together and broke out pretty low in the dusk, then descended further to remain out of the clouds. As the last of my adrenaline wore off, we flew literally *among* the burning remnants of the bombed-out facility. The scene was surreal; our night low-level lit by fires on the ground. "Bongo" passed the BDA to AWACS, and we climbed out to the south.

An hour later, in the familiar black skies south of the ship in holding, with little energy left for the night approach, we got a call from the boat saying one of our squadron jets had just launched and the landing gear wouldn't retract. "Ash" and "Zimby" had less fuel than we did, so we split up. While our wingman recovered, we found (visually, the *fun* way, of course—no radar) our troubled squadron mates overhead the ship at seven thousand feet, joined up, and then flew directly beneath them, ten feet below their belly in the darkness, while "Bongo" used his flashlight to check out their landing gear.

Detail of kill marking on F-14A side-number 103 or "Wolf" 103. *Broce.*

Seeing nothing out of the ordinary, they brought them down to land before us (they *did* have obligations over Kuwait that night). As it turned out the plane captain, trouble shooters, catapult crew, final checkers, and launch officer all missed the main gear down-lock pins, with large red flags attached, still in place on their gear. The pins were pulled, and they launched into the night again before we recovered.

I used much of my remaining energy and concentration snagging the two-wire in the darkness, six and a half hours after launch. They parked us right in front of the island, and after the chains were in place anchoring us to the flight deck, and the throttles went to cutoff, about fifty people emerged out of the darkness and surrounded our jet.

Skipper got out first, and when I hit the bottom of the ladder, Captain Jay "Rabbit" Campbell (Commander of the Air Group: "CAG") grabbed my hand, and patted me on the back in the darkness. About thirty other people shook hands with me, and tried to yell things above the noise of the jets. Someone handed me the piece of cable that had connected the Sidewinder to the aircraft, to keep as a memento.

Another maintainer on the flight deck came up to me and yelled, "Where's your tape?," referring to our ¾-inch videotape cassette that would have recorded the entire intercept and shoot-down.

"What?" I replied.

"The HUD tape. There isn't one in the recorder!"

Suddenly the skipper's silence every time I said, "Recorder on!" made sense to me. Not three weeks earlier, "Bongo" had made it very clear to every officer in the squadron that it was the RIO's responsibility and duty to bring a blank video tape to the jet, and ensure it was inserted into the onboard recorder. He had forgotten it on this flight. That would explain the silence and apparent distraction during the intercept.

We headed down to debrief the flight in CVIC (where the Intel guys work), and they had three video cameras set up and a bunch of people waiting, including a fired up Admiral Zlatopper. We spoke for about fifteen minutes, and headed down toward our ready room, where three more cameras and half the squadron were waiting.

We told the same story of the day to the guys in the ready room, then to the commander of the Navy in the Gulf over secure radio from the Admiral's office (he's got a big office with couches, a big desk, and a big TV). Finally, we made it to the wardroom to eat with the CAG. The skipper of the boat showed up to hear our stories and congratulate us. While we ate, CNN mentioned us on the big TV in the wardroom.

Of course, during each set of storytelling, the question of the video tape came up.

Two days later, my Intelligence Officer roommate (one of seven) gave me a couple of cryptic details about the helicopter gathered by Special Ops the day prior, increasing my suspicion that there was prior knowledge of, and extreme prejudice, towards the helicopter flight.

Three days later, the skipper went to Riyadh to meet with Dick Cheney (Secretary of Defense) and General Colin Powell (Chairman of the Joint Chiefs of Staff). I didn't go because I refused to shave off my earlobe-length, but legal at the time, sideburns for the trip.

Looking back, there were lots of mistakes made that day, not the least of which was taking a lame aircraft into combat. Our tactical intercept communication between jets was unacceptably near-nonexistent.

The good things: The systems and training of everyone from the young ordnance crew to my limited weapons knowledge worked. Speaking of limited weapons knowledge (at the time), I expanded the AIM-9 Sidewinder employment envelope that day

During the *USS Ranger's* 24th and final deployment, spanning 1 August 1992 through 30 January 1993, "Meat" Broce and VF-1 saw combat over Iraq (Operation SOUTHERN WATCH) and Somalia (Operation RESTORE HOPE). In this cruise photo,, the flight deck personnel spell out the latter. *USN.*

in a few ways, including, I believe, minimum range. Strangely, as far as I know, it was the first helicopter shot down in combat by an American pilot, and it was followed a few hours later by the downing of another Iraqi helicopter by an Air Force A-10.

Lt Broce went on to fly a total of 40 combat sorties during DESERT STORM. While still with the "Wolfpack" in 1992-3, "Meat" went back to the gulf for more Operation SOUTHERN WATCH (OSW) and RESTORE HOPE (Somalia) sorties. After joining the "Blacklions" of VF-213, he cruised again for more OSW. After leaving the Navy for a time Stuart rejoined the military, this time the USAF. He checked out in the U-2, and has flown two U-2 combat deployments for Operations IRAQI FREEDOM and ENDURING FREEDOM (but no night traps!). Stuart is currently a U-2 Instructor Pilot with the United States Air Force. With the retirement of the USN F-14s in 2006, this marks the last U.S. kill for the type.

Captain Robert "Swaino" Swain (USAFR)

706th TFS "Cajuns," A-10
Operation DESERT STORM
Bo-105 Kill
6 February 1991
Call-sign: SAVAGE 01

Captain Swain holds the distinction of scoring the first aerial victory in an A-10 Thunderbolt II. His squadron, the 706th TFS "Cajuns," was the only Reserve A-10 unit to deploy to the Gulf. Their home base was NAS New Orleans. The following account is from Col Swain.

It was the third sortie of the day for 1Lt Mark White and me, and the sun was setting for the day. We had already flown two sorties to the kill box located just west of Kuwait City, and were ready to finish the day and head home with fuel to make it all the way back to Al Jabr, Saudi Arabia. Another two-ship led by Captain Larry Merington (SHOTGUN Flight) had no luck finding any targets in his kill box, and asked if he could join us, since we had several tanks and trucks still moving. I also brought up the OA-10 just south of our target location, and asked if he wanted to join us to locate additional targets once I left and to work the additional fighters. My goal after expending six 500-lb bombs and two Maverick missiles was to stay as high cover for SHOTGUN, and allow them to expend and then return as a four-ship back to the home drone.

Sitting as high cover, I noticed two black dots running across the desert much faster than any trucks or tanks. They weren't putting up very much dust, and yet they were moving fast over the ground to the southwest. On the radio, I then directed the other four aircraft in the kill box that I was at 13,000 feet, and for everyone else to stay high and dry, because I was padlocked on possibly two helicopters. I called AWACS, and asked if they were working any friendlies in the area other than the four other aircraft I knew of in my kill box. The response was negative, so I then began to try and talk the rest of the flight onto the target. The forward air controller helped out and put down a white phosphorus (WP) rocket for a mark on the ground that allowed everyone else to get eyes on the targets.

A-10 77-205 shown after returning to NAS New Orleans. Note rarely used drop tanks, and the travel pods still on the jet from the re-deployment flight.
Don Logan collection.

Detail of the "Chopper Popper" nose art added after the kill. This aircraft is now on display at the USAF Academy in Colorado Springs. *Don Logan collection.*

Col Swain's "Chopper Popper" being placed on display at the Air Force Academy. *Gary L. Coots.*

Col Swain at the dedication of "Chopper Popper" at the Air Force Academy, 6 September 2002. *Gary L. Coots.*

I decided to get a closer look, and tried to get a visual identification by over-flying the two helicopters at 5-6,000 feet. They must have seen me, because then they split up and started taking evasive maneuvers. The one helicopter to the north broke away and headed to a known Iraqi police station/camp, while the other aircraft continued southwest. Once it was determined that there were no known friendlies in the area, and that one of the helicopters flew to a known enemy site, I determined that the remaining flying helicopter was also a bandit, and decided to destroy it. I gave the first shot to my wingman, Lt White, but his slant range was beyond two miles, and he misjudged his shot and missed. I then decided that, since I was overhead the target, I would take a shot. I armed my gun, but also un-caged my AIM-9 heat seeking missile. I was fairly steep (65-70 degrees), and tried to lock up the helicopter twice, but the missile kept breaking lock because of the size of the target, distance away, and the surrounding terrain. Prior to pulling off the target I decided to also shoot the gun and put about 75 rounds out, but thought I had missed. I then extended away from the target and tried a second pass. I noticed that the helicopter was flying erratically, but I still managed to miss to the left with my first burst of 100 rounds, retook aim, and fired another 100 rounds and missed right. Knowing I was pressing the minimum altitude for the kill box, I put another 100 rounds down, and the helicopter jinked right into the last burst; the helicopter looked like it had been hit by a bomb. We tried to visually identify the type of [helicopter] after we were finished, but it was just in a bunch of pieces.

Since all five aircraft were low on fuel we decided to return as a five-ship formation. We flew over the center of the airfield as a five-ship, and pitched up into the overhead pattern over the tent city in celebration of the first A-10 air-to-air victory. After the debrief my Squadron Commander, Lt Col Tom Coleman, came and asked me to accompany him to discuss the day's events with the two Wing Commanders, Col Sharp and Col Sawyer. Rumor was that a Special Forces helicopter was missing and not yet accounted for. Lt Col Coleman stated that, "There was a fine line between a

Two views of Capt Swain's kill from both the A-10 and helicopter's perspective. These paintings were created for the official USAF Art Collection program by artist William Lacy under the titles "Capt Swain And His A-10 Make History (From Pilots Perspective)" and "Captain Swain And A-10 Make History II." *via Col Swain.*

goat and a hero, and they were trying to decide which one I was." Your enthusiasm goes way down at this point, as you can imagine. As we entered the secure area I was then greeted by loud cheers, as confirmation had come that all friendlies were accounted for, and that I truly did shoot down an enemy helicopter.

Capt Swain went on to fly a total of 43 combat sorties during Operation DESERT STORM. After the war, the 706th Fighter Squadron transitioned to the F-16, and then back to the A-10 in 1996. The 926th Fighter Wing has flown in combat missions in Operation NORTHERN/SOUTHERN Watch, Operation DENY FLIGHT, ONE, OIF, and OEF. Col Swain was the 926th Wing Commander before moving to Robins AFB as the Air Force Reserve Command Assistant Director of Operations.

Capt Tony "ET" Murphy (USAF)

58th TFS "Gorillas," F-15C
Operation DESERT STORM
2 X SU-22 Kills
7 February 1991
Call-sign: CHEVRON 21

Tony "ET" Murphy graduated and commissioned through Oregon State University's AFROTC program in 1985. After a few months he was assigned to UPT at Sheppard AFB's Euro-NATO Joint Jet Training Program (ENJJTP), and was assigned to the F-15C. After completing initial training at Tyndall AFB, he was assigned to the 58th TFS at Eglin AFB, Florida. "ET" had recently upgraded to four-ship flight lead, and had approximately 550 hours in the F-15C prior to this engagement. The following account is taken from a phone interview with Lt Col Murphy.

My job in the squadron was the Electronic Combat Pilot position in the Weapons Shop. I deployed to Saudi on the second day of the deployment. Twelve jets went on the first day, and I was in the second wave of twelve two days later. Once we were settled in at Tabuk we were assigned into paired four-ships. In mine were three Lt Cols: Tommy Ayers, "Budge" Wilson, and Mike Crow. Tommy and myself took turns switching between the lead and the number three position. We had flown about 20 DESERT STORM

sorties up to the point of the shoot-down, and the only engagement I had been involved with was back in December, before STORM kicked off. Mike Crow and I were patrolling the border when three pairs of Iraqi jets took turns charging at the border. When one two-ship would turn around, so would we, then another pair would charge south. They were trying to get us to cross the border, and we were hoping that they would, but after 45 minutes of border-charging, they left. That was the closest action I'd seen prior to the shoot-down.

Capt Tony "E.T." Murphy (left) and Capt Pat "Pat-O" Moylan after a mission. *via Tony Murphy.*

Capt Tony "E.T." Murphy with F-15C tail number 85-0102. *33rd TFW Public Affairs.*

By 7 February our squadron had been patrolling along the Iranian border for a couple of days, and this was not my first time in this CAP. My paired wingman had to return to the States early, so I was a flight lead without a wingman. Instead of re-pairing me, the squadron kind of used me as a "pick-up" pilot for a special tasking, or just to fill in as needed. On this particular day the 33rd TFW Commander, Col Rick Parsons, was up to fly, so they put him on my wing. While most flights going to the CAP were four-ships, this was a short notice add-on two-ship to cover the border. We had flown together occasionally, so this was not our first STORM sortie together.

Brief and launch were uneventful, and we proceeded due east to bootleg a tanker that had a little extra gas. From there we wanted to go due north on the east side of Baghdad to avoid all the SAM sites around the city. Our standard load-out was three bags of gas and four each of AIM-7s and AIM-9s, plus the gun. Our plan was to get past the SAMs and patrol in a north-south pattern, versus the usual east-west CAPs we had been using.

We had passed just north of Baghdad when my wingman called out a radar contact. His radar was looking level, and mine was looking low to detect any close in, pop-up aircraft. I moved my radar up and saw the same. After we broke lock we started to build a picture. What we had were two groups heading southeast: the closest was about 70 miles north of us, with the second group 40 miles behind them. We asked AWACS if they could see them and they said no, so I asked if they could see us, and they confirmed that they could still see us. I asked them to help monitor our position and keep me in the right country, as I believed these contacts were heading for Iran. We worked our identification systems and did not get any friendly replies. AWACS confirmed that we were the only friendly aircraft in the area, so it was starting to firm up in my mind that these were hostile groups.

I called "Tapes On" to make sure we did that right, did a quick ops check to make sure both our wing tanks were empty, and then we jettisoned them. I started the intercept by leaning to the east to try to get some cutoff, and elected to target the lead group. At about twenty miles the lead group turns left to about a due east heading which puts us in the beam, looking at the right side of their aircraft. We were in the low 20s, and the bandits were pretty low, around two or three thousand feet. I was on the left side, and my wingman was line abreast on the right, to the east. They pushed it up, so we elected to climb in an effort to out-Mach them, and we end up in about a ten mile tail chase.

The radar was showing a blob; we could tell there were more than two, but could not break them out. As we reconstructed the engagement, the best way to describe what we saw on the radar is to take your left hand, and hold it up with your palm away from you. Your fingernails are roughly what we saw, and we both ended up locking the ring finger. After verifying he's in range, I launched an AIM-7. A few seconds later Col Parsons shoots at the same target, but we don't realize it at the time. My missile comes off, and appears to be tracking to the target. As the counter approached zero, I bunted over to center the target in the HUD, and I then see a bright flash and an aircraft rolling in the dirt. I'm still at about 20,000 feet, and my wingman is pointing down at the targets, so

he is getting below me and slung a little aft on the right side as we chase this lead group east. My wingman sees the flash before his missile had timed out, and though barely perceptible, his radar has transferred its lock to the "middle finger" target, who is just out of range. He is now closing in on this target.

As that is going on I see some movement to my right, and I see what I think is the "index finger" target. I turn right and lock this guy up. I check to see that he's in range and shoot another AIM-7, and it looks good, as well. Right then AWACS calls that the border is 15 miles on our nose, so I know we're getting close. As that missile counted down to zero I again bunted over, although this time there was no flash, no fireball—not a thing. I check his range again and shoot my third AIM-7. I then turn to the right, or more south, to preserve room to the border. This takes me across my wingman's nose as this missile is timing out. As I'm still running on this guy, I look out to my left and see another target, which I believe to be the "pinky" guy. I'm about two miles from the "index finger target" as I start a hard left turn towards the third. I check that the missile has timed out before I gimbal the radar. I boresight locked the "pinky" target, and at first I think about using an AIM-9. I thumb aft to HEAT and get a good tone, but I'm still WAY out of range, so I go back to the radar missile and shoot my last AIM-7. Meanwhile, my wingman has gotten into range of the "middle finger" target and shoots an AIM-7 at him. My last AIM-7 burned all the way to impact, and hit the target about five feet behind the cockpit on the right side. This is when I realized two things. First is that the distance from his aircraft to his shadow was the same as his wingspan! So he's at about 50 feet. Second, this is the first

Capt "E.T." Murphy with F-15C 85-0102, seen here at Tabuk loaded with the standard four AIM-7Ms, but also with two AIM-120s in-board of the AIM-9Ms above the tanks. *Dave "Logger" Rose.*

With my crew chief, SSgt Sniff. *33 TFW Public Affairs.*

time I realize that I'm at only 100 feet! That was the first time I realized I was low altitude. It shows you how focused you can get on the target.

There's a flash, and he rolls and hits the ground. There was no ejection. This was as close as I got to any of the targets, and I had my best opportunity to identify the type. My best description is it had a cylindrical fuselage with a swept, variable geometry wing and a single engine, so I thought it looked more like a Fitter than a Flogger. I call for a 180 degree turn to the right, as I'm not hearing anything from my wingman. As I'm in this turn, I see another burning aircraft off to my right. I know it was not my first target and not the last. Col Parsons arcs inside my turn and climbs up with me, staying on my right side. I tell AWACS that we have splashed two, possibly three bandits. We punch off our centerline tanks and execute our short-range radar plan and detect the second group—the original trailers. They have split up, and are showing a side-side radar picture. I do a weapons inventory, and determine that my wingman has two AIM-7s left, and I'm down to just heaters. We do our sort, and he takes the one on the right and I take the one on the left. I tell him to press, so he's running the intercept now. The bandits check off to the north, and now we're in a ten mile tail chase with this group.

Based on their direction of flight, our position, and our fuel state I decided to skip it. So we turned south and climbed up to 45,000 feet, and started calling for a tanker. We promptly have a tanker heading for us, and he comes WELL north of the border to give us gas. While we weren't as low on fuel as I thought we were, being north of Baghdad with 7,000 pounds didn't make me feel fat on gas. We did our battle damage checks and saw the aircraft were in good shape, so we headed back to Tabuk, came up initial,

and did a couple of aileron rolls. We were met on the ground by a host of maintainers, the Squadron Commander Lt Col Bill Thiel, and a reporter from AIRMAN magazine who just happened to be on base at the time.

I filed a claim that day for two kills, and confirmed Col Parson's kill. The wreckage I saw could have been from either of our AIM-7s; since I didn't see my missile time out, and my wingman took a valid shot into a target at the same place and time, I credited him with this kill. We each wrote two claim accounts that day: one of what we each did, and one of what we saw each other do. Based on this I was credited with two kills, and Col Parsons was credited with one.

I have a few observations to share with readers after having fought in DESERT STROM. First, I believe any pilot in that squadron when placed in the same position as myself would have emerged as successful or moreso. That is a testament to the equipment and training our leadership pursued for the 58th TFS. Second, the jets performed in a spectacular manner. In seven and a half months I only aborted two jets. The courage and dedication of the men and women who maintained those jets will never get the credit they're due. Third, the other aviators I was exposed to, specifically the tanker and AWACS crews, played a huge role in our success. I'm convinced there is no risk those folks wouldn't take to provide any form of assistance. Finally, the phrase "Train like you'll fight" is not something you pay lip service to. Aside from jettisoning wing tanks, everything we did on our engagement was almost automatic, not deliberate. Those habit patterns developed during training serve you well when you haven't run an intercept in weeks. World class athletes know this well, and fighter pilots need to continue to apply this principle to their daily training.

Since we can't choose when we will be called to fly in combat, we may not get the opportunity to spin up. Always be ready to go to war tomorrow.

Capt Murphy flew a total of 52 combat sorties for 283 combat hours. After returning home in April 1991, "ET" was assigned to Operational Test, and the 85ᵗʰ Test Squadron at Eglin. He was selected to attend the F-15C Fighter Weapons School in 1994, and after graduating served as an Instructor Pilot and Weapons Officer in the F-15C FTU at Tyndall AFB. From there it was a staff tour at the Pentagon, followed by another tour with the 33ʳᵈ FW as the Wing Weapons Officer. He commanded the 85ᵗʰ Test Squadron, and is currently the Deputy Group Commander of the Weapons System Evaluation Program (WSEP) at Tyndall AFB, Florida.

Captain Murphy with his wife immediately upon his return from Saudi Arabia. *LtCol Bran McAllister.*

Colonel Rick Parsons (USAF)

33rd TFW Commander, 58th TFS, F-15C
Operation DESERT STORM
SU-7 Kill
7 February 1991
Call-sign: CHEVRON 21

As the commander of the 33rd TFW ("The Nomads"), Col Parsons had already had an event-filled career. After several tours as a Navigator, including one in Vietnam, then-Captain Parsons was selected for pilot training. After graduating he was awarded an F-4 Phantom II slot, and again headed for combat in Southeast Asia, this time as an F-4 pilot with the 4th TFS. Upon returning to the States, he helped establish the new AT-38 Lead-In Fighter Training program at Holloman AFB, New Mexico. After transitioning to the F-15A at Langley AFB, Virginia, he went on to command the 32nd TFS "Wolfhounds" at Soesterberg AB, The Netherlands. Prior to taking command of the 33rd TFW at Eglin AFB, Florida, he was the Vice Wing Commander of the 31st TFW at Homestead AFB, Florida. This position required a check-out in the F-16. Col Parsons checked out again in the F-15C, and took command of the 33rd TFW. The following account is from Col Parsons.

My DESERT STORM mission on 7 February 1991 was to fly a two-ship Eagle BARCAP east of Baghdad. Capt "ET" Murphy was lead. We were to spend a couple hours on station preventing any Iraqi pilots from making it to Iran for sanctuary. At this point in the war the air force (Iraqi AF), which had been the world's sixth largest just three weeks prior, was suddenly very interested in preserving its rapidly diminishing fleet.

Our F-15Cs were loaded wall-to-wall with air-to-air missiles, plus three external tanks. Since we departed from south and well

west of Iraq, both pre- and post-mission inflight refueling were needed. It was a clear day above the desert, with no more than the usual blowing dust and sand. After refueling and heading to our CAP, we found that communications with AWACS was degrading. On station, at high altitude, we could barely communicate. AWACS, however, could only see us intermittently, and gave us no assistance with the air picture.

Our CAP racetrack to the northeast of Baghdad was uneventful until the "Eye of the Eagle" picked up low altitude hits some miles

F-15C 85-0124 used by Col Parsons during the last kills by the 33rd TFW. *Alec Fushi via Don Logan.*

to our west. These radar contacts were heading directly to the Iranian border. Efforts to confirm our radar contacts with AWACS were fruitless. We started our intercept and, with our wing tanks dry, jettisoned them as we descended. During our conversion to their six o'clock we were able to identify them as SU-17s. I thought "ET" and I had a good sort, so as I fired a Sparrow. I wanted to ensure that I captured it on film. (With nearly 25 years in the Air Force and two tours in Southeast Asia, I knew that I would not get a similar opportunity.) As I centered the target in my HUD I was surprised to see an explosion several seconds before my missile could have gotten there. I had just validated "ET's" first kill. What more could you want in a wingman?!

As I came off that debris I was able to acquire another target, and with "ET" engaged with his second, I fired another Sparrow. By this time the maneuvering had taken us close to the border, so even before the missile timed out, we had started pulling off to the west. I did not see my second missile impact. Between "ET" and I we counted three explosions; "ET" accounted for two.

As we climbed out and headed southwest to rendezvous with our tanker, we jettisoned our empty centerline tanks. At high altitude and further south, AWACS was able to help us find our tanker.

These were the last three kills credited to the deployed 33rd TFW, bringing the total to 16, the most of any unit in DESERT STORM. There should be no doubt that superior machines, realistic training, and top notch freedom loving supporters, maintainers, and jocks make an unbeatable force. Of those wing members that

Col Parsons upon his return to Eglin AFB after Storm. Even though F-15C 85-0102 was the "Wing King's" aircraft, and hence carried Col Parsons name and single kill marking, the aircraft actually flown by Rick on his kill was F-15C 85-0124. Note that tail 102 carries the three flags denoting the kills by "Logger" Rose and "ET" Murphy. *USAF.*

stayed behind, all wanted to be in on the action. Their support, and that of all our families, contributed incalculably to the success of those deployed.

Col Parson's kill marked the last for the 33rd TFW during DESERT STORM. Rick retired from the USAF after a truly unique and event-filled career.

Iraqi SU-7 on display at Nellis AFB, Nevada. *Gary Chambers.*

Major Randy "Rotor" May (USAF)

525th TFS, F-15C
Operation DESERT STORM
Helo Kill
7 February 1991
Call-sign: KILLER 03

Major May was not available for comment concerning this engagement. Sources close to this matter have varying views on the validity of the kill, and unfortunately, several years later, while serving as the 53rd FS Commander, Lt Col May was one of the two F-15C pilots to shoot down two U.S. Army UH-60 Blackhawks over northern Iraq. I am including the text from a now declassified USAF after-action report, and an excerpt from Steve Davies' book, F-15C Eagle Units in Combat (Osprey Publishing), with Steve's kind permission, to add one point of view on the DESERT STORM event. Unfortunately, the facts surrounding this engagement will probably remain a mystery.

Report date 7 May 1991, KILLER 1/2/3/4, one unidentified helicopter (U).

(U) Capt "Dutch" Masters (525 TFS) was leading a four-ship tasked to sweep two minutes ahead of a strike package attacking two northern airfields. His wingman was Capt "Nads" Fullerton (525 TFS). KILLER 3 was Capt "May Day" May (22 TFS) and his wingman was Capt "Gecko" Rockel.

(U) KILLER one led the four-ship across the border, sweeping south towards Mosul airfield. The plan was to turn east and clear a path towards Erbil for the strike package. The strike package, of twenty-four F-16s and eight Wild Weasels, was enroute to strike Mosul and Erbil airfields as well as a suspected SCUD site near

Syria. Shortly after turning the formation east, KILLER 3 acquired a slow moving target east of their position for forty miles. The four-ship continued east. KILLER 3 was the only member of the four-ship who had the target on radar. At twenty miles, KILLER 1 and 2 turned south and cleared KILLER 3 and 4 off to the east to engage the contact.

(U) At nineteen miles, KILLER 3 turned to put the contact on the nose. The target was at 2,000 ft., traveling northwest. KILLER 3 took his final radar lock-on at fifteen miles and called "engaged" at twelve miles. At eleven miles, KILLER 3 launched an AIM-7. KILLER 3's two-ship was at 20,000 feet. The missile pulled to a lead-pursuit trajectory and guided to the target. A second AIM-7 was launched at eight miles.

May's F-15C 80-0003 seen at the Fairford, UK, International Air Tatoo in the summer of 1991. *Pieter Taris.*

(U) KILLER 3's view of the target was obscured by clouds but KILLER 4 was able to see both missiles explode. The second missile created a large fireball which fell into a small military compound setting off numerous secondary explosions.

(U) The two-ship was at 16,000 ft. during the terminal stages of the intercept. They began to receive AAA fire from a gun complex northwest of Kirkuk airfield. KILLER 3 directed his wingman to abort left. During their flow northwest, they picked up the last strike package coming off target and followed them north into Turkish airspace.

Excerpt from Steve Davies' book, *F-15C Eagle Units in Combat* (Osprey Publishing):

"7 February saw Bitburg pilot Maj Randy May (in F-15C 80-0003) claim a helicopter kill. He fired two AIM-7s at what was claimed to be a Mi-24 'Hind' gunship. Both missiles impacted the target and fused as advertised, and May's wingman reported seeing the wreckage 'fall into a military compound.'

"Several interviewees have made reference to the fact that May shot through a solid undercast, and neither he, nor his wingman, actually saw the target. There was no post-kill intelligence to correlate the destruction of the helicopter either. Long-standing rumors in the Eagle community of a car traveling down a highway that was killed by an AIM-7 may well stem from this event, as it was widely believed, albeit in a closely-guarded way, that May actually 'shot down' a Mercedes. This kill certainly seems to warrant some independent verification, although this is unlikely, and the truth may never be known."

Cartoon by 525th TFS "Bulldogs" squadron-mate "Dutch" Masters depicting what *might* happen if you shoot AIM-7s at fast-moving cars! This is proof that there is no slack in a fighter squadron, Masters.

Captain Steve "Gunga" Dingee (USAF)

525th TFS, F-15C
Operation DESERT STORM
½ Mil-8 Helo Kill
11 February 1991
Call-sign: PISTOL 01

Capt Dingee's Bitburg tour was his third in the Eagle, having previously been an Instructor Pilot at Luke AFB, and also a Distinguished Graduate of the U.S. Air Force Fighter Weapons School F-15C Division. "Gunga" had about 1,700 hours in the F-15, and was an instructor pilot and qualified Mission Commander when he joined the 525th TFS. This engagement marks the only shared kill since the end of Vietnam. "Gunga" shares this kill with Capt Mark McKenzie. As Mark was not available for comment, "Gunga" has written the following account to reflect both pilots' participation in the kill. Also, leading off this piece is his flight lead perspective on Capt Prather and Lt Sveden's kills.

I was in the 525th TFS at Bitburg, the "Bulldogs." I was lucky enough to be involved in several engagements during Operation DESERT STORM; this is my background and story on those particular days.

I arrived at Bitburg in January 1991, spent a couple of days in Germany, and then flew down to Incirlik, Turkey, to meet up with the squadron on 8 January. Also deployed to Incirlik was an F-16 squadron from Torrejon, Spain (612th TFS), an F-4G / F-16 Wild Weasel squadron from Spangdalem, Germany (81st TFS), and F-111E and EF-111 squadrons from RAF Upper Heyford (79th TFS & 42nd ECS). Additionally, in the support package were E-3 AWACS, KC-135s, and EC-130s. The 525th was also assigned 24 hour standby alert to protect the airfield, as well as supporting the 24 hour a day air campaign in the northern Iraq, striking targets as far south as Baghdad. About halfway through the war we also picked up the DCA and CAP mission along the Iranian border to stop aircraft from fleeing across the border.

F-15C 79-0048, flown by "Gunga" Dingee during the mission on 11 February 1991. Tail number 048 is seen after the war (notice kill marking under canopy) at Bitburg, 15 March 1991. It is interesting to note that most USAFE units use the national flag to mark the kill, while stateside units used a star symbol. *Don Logan Collection.*

Capt McKenzie's F-15C 80-012, seen here in 1990 sporting only a centerline tank. *Don Logan Collection.*

We used a Composite Wing concept. That meant all 60-70 aircraft in any package would brief, fly, and debrief together. This was a little bit different than other areas, but it was significant for the way we operated.

My four-ship had three separate engagements, and destroyed a total of three enemy aircraft. The first day mission for our squadron was 19 January 1991. I was the F-15 four-ship flight lead and overall air-to-air mission commander. I had 12 F-15s under my command to conduct this particular mission. On this day our call signs were RAMBO, CONAN, and PISTOL—all flights of four. I took eight F-15s and put them out in front of the package in a wall formation, a very standard F-15 tactic. We had two miles between each Eagle in this eight-ship wall, and I positioned them 10 miles in front of the strike package. We also had AWACS and RIVET JOINT (RC-135) supporting the package, providing "picture" and intelligence calls. The target for the strike that day was Kirkuk airbase. We normally flew in the high 30s for altitude, but on this day there was a high overcast forcing us into the 20-25 thousand arena, so we wouldn't be highlighted by the clouds.

We were about 80 miles into Iraq when we were alerted to enemy aircraft airborne over an airfield in north-central Iraq (Qavyarah West). We didn't know anything about what kind of aircraft they were, just that there were possible "bandits" at that location. At that point they really weren't a factor to the strike package as of yet, so we continued south with the eight-ship wall in front of the strike package.

The flow plan for the mission was to have the F-15s out front, and bracket the target area at about 80 to 90 miles from the target. Each of the two four-ships were to check about 20 degrees away from each other, so as to not over-fly the target, the SAMs, and other air defense assets near Kirkuk. RAMBO flight was on the west side of this push, so when we checked the flight that put Qavyarah West on our radars. The enemy aircraft that had been in a racetrack pattern over the field were now hot on our radars.

They were now a factor for us, and if they had continued to the east would have become a factor to the strike package. At about 60 miles I made the call for RAMBO to engage these targets, so we checked further to the right to put these targets on the nose. We were setting ourselves up for a bracket attack, whereas the four-ship would check 30 to 40 degrees away from each other, splitting into two groups of two, essentially surrounding the targets from our ingress angle.

We had dropped down to 15-20 thousand feet. I assigned CONAN, the other four-ship, to continue on with the flow while we investigated these targets, which were now about 45 miles on our nose. At this point it was becoming obvious to me as the flight lead that we were actually going to have to engage these targets. When the targets were a hot aspect (pointing at us) we would see them on our radars. We would lose them when they turned cold in their racetrack pattern, but we were getting constant updates from AWACS. We had gone through our own BVR ID process to eliminate them as friendly, but we had not received word as of yet that they were enemy aircraft.

At approximately 30 nm they turned hot again, and we picked them up on the radars, seeing that there were two of them. We were also able to determine that they were actually enemy aircraft (Mirage F-1s). We jettisoned our external tanks, which left everyone with about 13,000 pounds of gas, except for me. I had about 10,000 pounds, as my externals had been slow to feed. We were all armed with four AIM-7Ms, four AIM-9Ms, and the gun. Our doctrine was to ID BVR, shoot BVR using a "shoot-look-shoot," where you shoot one missile, see if it's guiding, and follow up with another as necessary based on the probability of kill (Pk) for an AIM-7.

The targets were still hot aspect, and they were down around three to five thousand feet, so we had about 10,000 feet of altitude delta above them. On the right side of our formation, both RAMBO 3 (Capt Dave "Spyro" Prather) and RAMBO 4 (Lt Dave "Abby"

Sveden) had radar locks on the targets. I was in the middle with a radar lock on the southern contact; at my left, eight o'clock was RAMBO 2 (Capt Larry "Von" Ludwig). We got hostile indications at the same time that AWACS declares them "Bandits." Immediately, RAMBO 4 takes the first shot and his AIM-7 guides. It turns out he is actually locked to the southern contact. We figure that out in a little while. We see his first missile guiding; the AIM-7 has a boost, and the rocket motor smokes while burning, but after that you have to pay close attention to see the missile. The targets start to turn to the north, a left turn. "Abby" follows up with a second AIM-7, and this missile also appears to guide.

Meanwhile, Dave Prather in RAMBO 3 is locked to the north target, his assigned targeting responsibility. He fires an AIM-7 that appears to guide, then fires a second that appears not to guide. He follows this up with a third missile, and this one appears to guide. The targets turn a little bit more to the north, and while they know we are there, they can't find us on their radars, and they don't see us visually until the last second. The northern target is the flight lead, and he starts a right-hand turn back towards the east, which puts him hot on my nose. I now have a tally-ho on both aircraft, and I watch Lt Sveden's first missile guide to his target. The missile is a direct hit with a contact fuse detonation, blowing that airplane completely into small pieces.

The other target starts to turn hard back into me when I see Capt Prather's AIM-7 have a proximity fuse as it goes by him. It blows off his right wing, and makes a huge fireball three or four times the length of the airplane. The airplane does a couple of Dutch rolls and then impacts into the banks of the Tigris river. I call for the flight to come north, which puts RAMBO 3 and 4 out in front by a couple of miles. We've gone through all of our gas that we have to play with for this particular mission, so we start heading north looking for the air refueling tankers.

CONAN flight continues on with the mission flow plan. They get south of Kirkuk, and turn around in their CAPs to watch the strikers roll in and totally decimate the Kirkuk airbase. They can also see the fireballs from the destroyed Iraqi fighters from 40 miles away. RAMBO leads the strike package out of the area while CONAN brings up the rear after the last strikers dropped their bombs, and out we go. All aircraft recovered safely, and we got to call in to our squadron ops about 150 miles out that we had shot down two aircraft. We were met by a wild crowd of crew chiefs, pilots of other aircraft, and maintainers to see our aircraft with the missiles gone, the tanks gone, and big smiles on our faces, knowing we had gotten the job done and brought everyone home, and killed two Iraqis on that first day.

Our success on that first day was all centered around the training we had all had in the months and years leading up to that particular day. It was pure good fortune on my part to be part of that team, especially being a new guy in the squadron, and being given the opportunity to lead those twelve planes on that first day was a tremendous feeling. This mission was like any training mission, except this time when we hit the button, tanks came off. And when we hit the pickle button, missiles came off and enemy airplanes blew up. It was all the hard work and training—the blood, sweat, and tears—that got us to that particular day and time.

The other thing I would definitely highlight was the teamwork from all the different kinds of airplanes and the support on the ground, from the crew chiefs and weapons loaders to the AWACS, RIVET JOINT, and COMPASS CALL all providing the right information at the right time. Everyone stuck to the flow plan; not deviating just because there is an air-to-air engagement going on. The professionalism in my four-ship, and the total teamwork allowed us to find, ID, sort, shoot, and destroy two enemy aircraft, and prevent them from becoming a factor to the friendly forces.

We flew lots of sorties between 19 January and 11 February, which was the day I got my kill. The mission had changed significantly. We had destroyed the Iraqi Air Force in the air and on the ground. They then decided that, to save their air force, they would fly their aircraft to Iran. So we started flying CAPs along the Iranian border 24 hours a day to keep the Iraqis from being able to get out of the country. Numerous aircraft were destroyed that way. It was on one of these missions that we stumbled across a helicopter. We were down as far south as Baghdad. Helicopters were not a big threat to us in the air, and not worth engaging if there was something else going on, but if we detected one on the way home, we would definitely divert some assets to go take care of it.

This was the only day I ever flew with Mark McKenzie, as my usual wingman, Capt Larry Ludwig, was sick. We were PISTOL 1 and 2 that day in a six-ship of F-15s. We had previously seen the helicopter traffic, and as it was not a threat we had bypassed it. On our way out we found that he was still there, so I took PISTOL 1 and 2 to the west to engage this particular Mi-8 helicopter. He was heading from west to east, probably in an attempt to get back to an airfield. We dropped down to about 12-13,000, but wouldn't go any lower, because the AAA and SAMs became more of a threat at lower altitudes. We confirmed with AWACS that there were no friendly helicopters in the area, and with our own capability to confirm that this was not a friendly. I fired an AIM-7 from about 7 nm, and the rocket motor burned all the way to impact. The aircraft appeared to basically just fall out of the sky after my missile fused near him. There was not a big explosion and fireball like the Mirage F-1s. It hit the ground, and there was a plume of black smoke and dust from where it hit, probably 8-10 seconds after my missile detonated. My wingman also fired an AIM-7 that appeared to guide at that target as well. It was an awesome sight to see the smoke trails converging on the target. There was an RF-4, ironically flown by a college friend, at low altitude about 10 nm north of it, and they witnessed the engagement while they were taking pictures on a post-attack mission.

Again, it was all good training, good execution, and professionalism that put us in the right place at the right time to ID and destroy an enemy aircraft.

Capt Dingee went back to the F-15C Division of the Fighter Weapons School at Nellis as an instructor, and later as the Commander, following his tour at Bitburg. "Gunga" retired a Lieutenant Colonel with 3,500 hours in the F-15. He currently flies a corporate aircraft and consults for a defense contractor.

Capt Richard "TB" Bennett (USAF)
Capt Dan "Chewie" Bakke (USAF)

335th TFS, F-15E
Operation DESERT STORM
Helo Kill
13 February 1991
Call-sign: PACKARD 41

Dan Bakke graduated Hawthorne College in New Hampshire with a degree and a Private Pilot certificate. After completing Officer Training School Dan went to Navigator training, and was selected for follow-on Weapons System Officer (WSO) training in the F-4 Phantom II at Homestead AFB, Florida. He had operational tours at Taegu, Korea, Moody, and Seymour Johnson (SJ) AFBs in the F-4 serving as an Instructor WSO, Check Airman, and flight commander. While at Seymour, "Chewie" was selected to transition to the F-15E Strike Eagle in December 1989. After completing transition at Luke AFB, Arizona, he returned to the 335th TFS in early 1990. He had about 1,900 hours in the F-4 and about 500 hours in the F-15E prior to DESERT SHIELD. He is a 4-time Warrior of the Year winner, Long Rifle Best Crew Award winner, and 4th Fighter Wing TOPGUN. The following account was written for this publication by Dan Bakke, then reviewed and contributed to by Richard Bennett.

December 1990, just after Christmas—the day of the deployment was one of the most miserable weather days at Seymour that we could remember. In fact, I don't think we even really had "mins"; it was close. But the squadron was fired up to go, we were ready to go, and most felt we should have been deployed earlier, like in October or September.

Lt Col Steve Pingle was the Squadron Commander. Steve is one of the most level-headed men, capable aviators, and sharpest commanders I ever had the pleasure of serving under. Just a great,

great guy. I always enjoyed flying with him, and learning from him. As we took off that morning in December from Seymour it was MISERABLE, and Steve and I were in the lead aircraft; I think we, or more importantly he, knew the gravity of the situation. As we looked to the right of the runway prior to take-off, the 4th Wing leadership had brought all the wives and families out to the end of the runway—not the taxiway, but the end of the actual runway. They were all there, waving American flags, holding up signs, in freezing rain for what seemed like forever—without a doubt the

F-15E 89-0487, seen at Seymour Johnson AFB after the war. It was in this aircraft that "TB" Bennet and "Chewie" Bakke scored their unique air-to-air k[ill] the only to date for the F-15E Strike Eagle community. *Al Fushi via Don Logan.*

best of America stood there to say goodbye to us. I saluted my wife, Rita, as we started rolling down the runway. We got airborne and climbed above one layer, and another, and the weather just got worse.

So we were off for war, and we were ready. I know I felt ready. We had a great pool of talent in the 335th (I'm sure the Rockets, our sister squadron, would say the same of their squadron) with the likes of Steve Pingle, "Slammer," "Taco," "LC," "Dimple Balls," "Teak," "Chairman," "Ghengis," "Catman," "Radar," "Norbs," "Spitter," "Slug," "Snaggle Tooth," and "G-Man," and that's to just name a few. Man, what a great group of aviators and American patriots.

The bad weather persisted all the way across the Atlantic, and halfway across the Med. Let me just say that the tanker guys did an OUTSTANDING job. To each of them—aircrew, boomer, load-masters and maintainers—I'd like to offer a word of gratitude. Finally, around Crete, maybe a little further east, but about sunrise, we got some good weather. I think it was also about this time that one of the guys fell asleep and ended up near inverted over the

"Chewie" Bakke bravely displaying some of the local Saudi wildlife; these lizards were about the only animal for a thousand miles that didn't actively try to kill you! *via Bakke.*

KC-10! The tanker guys asked, "Chief One, is there something here we should be concerned about?" We all started shouting on the radio, "WAKE UP, WAKE UP!!!" He does, and immediately pulls max G and ends up 180 out to the flow and 100 miles behind us. Actually, besides this minor situation and the weather, it was a seamless nonstop 15-plus hour deployment of all 24 aircraft directly to "Al's Garage."

When we landed, the tallest thing on the whole base was a concrete apron structure called "Texas Stadium," where the F-15C model guys were parked. That was it. There were some frames up for hangars. They picked us up in a flatbed truck and pickups, took us to "Tent City," and there they dropped us off. "There's your tent"...big boxes and pallets of boxed furniture...by and large the frames were up, but it was up to us to finish and secure the liners, build the furniture, and put the flooring in. But that tied everyone together. It was like the TV show M*A*S*H, when they would bug-out. It helped bond us as a unit. Everyone was working together, and of course we had our own "Radar" that always seemed to be able to "find" things we needed. In our tent we had "Mohammad," "TB," "LC" Coleman, "Snaggletooth," and myself—a whole lot of stories to be told there.

Almost immediately, by January 1991 we had started turning jets, and flew mostly local area orientation flights. We quickly learned that the Terrain Following Radar (TFR) in our LANTIRN NAV pods was having extreme difficulty "seeing" the very fine, silty sand dunes. We also had to start working some tactics that we didn't think we would need, but became a necessity. These were buddy-lasing tactics, since we did not have enough TARGETING pods for every jet. These pods were not fully integrated into the F-15E, as they are today, and on top of that, we only had about 16 for the whole Wing. This meant that each four-ship would get one pod, and have three "mules" to carry Laser Guided Bombs (LGBs) or other munitions. It was up to Steve Pingle and "Steep" Turner (336 TFS Commander) to work out when and where these pods would go. So we had to develop tactics that would work around this issue.

We also didn't have any LGBs at first, so the best we could do was drop "dumb" bombs using the laser designation through the pod. This was the most accurate way to develop a bombing solution, using the laser in the pod. So with this in mind, we were developing our comfort level for flying at 200 feet in this environment, since we firmly believed we would employ almost exclusively from low altitude.

We actually found out about night one on about day one—there wasn't a whole lot of lead time. Maybe about twelve hours prior, Pingle called an aircrew meeting and told us they were getting ready to kick this thing off. What was interesting, of the items I remember him briefing, is he told us that the powers-that-be estimated that we would experience (again recollection) over a 20% loss rate. He said, "Gentlemen, look at the person next to you, because you may not see him tomorrow." Not a head moved. We got it, we understood. Salute smartly and carry-on. I had been crewed with one of the most capable fighter pilots I knew at the time; in fact, we had been crewed together in the F-4 Phantom, through F-15E FTU upgrade, through our initial Check in the

"Mud Hen," and now in combat. We worked very well together—a true team. To this day we are Brothers in every sense of the word.

The preponderance of the initial sorties on Day One were Rocket missions; we rolled-in to the second phase, which included our attack on the Basra Hydroelectric plant. There were three distinct flights executing in our package, with three distinct and different target sets: a Rocket mission to interdict some bridges up by Basra, our flight was on the hydroelectric plant, and the last flight was on a refinery south of Basra. It was on this first mission that we lost "Teak" and "Dimple Balls." That was devastating. Anyway, we are down low getting hammered by AAA and SAMs. "Ghenghis" and "No-Cap" get lit-up and have to do a SAM break, which gets them out of the flow to the target. They ask "Chairman" for permission to reattach to the end of the package to execute their portion of the mission...it isn't until debrief that it's seen that while doing this...all at low altitude...200-400 feet...pitch black... you can see an aircraft going down the left side of his HUD. Just after the aircraft leaves the field of view of the HUD there is an IR bloom...at the same time "Ghenghis" sees a splash of flame and says, "Man, somebody dropped short there." Actually, that was our first loss. I don't think we'll ever know what happened or the cause, but it was a significant loss to us.

Our six-ship was led by Steve Pingle, with "Taco" Martinez in his pit. Number two ground aborted, so "TB" and I moved up to fill number two's position. We were carrying four Mk-84 2,000lb "dumb" bombs and, by using a laser designation, we put them right into the plant, completely destroying it. What Intel had failed to mention, or didn't know, was the amount of AAA in the area. We were told to expect no more than two AAA sites in the area, but this was along the road that goes between Basra and Kuwait City. The entire Republican Guard was set up along this road with every known type of AAA and mobile SAM imaginable. It got kind of sporting there for a while. Not throwing stones; we were all learning as we went.

On 13 February "TB" and I launched out with "Box-of-Rocks" Johnson and "Baron" Von Luhrty on the wing as PACKARD 41 flight. It was planned to be a relatively benign SCUD patrol, and

Capt "TB" Bennet seen with a 335th TFS F-15E at Al Karj. The weapon is a 2,000 pound GBU-10 Laser Guided Bomb (LGB), the same type of weapon used to down the helicopter. *via Bakke.*

we had several alternate targets lined up. Since there was not a lot of SCUD activity that night, we were in the process of prosecuting an attack on one of our alternate target sets, an SA-3 site located halfway between Baghdad and Al Quaim. It was not an active SAM site, as it had already been hit by the very, very capable F-4G Wild Weasels. We were attempting to hit the individual missile launchers to keep the site off the air, permanently. We were carrying a LANTERN targeting pod and four GBU-10 2,000lb LGBs, and "Rocks" and "Baron" were, on this sortie, pod-less, and carrying twelve Mk-82 500-pounders.

We were just coming off our first attack, at about 0200 hours, when the AWACS, callsign COUGAR, came up on the radio with, "PACKARD 41, COUGAR, we have immediate priority tasking." We knocked-off the attack and, as we got number two on board, came back to AWACS and asked, "State nature of tasking?" The answer was an urgent, "PACKARD 41, we have three enemy helicopters dismounting troops. Possible troops in contact. Kill all helicopters." We "copied kill all helicopters," and asked for secure radio to get the location. This entailed "going green," or using the KY-58 secure radio. This is a very secure UHF capability, but makes your voice sound like you're talking into a garbage can. COUGAR passes the coordinates, and I do my best to get them loaded into the jet quickly; sure enough, they are located right in the middle of one of our "no-drop" zones. I surmised, since this was a no-drop zone *and* they were reporting possible troops in contact, that there must be some of our Special Forces deep in Iraq hence the no-drop zone designation.

I reconfirmed the "kill all helicopters" call from COUGAR several more times. Use of the word "kill" was very rare at this time; we were used to hearing "identify" or "investigate" in conjunction with AWACS' taskings, so the "kill" directive made me a little uneasy. On every radio transmission with her (AWACS controller) I continued to reconfirm the clearance to kill. We turned southwest towards the location of the coordinates, which were about 80 miles from our current position. The area was due south of H2/H3 airfields, out in the middle of nowhere.

On the way down to the area I start to get very intermittent contacts on the radar, but they would come and go off the radar. I tried tightening down the search to a single bar scan to break out the targets, and I was getting hits on and off. What the radar was seeing was the rotation of the rotor blades, but it couldn't hold a lock. So I decide to see if I can see them in the TARGETING pod. I'm doing good ol' F-4 radar "tilt and gain," but with the pod, and this is with an extremely limited LANTIRN pod air-to-air capability. I would look at the intermittent hit on the radar, and see it, extrapolate two degrees low and ten degrees left. I could then command the pod there. Training counts for everything... there they are! We're at 50-60 miles, at about 8,000 feet, and I can see two of the helicopters, or more correctly their rotors spinning in the pod. So I transition almost entirely to the pod, since the radar wasn't much help at that point. Our mindset was turning to a ground attack...with what we're seeing and the information from AWACS, I don't think either of us were thinking anything else.

At about 40 miles we started to pick up a bit of an undercast so we started to take it down. "TB" directed number two to remain

Capt Dan Bakke pictured with a 335th TFS F-15E. Note the light grey drop tanks that were commonly used for both the 53rd TFS F-15Cs and the 335th F-15Es. *via Bakke.*

up in a high-cover in air-to-air mode, using the radar and eyeballs to clear the area around us, and to act as a comm repeater if we lost contact with COUGAR down low. As we ducked under the weather, I'm not sure that anybody saw us—more like noise activated AAA—but we started to pick up some light AAA, nothing heavy or accurate. I pass to COUGAR that I have contact with two helicopters, and I reconfirm that we are to KILL all helicopters... Still affirmative...by now we are down to about 4,000 feet and smokin'. We're doing a little over the Mach, and our manuals tell us that we are not to drop these babies at anything over .9 Mach. The fact of the matter was we still had not totally committed to dropping a GBU-10.

We knew they appeared to be on the ground in the radar. AWACS is telling us they are on the ground dismounting troops. So by 15 miles we are of one mind; this is going to be a ground attack. We confirm one more time with COUGAR that, "These are helicopters, dismounting troops, that there are troops in contact NOW, and KILL all helicopters." Okay, light em' up! We're doing Mach 1.2ish, and I get the first release cue. "TB" queries me as to whether I'm good for a release. I've got good laser ranging to the target, but I hold off for just a little bit—no technical reason, just a gut feeling. Finally, I call "Cleared to Pickle," and when "TB" pickles-off 2,000 pounds the aircraft immediately responded by shuttering and lurching upward.

After release "TB" executes a 30 to 45 degree left designator turn. Not much more than that, as we are inclined to stay close and immediately support the extraction of the friendly Special Operations forces, or engage the second helicopter, if necessary. I keep the laser spot right on the base of the rotor mast, where the heat from the transmission is very bright in the IR return. The Time-To-Impact counts down to zero, and "TB" says, "Keep it going Chewie, no impact." It seemed like it was easily 10 more seconds before "the GBU-10 that could" came into view on the display. It appeared to be angled nose high, then starts down and penetrates through the rotors, and the scintillation of the rotors as they disintegrated was easily discerned in the LANTIRN pod. The

GBU then enters into, or very near to, the cockpit of the helicopter, and is just exiting the bottom of the aircraft when the fuse delay functioned.

Through the entire TOF of the weapon, there was nothing to lead me to believe this aircraft was airborne or even moving, nor was I looking for any clues. It was an easy, easy track. I perceived no line-of-sight rates, and no shadows. I had fantastic IR contrast and was continuously lasing, so I was *very* focused on the aimpoint. It wasn't until I saw the weapon exit the *bottom* of the helicopter that I realized it was airborne. I'm still in the pod when the 2,000 lbs of GBU-10 "whupass" functions and the IR signature blooms.

There was a tremendous explosion, and the helicopter just disintegrated in a huge fireball. We are looking at right 2:30 when we see a pillar of flame of almost Biblical proportions. "TB" immediately gets us into a hard turn to the left, and is already setting up to engage the second helicopter while I'm on the radio transmitting, "COUGAR, PACKARD. Splash one helo, expect second splash in 30 seconds!"

An unbelievable and equally unexpected response from COUGAR, "PACKARD 41, confirm you VID the helicopter as Iraqi." ...YGTBSM!

So much for elation...I admittedly went into a tirade on the radio. I can't even begin to tell you what was said! We had to curtail the attack on the other helicopter even as it was airborne and running north at (relatively) high speed. "TB" had precisely intercepted it, and was set up to kill it with an AIM-9, but because of the injected uncertainty we are now "saw-toothing" to stay behind it. While we're doing this there is another miscommunication somewhere, and another flight from our sister squadron engages this helicopter by dropping bombs on his position, which is also OUR position. So we break turn to get away from this mess and the frag.

So now we're trying to figure out how we went from total elation to, "Oh my God, what have we just done?" in a matter of seconds. All the way through the execution of the detection, target, prosecution of the attack, the designation, through TOF of the weapon, the impact, reposition for follow-on attack...all through this we performed as trained, without error. 45 degrees of turn later, it had all turned to crap when COUGAR's response was, "Confirm you VID that helicopter as Iraqi?" She had removed any requirement to VID when she issued the directive radio transmission, "Kill all helicopters." The first time "VID" was ever mentioned was off target. Because we no longer understood the tactical situation we could not engage the second helicopter. It was a very quiet cockpit on the way home. I don't think either of us said a word.

About eight hours later, back at the "Garage," I'm on the phone to the HQ, or "Black Hole," up in Riyadh. That's when I start to hear the story of what was going on. Apparently there had been a Special Forces team inserted in the area, and they were subsequently found out. They had sent a distress call via a microburst to their HQ, or command and control facility, in Crete. They in turn had contacted Riyadh, who forwarded the message to ABCCC (airborne command, communication, and control), who had sent it to AWACS, who made it sound as if they were talking

"Chewie" Bakke clowning on a "liberated" Iraqi (Soviet-built) ZSU quad 23mm anti-aircraft piece outside the tents at "the garage." This gun was shipped back to Seymour, restored, and now sits in front of the 335th FS. *via Bakke.*

to the troops on the ground at the time they were talking to us. Actually, this information could have been up to twenty minutes old at the time.

While shooting down the helicopter was a cool thing, the coolest thing was the next morning talking to the guys in the Black Hole. We relayed that we had shot down an Iraqi helicopter in this area of Iraq. I asked if there had been any of our Special Forces in the area, and the answer was, "Yes, and by the way, we wanted to thank you for saving 17 members of the Special Forces. They all made it out, unscathed and unharmed. And when we get back to the States, they would like to buy you a couple of cold, frosty, malted beverages!" I've actually gotten to collect a couple of those drinks over time. But that was the "Hooah!" of the whole thing, just knowing those guys made it back safe and alive.

As a final anecdote to our DESERT STORM story, I'd like to add this as the finale. Since the 336th had been in theatre since August, they were the first to go home in March. The "Chiefs" stayed until July waiting for the 334th TFS to finish transitioning and achieve full operational capability so that they could relieve us. We were among the last "Chiefs" aircrew to leave Saudi, and got as far as Zaragosa, Spain. Upon landing there our left brake seized, and we trashed the left wheel brake-stack. We flew back to the States on a KC-10, to Barksdale, if I'm not mistaken. Then

335th TFS F-15E seen over the burning oil fields of southeastern Iraq at the end of the conflict. *Bakke.*

we continued on home, thanks to American Airlines. We got on the airplane, still in our flight gear! A flight attendant came to us prior to takeoff, and asked if after we got airborne she could offer us a libation. "TB" looked at her and said, "I'd like a six-pack of Budweiser." That sounded good to me, so I said, "I'd like the same." She said "I can't give you a six-pack!," to which "TB" said, "Ma'am, we've been living in the desert of Saudi Arabia for seven and a half months, without the opportunity to enjoy an ice cold, frosty, malted beverage. I WANT A SIX-PACK OF BUDWEISER." That was the last we see of her. We get airborne, and they close the little curtain to first class. Then the captain comes on the PA and announces, "Folks, I'd like everyone to welcome two American heroes, from DESERT STORM, who haven't seen their loved ones yet. Capt's Bennett and *Bake*." The passenger compartment breaks into applause, the little curtain opens up, and everyone from first class comes out; we're escorted up to first class and seated on opposite sides of the aisle, then a (full) beverage cart was parked between us for the rest of the flight home. The only way to fly!

Capts Bakke and Bennett flew a total of 43 combat sorties during Operation DESERT STORM. "Chewie" left SJ in 1992 for a Pentagon tour in the CHECKMATE cell. After Air Command and Staff College "Chewie" returned to SJ, serving as the Operations Officer of the 334th FS and the Commander of the 333rd FS "Lancers." He retired in 2001, and is currently a defense contractor, supporting America, and still fightin' the good fight!

Tim "TB" Bennett went on to fly with UPS and the South Carolina Air National Guard, where he is flying F-16s, and is currently the "Swamp Foxes" acting Squadron Commander.

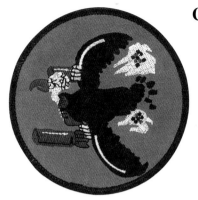

Captain Todd "Shanghai" Sheehy (USAF)
Thunderbolt Triumph & Tragedy
A Hog Driver's Story

511th TFS "Vultures," A-10
Operation DESERT STORM
Mi-8 Kill
15 February 1991
Call-sign: SPRINGFIELD 27

Capt Sheehy was posted to RAF Alconbury and the 10th TFW, where he promptly joined the "Vultures" of the 511th TFS. Capt Sheehy was one of only two A-10 pilots to achieve an aerial victory. The following account is from Capt Sheehy.

As the first few rays of sunlight crept into the small, sparse room, I lay on my cot staring at the ceiling, frustrated and unable to sleep. It was Friday, 15 February 1991, the final day of my stint at the forward operating location (FOL) known as Al Jouf airfield, Saudi Arabia.

During the previous five days the weather had been good, the targets plentiful, and the defenses relatively light. With eight A-10s forward deployed from King Fahd International Airport, home to the 144 "Warthogs" of the 354th Tactical Fighter Wing (Provisional), we were successfully deterring the Iraqis from launching Scud missiles toward Israel, as well as pounding a wide variety of other targets, notably radar sites and ammunition storage facilities. Although not fun by any stretch of the imagination, it had been a pretty good week of combat flying, and I found myself strangely sorry it was coming to an end. I was doubly frustrated by the fact that, except for ferrying a broken airplane back to King Fahd, I was not on the day's flying schedule.

Three days before, while strafing an artillery site in southwestern Iraq, I had been hit by anti-aircraft artillery (AAA), causing some of my A-10's 30mm ammunition to prematurely explode inside the barrels, severely damaging the gun, and spitting pieces out the left side of the fuselage and down the left engine's intake. The aircraft flew home like a champ with the left engine still running; although the maintenance troops did a super job changing the engine under very austere FOL conditions, the gun was damaged beyond repair. Even though the engine had been replaced, the inability to use the gun prevented the aircraft from being flown into combat, and as such, a wrench was thrown into the daily flying schedule. I personally wasn't affected too much, because as an experienced flight lead, I was able to fit into the schedule in any position and on any mission. I had flown at least one combat mission each day since then, and was disappointed that I wasn't going north that day. It wasn't that I enjoyed getting shot at, nor that I received any great "high" from risking my life flying combat, but part of a fighter pilot's nature won't let him be content with sitting on the sidelines while others do the job he's been trained to do.

Capt Sheehy with A-10 81-0964 sporting the kill marking. *via Todd Sheehy.*

Capt Sheehy after landing, briefing pilots in the crew van on what to expect on their mission. *via Todd Sheehy.*

The guy who had really gotten the short end of the stick was my combat pair, and fellow Royal Air Force Base Alconbury, England, 511th Tactical Fighter Squadron "Vulture," Captain Scott "Sparky" Johnston. "Sparky" wasn't qualified to lead formations yet, so he wasn't as easy to fit into the schedule as I was. Consequently, he had only flown once in the last three days and, like me, except for our trip back to Fahd, wasn't flying today, either. Apparently "Sparky" had come to grips with his frustration, though, because he was sound asleep on the cot next to mine. The two other pilots who shared our small room, Lt Col Johnnie Alexander and Captain Jim Calloway, both 706th TFS "Cajuns" reservists out of New Orleans, Louisiana, had been up for over an hour now, and were undoubtedly already briefing to fly their combat missions.

As I lay there wrestling with these thoughts and emotions, I tried to console myself with the fact that I had made a contribution already, and since no immediate end to the fighting was in sight, I would likely get several more opportunities to help defeat Iraq and free Kuwait. Additionally, I reasoned, there were certainly fighter pilots all over the world more frustrated than I, namely those who didn't get to participate at all, and those who had been shot down up north and were starting another day as prisoners of war.

Suddenly, I was startled out of my restless self pity by the imposing form of Lt Col Seth "Growth" Wilson as he burst through the door. "Growth" was also a "Cajun"; a reservist who had flown fighters for around 20 years, including many combat missions in Southeast Asia. Like me, he was happy to be in the fray. He was a large physical presence and a great fighter pilot. He was also a super nice guy, and the operations officer for the forward operating location.

"Shanghai," let's go, you're flying two sorties this morning before you leave for Fahd," he said.

"I thought I wasn't on the schedule, sir," I retorted a bit defensively, thinking he sounded as if I were late for a scheduled briefing.

"You weren't, but Colonel Efferson can't fly today, so you're his replacement. You're leading a two-ship. Briefing's in 15

minutes. I'll give you a ride over to Intel if you hurry up and get ready," he continued.

I certainly didn't have to be asked twice. I jumped up off the cot, grabbed my towel and shaving bag, and hurried out to the shower room. As I sprinted out of the room, I called over my shoulder with a typical fighter pilot exclamation; "Shit hot!—I'll be ready in 10 minutes."

Exactly eight minutes later I had shaved, showered, and dressed in my flight suit and boots. With map bag and ever-present gas mask in hand, I headed down the hall toward the small room where we kept our helmets, harnesses, and anti-g suits. Quickly grabbing up all my gear, I awkwardly made my way to the front door of the small dormitory building originally built for the workmen who maintained the airport facilities, and now home to some 20 U.S. fighter pilots. "Growth" met me in the hallway and relieved me of some of my burden.

"Looks like a great day for combat" he mused, as we walked out into the sunny desert morning.

"Yes sir, sure does!" I replied cheerfully.

We drove across the airfield quickly, and I soon found myself immersed in preflight planning and briefing. My wingman for the missions was to be First Lieutenant Jay Keller of the 76th TFS out of England AFB, Louisiana. The Intelligence Officer told us of recent activity and briefed us on our targets. We were to search for and destroy any Scud missiles or associated equipment within an area in far northwest Iraq known as "Scud alley." In the event we had ordnance left after our search, we were to expend it on "home depot," a huge ammunition storage facility in the Scud alley area, or on a mechanized infantry regiment which I, along with "Growth" and Col "Eff," had found two days earlier dug in near the Nukhayb Sector Operations Center complex in an area we called "East TAC," after a popular practice bombing range near Davis Monthan AFB in Tucson, Arizona, home of all A-10 initial qualification training. In addition to target and threat information, we reviewed search and rescue and escape and evasion procedures, and memorized the day's various codewords.

During the Intel briefing Jay mentioned that the previous day, he and his flight lead had found four SU-7 Fitter jet fighters parked in makeshift sand revetments about two miles north of Mudaysis airfield. He indicated that they destroyed three of them for sure, and one was probably still intact. The Intelligence Officer and "Growth" both agreed that any remaining fighters were priority targets, so this became our primary target should we find no activity in Scud alley.

Next we spent about fifteen minutes copying target details on our maps and administrative data onto our lineup cards, such as our callsign and mission number for the day—SPRINGFIELD 27, and our mission number, 5127. Because Jay and I were from different squadrons and had never flown together, I spent the next 15 to 20 minutes briefing him on my tactics, what I expected of him as my wingman, and what he could expect of me as his leader. Satisfied that we were ready to function as a fighting team, I ended the formal briefing so that we could each take care of any last minute personal business before we rode out to our jets. For me that meant something to eat, so I rummaged through a couple of cardboard boxes full of MREs (meals ready to eat) until I found one that sounded palatable for breakfast. The thick, room temperature beef stew mixture was actually fairly tasty, all things considered, and washing a few spoonfuls down with some water, I was ready to go.

Jay and I donned our flying gear, and caught a ride to the flightline with the maintenance supervisor. My crew chief greeted me at A-10 serial number 81-0964 with a salute, and I exchanged my gas mask, map, and helmet bags for the aircraft forms he held out to me.

"How's the jet, chief?" I asked.

"Ready to go get 'um, Sir," he replied.

"Outstanding" I said, as he scurried up the ladder to place my gear in the cockpit.

After reviewing the aircraft maintenance forms I carefully performed my preflight walk-around, paying particular attention to the six CBU-58 cluster bombs, two AGM-65D infrared Maverick missiles, two AIM-9L air-to-air missiles, and ALQ-131 Electronic Countermeasures (ECM) Pod loaded under the wings. As was typical, the bombs had a variety of names and short messages scribbled onto them by the weapons loaders. As had become my habit, I removed the grease pencil from the pocket on my left sleeve and added a message of my own to the side of one of the CBUs. On that day, I chose to acknowledge my departure from Al Jouf with, "Adios Western Iraq, It's been no fun!!"

Satisfied that everything was ready to go, I climbed up the ladder, took a look at the top of my Warthog, settled into the ejection seat, and began strapping in. The crew chief climbed back up the ladder to help me with the shoulder harnesses, then descended, donned his headset, checked in with me on the "hot" microphone, and together, we started the engines and got the jet ready to go.

Five minutes later I checked Jay in on the UHF, VHF-AM, and VHF-FM radios, and we taxied toward the runway. After a quick, but thorough, end-of-runway (EOR) check and a thumbs-up from the chief of the weapons crew, I was ready for combat.

A quick call to the control tower and we were cleared for takeoff. I taxied onto the runway, with Jay pulling up along my right side. As I looked over at him he gave me a big head nod, indicating he was ready to run up his engines. I signaled run-up of both engines, and advanced my throttles until the twin RPM gauges read 90 percent. After checking over all the engine instruments, and taking one last look around the cockpit to ensure all the switches were set correctly, I looked over at Jay again and noted another big head nod, which indicated he was ready for takeoff. I saluted him sharply, released my brakes, and pushed the throttles forward to the stops. Slowly at first, then faster and faster, I hurled down the runway wrapped in 45,000 pounds of steel and explosives.

Passing 145 knots of airspeed, I gently pulled back on the control stick and my craft lumbered skyward. Immediately, I reached for the wheel-shaped landing gear handle and lifted it up to retract the gear. I then retracted the flaps from their takeoff position and pulled the throttles back to 93 percent RPM in order to give Jay a power advantage, so he could catch up to me in the climb. He released brakes 20 seconds after me, and as I looked over my left shoulder, I saw him just lifting off the runway behind me.

Within a couple of minutes Jay slid into position on the left about a mile out and slightly aft. I then directed a channel change to the Airborne Warning and Control System aircraft, or AWACS, frequency.

"SPRINGFIELD, go amber six."

"Two." Jay replied.

Switching over to the UHF frequency that corresponded to the codewords amber six, I checked in with the air weapons controller aboard AWACS, whose callsign was COUGAR.

"SPRINGFIELD, check."

"Two." Jay replied.

"COUGAR, SPRINGFIELD TWO-SEVEN, mission fifty-one twenty-seven alpha," I transmitted.

"SPRINGFIELD, COUGAR, radar contact. Picture clean." the controller replied.

"COUGAR, SPRINGFIELD, sweet-sour," I added, indicating I wanted a check of my identification friend or foe (IFF) systems.

"SPRINGFIELD's sweet all modes," was the answer.

After this short banter, I armed up my chaff and flare systems for an in-flight check, and directed Jay to do the same, which was followed by a systems check of our Maverick missiles.

As we cruised along at 20,000 feet, I split my attention between keeping a good look out for other aircraft, keeping an eye on Jay, and cross checking the steering cues to the target area on the heads up display (HUD) with my map, and the few ground references on the otherwise featureless desert. I also took the time to title my videotape, as the aircraft was equipped with a video tape recorder (VTR) that could record the HUD display or the Maverick missile screen.

About twenty miles from the border, AWACS alerted me to the presence of the border combat air patrol (CAP) ahead and above me.

"SPRINGFIELD, two friendlies, three-four-zero for ten."

"SPRINGFIELD's looking, no joy, say angels," I replied.

"SPRINGFIELD, friendlies are at base plus thirteen."

Since the day's base altitude was twelve, base plus thirteen put them five thousand feet above me at twenty-five thousand feet. They were obviously searching for me now too, as my radar warning receiver indicated friendly air-to-air radar at my twelve o'clock. After a couple more seconds of scanning the sky ahead and above, I saw two F-15 Eagles traveling in a wide line-abreast formation about five miles away.

"Two, one's got two Eagles off the nose, 20 high, five miles," I informed Jay.

"Two's tally," he replied.

"COUGAR, SPRINGFIELD's tally-ho," I transmitted.

"Roger SPRINGFIELD," was the reply from AWACS.

Remembering a mission a couple days earlier when "Sparky" and I performed defensive maneuvers while being chased by two Iraqi MiG fighters, I was comforted by the presence of the Eagles. I rocked my wings to say hello as we passed below the F-15s and pressed north toward Scud alley.

Approaching the border, I directed Jay to "fence-in," which entailed, among other things, turning off external lights and some of the IFF modes, and turning on the electronic countermeasures

(ECM) jamming pod. Also, as we crossed the "fence" into bad guy territory, I began flying a less predictable flightpath which, although harder for Jay to follow, made it even more difficult for the enemy's anti-aircraft artillery (AAA) gunners. We had over fifty miles to fly to the southern part of Scud alley and, although the defenses in this vast, open part of southwestern Iraq were light compared to those closer to the population centers, there was always the possibility of AAA and heatseeking missiles.

Upon reaching Scud alley, I descended to approximately 15,000 feet and began a methodical search pattern, starting at the southwest end of our assigned sector and working our way east and north. We were mainly looking for any signs of movement, and particularly the large vehicles associated with Scud activity. Jay was primarily clearing for other aircraft and looking for threats coming up, as I concentrated on looking for targets. Occasionally, when I thought I saw something of interest, I would pull my binoculars out of the map bag secured on top of the glare shield in front of me and take a closer look. Unfortunately, after about 20 minutes of searching, we didn't find any activity, so I decided to head down to Mudaysis and check out Jay's Fitters. I turned south and toggled up the inertial navigation system (INS) steer point that I had loaded the airfield's coordinates into. The cues in the HUD showed twenty miles to the airfield as I climbed back to 20,000 feet. Less than five minutes later, as we approached the airfield, I checked Jay's fuel and directed him to prepare to drop the CBU.

"SPRINGFIELD, fence in bombs. Ops check. One's seven point zero."

"Two's six point nine," Jay replied, indicating his six-thousand nine-hundred pounds of fuel remaining.

Looking ahead, I could see the buildings, hangars, and revetments of a once-busy fighter base. Now it appeared deserted, and it was visibly black and cratered after numerous coalition air strikes. The fighters we were looking for were, according to Jay, about a mile from the airfield perimeter. They had apparently been towed north along the only paved road leading to the base in an effort to spare them from the first attacks. As we got closer to the airfield, I was able to make out four widely spaced earthen revetments. A quick radio call to Jay confirmed that between those walls of sand was where the fighters were parked. Jay also indicated that the previous day they had only seen four, and after a few passes three of them had exploded and burned. They had left without destroying the one closest to the airfield due to heavy AAA fire coming from the base and low fuel state. As these thoughts quickly passed through my mind, I looked again around the deserted-looking airfield and found it hard to believe that there were actually people down there who, as soon as they discovered my presence, were going to try to kill me. With these thoughts in mind, I called to Jay that we were going to set up an orbit at our present position, about two miles from the target revetment.

The next 10 minutes were some of the most frustrating I've ever experienced in an aircraft, as Jay and I collectively made four passes, and expended 12 CBUs and several hundred rounds of 30mm into the revetments containing the Fitters with no more to show for it than a bunch of sand blown around the target. With fuel running short, the AAA zeroing in on our position, and no doubt the gunners on the ground getting wise to our task, we had no choice but to head home with our Warthog tails between our legs.

During the 15-minute flight back across the border I kept the flight maneuvering randomly, as we scanned the sky and ground around us for threats and for potential targets to report to the Intel guys. Once south of the border, we performed mutual battle damage checks and settled in for the boring 20-minute flight south to Al Jouf, during which time I replayed the events of the first target area over in my mind several times. I could see the CBU bomblets and bullets impacting directly inside the revetment, and yet there were no secondary explosions at all?

Perhaps that one wasn't fueled, I thought. But what about the oil and hydraulic fluid? Of course, the CBU-57 bomblet was pretty small, and the 30mm armor piercing ammunition would rip right through the soft skin of the fighter, so it would take a direct hit on a critical area to cause a fire, I reasoned. Maybe we would get another chance, I hoped.

Twenty minutes later, with the single runway and few buildings of Al Jouf in sight, I thanked COUGAR for the help and checked in with Al Jouf tower. They cleared us for the now-standard 90 degree to initial entry to the overhead landing pattern, so I directed Jay to line abreast on the left side and started a descent to 500 feet above the desert floor. As Jay pulled alongside and a mile off my left wing I radioed I was "pushing it up," as I put the throttles forward to the stop, then inched them back slightly so Jay could keep up. I then aimed directly at the control tower. The goal for what had become the standard "arrival show" after a combat mission at "AJ" was to level out at 500 feet with the maximum speed possible, just prior to crossing over the top of the tower and pitching up to a 1,500 foot right downwind for landing. The ground personnel got a kick out of it, and it was pretty fun for us, too, after the tension of combat flying. Also, as something we could never do at the very busy home base of King Fahd, the AJ arrival was a nice "perk" at the austere forward base.

I noted my speed at 415 (pretty fair for the 'Hog) as we roared over the tower in line and simultaneously pulled up into a bone-jarring climbing, right-hand turn. As I rolled out parallel and slightly offset to the runway, I yanked the throttles back and put the A-10's massive speed brakes out halfway to slow to gear extension speed; with the deceleration pushing me forward against the ejection seat's shoulder straps, I lowered the landing gear and the wing flaps, and started a descending right turn to the runway. Rolling out to align with the runway, I slowed to 150 knots and aimed for the numbers. Once over the concrete I flared slightly, touched down with a "thud," and put the speed brakes out fully, holding the nose off the runway until 100 knots. Lowering the nose, I touched the brakes to ensure they worked, and then rolled out to the end to be de-armed.

After the weapons troops insured the jets were safe, we stopped in the hot-pits for gas, and then returned to the parking area and, with the engines still running, the arming crews swarmed over our aircraft to replace the CBUs, bullets, chaff, and flares. As they did this, one of the Intel guys arrived and plugged his headset into my intercom system. He took the debrief of my mission events and briefed me on my next targets. He indicated that other flights were adequately covering SCUD alley, so we were free to concentrate on the Nukhayb area and, if we wished, could take another crack at the Fitter.

Within 30 minutes of landing Jay and I were airborne again, and heading north on my last combat mission out of Al Jouf. All was uneventful enroute to the border. We talked to COUGAR and to a couple of flights of A-10s who were headed home. They talked of continued activity at Nukyhab, increased AAA, and even occasional movement on the ground. Apparently, even the boys in SCUD alley were getting some action, as they had located and dispatched a couple of fuel trucks on the highway between Jordan and Baghdad. I was looking forward to good hunting as we coasted across the border and fenced in for bombs. I was heading to the airfield first for one last attempt at bagging the resistant Fitter.

Arriving at Mudaysis from the south, I gave the airfield defenses a wide berth, skirting to the east. As we approached the revetted fighter I turned the VTR on, and immediately rolled in and put all six CBU-58s onto the target. Again, it appeared to be a decent pass, but with no visible effect. Jay followed with his six cluster bombs, also a good pass, but to no avail. Now I was really frustrated. I really wanted to kill this target.

23mm AAA started up, but with no signs of anything bigger or any missiles, I decided one strafe pass would be prudent enough. Determined to make it a good one, I carefully picked my run-in heading to eliminate any crosswind. I decided that I would begin firing at 10,000 feet, and fire a two to three second burst while trying to keep a good aim-point in order to get a lot of bullets in the revetment. As I rolled in everything came together, and it was looking like a really good pass. As I took aim and squeezed the trigger, I could almost feel the bullets heading to the target. As I recovered Jay reported good hits, so as I rolled out of my turning climb, I fully expected to see a large fire in the revetment. Again, I was disappointed. No secondaries. It was almost laughable: 2 sorties, 24 CBUs, some 600 rounds of 30mm, and still no visible damage. Jay was ahead and east as I passed through 10,000 feet. Without even thinking about it, I knew I was going to make another pass.

In retrospect, this obviously wasn't too smart, as it wasn't an important enough target to risk an A-10, let alone Jay or myself, but it was a quest now, and I didn't want to just give up. I told Jay to keep pressing toward East TAC. I didn't even tell him I was rolling in again; I just "whifferdilled" over into a 30 degree dive, took aim, and started firing at 8,000 feet. Everything seemed to be moving in slow motion as I fired, subconsciously surprised at my impetuousness.

After about a three second burst I pulled and jinked, climbing to the east after Jay. He had turned to the north to cover me as I egressed from the first pass, and had undoubtedly seen me roll in and shoot. Suddenly, he called out, "It's burning!" I looked over my right shoulder as I climbed and saw thick black smoke rising from the revetment. The quest was over and, although excited to see the target finally destroyed, I was feeling pretty embarrassed about the whole thing, with the realization that it was a dumb stunt sinking in. I turned the VTR off and vowed to save the tape as motivation to never be so stupid again.

Arriving at East TAC, we found MARLIN flight finishing up dropping bombs on what they thought was the command post for the regiment, and another flight just arriving from the south. Since we were fat on gas, and I had a good handle on where the live targets were, I said we would hold "high and dry" while the other flight employed. I put Jay into a big, loose wheel and climbed to 20,000 feet to save gas. As we watched the show below us, COUGAR called for MARLIN. After two more calls, I piped up and informed COUGAR that MARLIN had departed the target area approximately 15 minutes ago. COUGAR replied that they had a low, slow contact on their radar bearing 060 degrees for 27 nautical miles. I immediately thought helicopter, and told them that I had the gas to check it out. I sent Jay to wedge as I picked up a 060 heading and reached down to turn the VTR back on. Over hot mike I brought the tape up to date with what we were doing. My excitement grew over the prospect of engaging a helicopter in air-to-air combat, and I directed Jay to cool down his AIM-9L missile seeker-heads as I reached down on the weapons panel to turn my AIM-9 switch to the cool position. As I started a steep descent, I started thinking about where the vector was taking us; 30 miles further northeast than A-10s usually worked, and very close to the heavily defended city of Karbala. Something just didn't seem right to me, as I knew that there were F-15s patrolling over Baghdad.

Why don't they check out this contact? I wondered.

Thinking that COUGAR might have given me MARLIN's vector based upon MARLIN's position on their radar (at least 30 miles south of East TAC), I queried COUGAR.

"COUGAR, confirm you have positive radar contact on SPRINGFIELD 27 and 060's the vector?"

I was answered by only a long silence.

Then, "SPRINGFIELD..." was the only reply.

Another long pause followed, which told me that my suspicion was right, and they were busy finding me on their radar.

"Okay, 27, look 280, two," was the frenzied response I finally got.

280 for two! I thought, my adrenaline pumping even faster now. *I'm right on top of him!*

I put my jet into a left slice-back maneuver, which would get me heading the other way while rapidly losing altitude and, after noting Jay's position in a deep, high wedge, I began methodically searching the desert below. Unfortunately, my maneuver into Jay left him pretty much out of the fight, as he had to go high and to the outside of my slice-back to both avoid and keep sight of me. I rolled out of the turn to a southerly heading at approximately 12,000 feet and shallowed my descent. Still searching, at about 10,000 feet I radioed COUGAR again.

"COUGAR, SPRINGFIELD. Update."

"Uh, SPRINGFIELD, contact's faded," was the reply.

At the instant that COUGAR told me the contact had faded, I saw some movement out of the corner of my eye. Looking more closely, I saw a dark object moving quickly across the desert floor in a cloud of dust. Instantly, my heart went into overtime, and my mouth went dry.

Simultaneously I told COUGAR I was rolling in, and I sliced toward the helicopter and began pulling the gun cross toward it. As I rolled out, I told Jay on FM what I saw.

"Two, one's in, off my nose across the road there," I babbled excitedly.

"Beware that triple-A, it still might be there," he admonished, referring to the heavy AAA that had been reported north of Nukhayb.

"Roger," I replied, fully aware of it, since I had been shot at furiously in this same area two days before by 23, 37, and 57mm AAA.

Things were happening fast; the helicopter moving quickly across my canopy, the altimeter unwinding and approaching 8,000 feet, and the potential threat all distracting me as I settled the gun cross out in front of the target.

No friendly helos would be in this area, I thought.

What about the AIM-9? No, the desert sand is probably hotter than the target—it's a good gun shot.

I can see it pretty clearly now... Man, that IS an enemy helicopter—looks like an Mi-8 "Hip" with rocket pods... Pull the trigger!

As my heart pounded in my chest and all these thoughts surged through my mind I was pulling the trigger. The gun was firing, but it seemed distant. Suddenly the distortion of time and space stopped, and I fully realized what was happening; the altitude in the HUD was rapidly passing five thousand feet as I came off the trigger and pulled and jinked to the right, away from the big guns.

"Looks like the second half of the burst got it," Jay reported excitedly, as I jinked for all I was worth while aware of all the small white "clouds" of exploding AAA around my canopy.

As I reached 8,000 feet in the climbing, jinking turn, I looked for Jay. He was still quite high, and about two miles northwest of me. I quickly asked COUGAR if he had any further contacts, to which he answered negative. I then told him I had found the contact, as I got my first look at the target since rolling in and pulling the trigger. Through the smoke and dust, it appeared to still be intact and flying, although more slowly than before, and trailing thin white smoke.

"Was that a helicopter?" Jay asked.

"Ya," I answered curtly, realizing I needed to attack again quickly before it got behind a battery of 23mm guns whose revetments and muzzle flashes I could see clearly from my relatively low altitude.

"One's back in," I transmitted, rolling in from 8,000 feet.

"Last pass," I added, perhaps to ensure I didn't repeat my "kill the target at all cost" performance like with the Fitter.

As I rolled in again, I was keenly aware of my low altitude and my proximity to the threat. I rolled out quickly and took aim, leading the helicopter more than during the last pass. I squeezed the trigger again, and as I watched the helicopter fly through the bullets I realized the ground was coming up fast. As I took in the altitude readout on the HUD, the gun suddenly stopped.

Did I let off the trigger? I briefly wondered. *Er!! 4,000 feet... Climb now!!*

Again, I pulled hard and rolled to the right. Jinking, I climbed. My lungs were straining to pull in enough air as I labored to breathe under the G forces, which pulled at every part of me. I climbed away to the west, twisting and slipping my jet through the sky with the 23mm AAA airbursts trailing behind. Somewhere in the distance I heard Jay proclaim "Great hits!!" *8,000 feet*, I eased off the G and looked over my shoulder at the target. It was gone. In its place a ball of flame and thick, black smoke. Many emotions went through me that instant: excitement, pain, fear, relief, and pride all at once.

It was a great moment. Unfortunately, I couldn't come up with anything momentous to record for posterity on the VTR. Through the still labored breathing of my adrenaline surge I said, "Well, it was... It's burning now!"

I directed Jay to wedge and pointed my nose southwest. I continued my twisting climb, moving the aircraft every few seconds as I caught my breath and called COUGAR to pass the battle damage.

"COUGAR, we found a medium sized helicopter moving along the road...and it's been destroyed," I said, trying to sound calm and collected, saving the details for a secure debrief with the Intelligence Officers back at Al Jouf.

The flight back seemed to take an eternity. Jay was more excited than I was. He congratulated me several times, but my "tired" had set in, and I wasn't very talkative. I did realize why the gun stopped firing so abruptly, however; when I safed it up, I found that the cockpit rounds counter read 0000. I had emptied it.

I was very tired, and spent physically, mentally, and emotionally. Approaching AJ, however, the realization of what had happened began to sink in. I had just become only the second A-10 pilot in history to score an air-to-air kill, and one of the very few pilots in modern history to do so with a gun rather than missiles.

I shot down another aircraft!! Again, I was excited. *Not a bad end to my AJ tour*, I thought.

And to think, just seven hours ago I was feeling sorry for myself because I wasn't scheduled to fly!

Todd's instrument panel, showing the rounds counter at 0000 after the sortie. *Todd Sheehy.*

Group photo of the 511th TFS "Vultures" in front of the squadron commander's A-10. Lt Col Mike O'Connor designed the artwork for his jet, "Fightin Irish." Capt Sheehy is second from the left, kneeling. *via Todd Sheehy.*

We put on a pretty good arrival show. 425 over the tower, and a good landing. Word spread fast on the ground, and I had my moment in the sun. It was great. I debriefed Intel (and everyone else), and then got my stuff together for the trip back to Fahd.

Sparky and I took some "hero pictures" in front of our jets before we left, and I basked in my newfound celebrity status for a few minutes before getting back in the jet for our flight home.

It was a beautiful sky that we flew through, and a peaceful desert below us as we made our way back across Saudi Arabia. The whole scene was surreal, considering the hundreds of tough combat sorties going on just a hundred miles to the north.

Although tired, I was feeling pretty good. It was calm and silent. We weren't going north, so I had the VHF-AM threat warning frequency turned off. Unfortunately, the peace was broken by the shrill, piercing sound of an electronic locator transmitter (ELT) tone on the UHF guard frequency. Someone had ejected out of a jet, and the automatic warning device built into the ejection seat had been activated. Instinctively, I wanted in on the SAR (search and rescue). I didn't have the gas or munitions for it, and besides, I was likely quite far away from the crash site, and was sure the guy would have more help than he needed anyway, as anytime someone went down, every fighter pilot within 100 miles would stop the war to go help their brother out of a jam.

Back at Fahd there were no fancy arrival shows. With 144 A-10s at one base, it was much too busy a place for that. On the ground again, word spread fast about my luck over Nukhayb, and I was the center of attention. For about 30 minutes, that is. Right up until we learned the ELT on guard belonged to an A-10.

Not only did we lose Dale Storr, but his flight lead, Steve Phillis, had also been shot down while running the SAR. Dale was captured (by the guys he had been bombing moments before) the minute he hit the ground. Needless to say, Dale's next few weeks were anything but pleasant, as he survived capture and torture before his release after the end of hostilities. Even worse, though, Steve Phillis, one of the A-10 community's most respected instructor pilots, never made it out of his Hog.

That's the thing about war; it's not glorious. It's not just about targets destroyed, arrival shows, and moments in the sun. Much more, it's about good men fighting and good men dying. It ain't any fun, and although a few weeks after this bittersweet day a great victory was secured, as Kuwait was liberated by the Coalition ground forces, I hope I don't "get" to do it again.

Besides being the last A-10 kill to date, this is also the last gun kill by U.S. forces.

Captain John "Nigel" Doneski (USAF)

53rd TFS "Tigers," F-15C
Operation DESERT STORM
SU-22M Kill
20 March 1991
Call-sign: AMOCO 34

*Capt Doneski was not available for comment on this engagement. His flight lead
for this engagement was Capt Tim "Duff" Duffy, and "Duff" was gracious enough
to supply all the information used in this account. Tim gave a flight debrief the day
after the engagement, and it was videotaped. He supplied me with this tape, and I
have transcribed it here after "Duff" edited and supplemented the information.*

Even though the active combat was over, we were still flying CAPs over Iraq. The ROE for this period allowed helicopters to fly, but precluded any fixed wing flying by the Iraqis. We had a six hour Vul from noon till six pm, and expected to be back on the ground by 8:00. While we were on the tanker the previous six-ship was coming out, and they told us there were multiple Iraqi aircraft on the ramps, and that there were fuel trucks and maintenance guys working on them, so they appeared ready to launch. AMOCO 31 and 32 were already cycling back to the tanker as we headed north. We proceeded around the northeast of Baghdad up near the dam. We proceeded west towards a couple of airfields, where there had

been a lot of activity, to take a look, and then we were going to head over to Al Asad for a look. We were cruising at about 20,0000 feet.

We started picking up a lot of contacts with the radar, but they were all low and slow. I get a contact at about 40 miles of a target at 4,000 feet doing 520 knots, fluctuating between 480 and 520 true. I talked to AWACS, but they were clean all around, so I advised them of the contact and continued to monitor it. "Nigel" had been on the right, or north side of the formation, but since we were passing to the north of Balad SE Airfield I directed him to check left, so that he had better radar coverage of this threat axis

"Nigel" Doneski's F-15C seen back on the ramp at Bitburg immediately after DESERT STORM. *via Don Logan.*

Two variants of the SU-17/22 Fitter are seen in late 2003 at an airfield outside of Baghdad. The aircraft in the foreground, minus the outer wing panels, is a SU-17, and the Fitter behind it is a SU-22. *Gary Chambers.*

while I was working my contact. He floats to tactical formation on the left and sanitizes the area south and west of us. At about 35 miles I'm able to get an onboard indication that this is a bandit, so I call "Tapes on." He is heading southeast and we are going due west, so I check to the left to start to pull some lead. He turns more to the east and points at us, and after a couple of seconds I get my second onboard indication that this is a bandit. He continues his left turn to northeast, so I come back to the northwest and start to ramp down. At this time AMOCO 34 reports multiple contacts off to the north coming down the Tigris River, so I cross him back to the right so that he floats to about a 330 heading.

My bandit is continuing to slow and descend, and continues his left turn. This turns out to be his approach and landing. I only get a Tally-Ho on him after he has landed on runway 32 Right at Al Sahra (Tikrit), and as I over-fly the airfield at about 300 feet and 480 knots I realize that I don't want to be there. I start a hard left turn and start to climb, and just as I'm crossing runway 32 Left I see a Fitter taxiing out on one of the hi-speed taxiways, so I climb up to 10,000 feet still in the turn to keep this activity in sight.

Meanwhile, to the east of the airfield, AMOCO 34 has picked up multiple contacts just northeast of the field. He samples a couple of guys and finds helicopters, but digs out one contact at 1,000 feet doing 320 knots true. 34 is pressing north to investigate this contact, and I'm at 10,000 feet still watching the Fitter, which is now on runway 14R, and it looks like he is getting ready to takeoff. 34 gets an ID on an aircraft, and does a high-to-low conversion in a left hand turn to roll out behind the contact, which is heading south. As he closes in he gets a VID on a Fitter, and calls this out to AWACS. They acknowledge the call, but don't say anything.

Mid-war photo of the 53rd TFS flight line at Al Kharj, in "Texas Stadium." The four jets farthest from the camera are "hot-cocked," and sit ready on ground alert. *via 1Lt Bob "Gigs" Hehemann.*

Meanwhile, the guy that was on the runway either saw me go by or got a call from somebody, because he turns off the runway and does a high-speed run into a shelter. He was going so fast he had to have wrecked in the back of the shelter!

AMOCO 34 is continuing to run his guy down. I point east towards them in AUTOGUNS, and 34 is down to 3,600 feet, and is following the Fitter on what is basically outside downwind. I get an AUTOGUNS lock on the Fitter, and 34 is at his dead six. There is no doubt in either of our minds that this is a Fitter; "Nigel" calls "Tally-ho Fitter," and AWACS again only acknowledges the call. Since I had my eyes on the target and could confirm it was hostile, I called "AMOCO 34, cleared to fire." Before I can finish saying the word "fire" "Nigel" takes a bore-sight FOX-2. At first all we see is a small flash in the burner can of the Fitter, and it didn't look like it was going to be enough to knock him down. I go to GUNS and get ready to gun this guy. About two seconds later there is a big fireball out the front as the engine is trashed. Two seconds after that the canopy comes off, then the seat goes. The Fitter hits the ground and the parachute was just opening—maybe two or three sleeves had filled as it hit the ground without fully opening. I call "Splash one MiG, two miles east of Al Sahra." With that we climb it up to the east to clear for other targets.

Overall, pulling lead ended up putting me in a bit of lag as the original bandit continued his left turn, probably delaying the ID, and could have delayed getting any shots off. Meantime, two did a nice job of sorting through the slow contacts and picking up the hot one, rolled in, got the early VID, and popped him. To take away from this, the ROE was still a little fuzzy, we really weren't in a peacetime situation; really just a cessation of offensive operations. We spent a lot of time in the brief going over the ROE so that we understood exactly what we were going to do, so that we would do everything by the book, and that we could live with it when we came back. Had the ROE been different, the first bandit we saw was ID'd as a bandit and was a fast-mover; I felt pretty comfortable with the ID, and could have had some shots in there.

We were both very clear of the need to VID, and we wanted to insure that throughout the intercept we had followed the ROE, and the higher-ups all knew what we were doing before we came

F-15C 84-0014, seen later at RAF Lakenheath while assigned to the 493rd Fighter Squadron. The second kill marking was applied by mistake after being flown by "Claw" Hwang's wingman during that engagement. It was later determined that "Claw" got both MiGs, but the kill marking on 84-0014 remained. *via Shower.*

down on the hammer. So that was going through our minds as we came in on the intercept, that we did everything by the book, and we could stand the heat once we were back on the ground. AWACS was clean the entire time, even with 4,000 foot bandits doing 520 knots, so they were missing quite a bit there. We also saw that they were flying their aircraft to different fields, as the numbers would change from what we had seen, so we were missing some radar coverage of this activity.

Capt Doneski went on to attain the rank of full Colonel in the USAF. Capt Duffy later left active duty and joined the Massachusetts Air National Guard and, interestingly enough, was the flight lead of the two F-15s that were scrambled over New York City on 9/11. "Duff" has since left the Guard and moved over to the USAF Reserves, where he is still active as an O-6 (Colonel).

Capt Thomas "Vegas" Dietz (USAF)

53rd TFS "Tigers," F-15C
Operation DESERT STORM
SU-22 Kill
22 March 1991
Call-sign: ZEREX 21

These two kills marked the last two kills accredited to DESERT STORM, and also were the third kills for the very successful team of "Vegas" and "Gigs."

March 22, 1991, was a beautiful day in northern Iraq. The DESERT STORM cease fire had been signed, and "Gigs" and I were enforcing the "no fly zone" north of Baghdad. If the war was boring, this was unbearable. Iraqi fighters and bombers were to stay on the ground, but helicopters were permitted to fly. The challenge was to patrol an enormous amount of airspace efficiently, and quickly sort out the helicopters just in case a fighter dared to fly.

We were just about out of fuel when I found a couple of targets traveling over 350 knots. They were too fast to be helicopters, and the adrenalin immediately ran through my body, as I thought this couldn't be. Skeptical that my radar may be lying to me, I broke lock and then reacquired one of the targets. Sure enough, 350 knots. I advised "Gigs" of the group, and we proceeded after them.

Ten miles from the targets we locked our radars for the last time. I locked the northern aircraft, and "Gigs" the southern. We rolled in on them from the south, and about five miles out with my target in sight I could make out a camouflaged paint scheme, a sloped vertical tail, and pointed nose. I was convinced the target was "fair game," but wanted to know exactly what type of fighter for the record.

I was so focused on identifying the aircraft that I misjudged the amount of closure between us as I rolled out slightly high at the enemy's six o'clock, and less than one mile away. The target appeared to have a variable geometry wing set in the midrange position, but I still wouldn't bet a paycheck whether it was a MiG-23 Flogger or SU-22 Fitter. Not to worry, I thought, I will shoot

"Vegas" Dietz's F-15C seen on final, but notice the AIM-120 inboard of the AIM-9. *via Don Logan.*

My regularly assigned four-ship in front of "my" F-15C prior to DESERT STORM. Left to right: myself ("Gigs"), "Vegas" Dietz, 53 TFS/CC Lt Col Randy "Bigs" Bigum, and Capt Lynn "Boo Boo" Broome. *via 1Lt Bob "Gigs" Hehemann.*

the missile, pull up to control the closure, and then roll over to get a good look at him from above for the precise identification. After all, in my earlier engagement, it seemed to take an eternity for the target to catch fire and ultimately impact the ground.

I fired as planned and pulled up, easily controlling the excessive closure, and stayed behind the target. As I rolled over and looked down, however, all I saw was a huge ball of fire. The heat seeking missile flew right up the target's tail pipe, and it blew up like in a Hollywood movie. The target was now in a million tiny pieces, and any hope of a precise identification was gone.

"Gigs" meanwhile had rolled in behind the southern target. He saw the missile fire from my jet, but was still unsure of his target's type, so he held his fire. To his astonishment, the enemy pilot ejected from his aircraft less than a mile in front of "Gigs." As he described this event on the radio I looked over to see "Gigs" roar by the enemy pilot descending to earth under his parachute. The now

pilotless aircraft flew on for a few more miles before impacting the ground. Knowing what we know now about Saddam's regime, I can only imagine the fate that befell that Iraqi pilot.

We visually identified the second aircraft as a PC-9 turboprop. It was not a valid target in accordance with the post ceasefire rules of engagement. "Gigs" displayed great discipline to not shoot after seeing a missile fire from my jet.

In hindsight, I should not have fired when I did, but waited for both of us to confirm the exact aircraft type. We were not immediately threatened, and could easily have maintained an offensive position on the enemy. My heart sank when I realized the second aircraft was a turboprop. I began to second guess my identification of the first aircraft as a Fitter or Flogger. Fortunately for me I was lucky, and intelligence sources later confirmed my claim of a Fitter.

As I reflect back on my DESERT STORM experiences, without a doubt the lion's share of the credit for our air dominance goes to the people that trained us. The iron Majors that established RED FLAG and the Fighter Weapon School created the "déjà vu" feeling that swept over me when I crossed into enemy territory the first time. The instructor pilots that set the standard, never gave up, and never lowered the bar, from post Vietnam to the start of DESERT STORM made our success a given.

Furthermore, by the time I flew in DESERT STORM I had more than 1,000 F-15 sorties under my belt. It took literally thousands of Air Force aircraft mechanics to produce those sorties. In the middle of the night, pouring rain, searing heat or freezing cold, these men and women ensured I had a fully functional, safe, and incredibly good looking airplane to fly. While I tried to, I know I never said "thank you" enough. In truth, they are the real "heroes" of modern air-to-air combat.

Capt Dietz went on to fly three more tours in the F-15C, and eventually commanded an F-15C squadron. Subsequently, he joined the Air Force Reserve, working principally to help integrate the Active and Reserve Combat Air Forces, spearheading the new Associate Reserve Program. "Vegas" is currently a full Colonel, serving full time in the Air Force Reserve.

1st Lt Robert "Gigs" Hehemann (USAF)

53rd TFS "Tigers," F-15C
Operation DESERT STORM
PC-9 Kill
22 March 1991
Call-sign: ZEREX 22

Lt Hehemann's second kill marked the third maneuver kill of DESERT STORM, and the last maneuver kill in U.S. history. He is also one of only three individuals to achieve three aerial victories since the end of Vietnam. "Gigs" penned this account for this publication.

By March 1991, after the ceasefire, we were still flying our patrols over Iraq, but the ROE was now significantly different. We were not allowed to shoot anything but Iraqi fighter type aircraft: no helicopters, trainers, or transports. We could tell that the fighters were being moved on a regular basis, mostly at night. "Nigel" and "Duffy" had stumbled onto the MiG-27 and Fitter on 20 March and killed the Fitter, so we knew the opportunity was there to catch them in the daytime, also. "Bigs" and "Vegas" did their usual world class mission planning to develop a route of flight that would give us the best chance to monitor most probable MiG bases.

On 22 March we were flying in two-ship elements to spread the firepower around and cover more area. "Vegas" and I were up near Al Samhra (Tikrit) when my radar decided to stop working. I ran a built-in test (BIT) on it, and just as the BIT was finishing "Vegas" started calling out contacts. My radar came back fully functional about 20 miles from the merge, and we continued on in, as our mission was to VID these guys. We were ramping down heading southeast, and they were heading northwest, so we started our stern conversion in a left turn. About this time we got a good VID on a Fitter. We rolled out behind the two aircraft, and I saw "Vegas" fire on the guy on the left, so I was very comfortable that the ROE had been met. I un-caged and cooled my AIM-9 (we didn't fly these long patrols with the missiles cooled to save the argon gas), and was about to fire when the pilot ejected. It surprised the hell out of me; he was only 6,000 feet off my nose, and I had bags of closure. I was about to spear the guy in his chute when I pulled hard off to the right. He passed a couple of thousand feet away down the left side, and I could see his little goggles—his legs were moving, so I knew he was alive.

"Gigs" Hehemann's F-15C 84-0015, seen back at Bitburg sporting the single kill marking. *via Don Logan.*

Close-up of kill marking on F-15C 84-0015. *Ed Groenendijk.*

"Preset Freqs" was our Fighter Pilot (lead singer was a crew chief) rock band that played in the mess hall after the cease fire. We also played regularly back at Bitburg before and after the war, including a HUGE partay we put on in the O Club upon our return, dubbed "The MOTHER of all Parties," in honor of Sadam's "Mother of all Battles." We celebrated all the stuff we missed while we were gone: Christmas, New Years (highlight of the evening), Easter, Birthdays, Memorial Day, etc. Most Excellent. *via 1 Lt Bob "Gigs" Hehemann.*

I looked back forward, and his aircraft was continuing ahead, straight and level, all trimmed up. I chopped it to idle and managed the closure to rejoin on the left wing in close. It was a Pilatus PC-9 straight wing turboprop, camouflaged, with missile rails and no one in it. I flew formation off the wing, with "Vegas" flying cover, for almost two minutes as it slowly descended, and then impacted the ground and exploded. It was pretty amazing!

By the time our Vul period was over and we were returning to Al Kharj a sand storm had blown up, and we couldn't see the hood ornament on the jet, let alone the runway, so we diverted to Riyadh International. We were escorted over to the command center, the "Black Hole." We debriefed the engagement, and were patting ourselves on the back when someone came up and said Gen Horner would like to see us in his office. This was quiet an experience. I could tell by the tone of the conversation that his primary concern was that the ROE had been strictly adhered to. He started rattling off questions to "Vegas" about the altitude, speeds, and headings, and "Vegas" machine-gunned the answers right back, knocked them all out of the park. He then turned to me and said, "Lt, let me get this straight, there's a jet fighter flying tactical formation with a straight-winged turboprop?" I said, "Yes sir, General, it was the strangest damn thing I've ever seen." At that point he stood up and leaned across the table and said, "Well shit hot, but how come you didn't gun those bastards!?" At that point I knew he was satisfied that we had followed the ROE to the letter.

We hung out in his office for another 45 minutes talking about the war and catching up with some CNN. He asked about the squadron, and the conversation naturally turned to the success of the 53rd and the number of kills. He asked how many the 53rd had, and we told him this made 11. He asked how that could be if "Nigel's" had been number nine and our guy today was number 10. I then realized he had no intention of giving me a kill for a guy who ejected prior to my firing any ordnance. I told him it was my understanding that in Vietnam, when F-4 crews maneuvered behind MiGs that then flew into the ground, that those F-4 crews were awarded a kill. He then made it clear to me that there was no way in hell that I would get a kill for this, and he is famous for some colorful metaphors, and I heard several right then. But two weeks later, when we sent in the HUD tapes and documentation, he did indeed sign off on this as a maneuver kill. But what a neat experience to sit in his office and know that he was concerned that we were doing the job right, and of course, if you know "Vegas," you know that everything he does is always world class and done by the book. We had a great time flying together, and I can't think of anyone else I would have wanted to have shared these experiences with.

"Gigs" flew a total of 49 combat missions for over 250 Combat hours during DESERT STORM. "Gigs" left Saudi for Bitburg in April 1991 to be home for the birth of his first child. He left Bitburg in February 1993 for an active duty Program Total Force position with the 131st Fighter Wing, Missouri Air National Guard. "Gigs" left active duty, but continued to fly F-15As with the 131st FW as a traditional Guardsman until May 2000. He currently serves as a Reserve Lt Col in the North American Aerospace Defense Command (NORAD), and also flies for United Airlines.

Lt Col Gary "Nordo" North (USAF)

33rd EFS, F-16D Block 42
Operation SOUTHERN WATCH
MiG-25
27 December 1992
Call-sign: BENJI 41

Gary North was commissioned in 1976 after completing East Carolina University's ROTC program as a distinguished graduate. He was selected from Navigator training to become an F-4E WSO at Kunson, Korea, and later trained as an F-4G Wild Weasel Electronic Warfare Officer (EWO) at George AFB, California. "Nordo" was then selected for UPT, and was assigned to the F-16 and the 19th TFS, Shaw AFB, South Carolina. During this assignment he graduated the F-16 Fighter Weapons Instructor Course (FWIC), and went on to another Viper tour at Ramstein AB, Germany. After several staff tours he made it back to the Viper just in time for Operation DESERT STORM, where he flew over 50 missions, and was the Chief of Wing Weapons for the 363rd TFW deployed from Shaw AFB. "Nordo" went on to command the 33rd FS by the time of this engagement. This account was originally published in The Washington Institute for Near East Policy; Military Research Papers under the title "Crisis After the Storm" by Lt Col Paul K. White. It is reprinted here with the kind permission of both the Institue and Lt Gen North.

On December 20, 1992, the Thirty-third Tactical Fighter Squadron from Shaw Air Force Base (AFB), South Carolina, commanded by Lt Col Gary North, arrived in Dhahran, Saudi Arabia, with eighteen F-16s outfitted with Low Altitude Navigation and Targeting Infrared for Night (LANTIRN) equipment for a ninety-day tour with Operation SOUTHERN WATCH (OSW).

The mission of the squadron during the deployment was to patrol the skies of southern Iraq in support of the relevant United Nations (UN) resolutions, and to display a constant U.S.-led coalition air presence south of the thirty-second parallel. The Thirty-third Squadron, although very experienced in terms of total flying hours, included only three pilots who had participated in combat

Col North at the controls of his MiG-killing F-16D in 1993 at Shaw AFB, SC. *David F. Brown.*

during Operation DESERT STORM. Despite being away from home for Christmas, the unit was motivated, and looked forward to fulfilling its time in what many U.S. military personnel referred to as the Saudi "sandbox" during the squadron's first Operation SOUTHERN WATCH deployment.

During the squadron's initial intelligence briefing, the pilots were informed there had been an unusual amount of Iraqi air activity near the southern no-fly zone border in recent weeks. In fact, E-3 Sentry Airborne Warning And Control System (AWACS) radar had observed Iraqi fighters occasionally flying into the no-fly zone before quickly returning north of the thirty-second parallel. The Iraqis initiated nearly all of the border incursions in the early morning hours, or when no U.S. fighters were present. No provocations involving U.S. aircraft had occurred, but the activity was unusual, and pilots were warned to be alert during their sorties.

The squadron flew its first mission into the no-fly zone on 22 December. During the days that followed, the squadron became

familiar with their Operation SOUTHERN WATCH taskings. The squadron's instructor pilots, who had DESERT STORM experience, led most of these initial sorties. The missions were relatively simple, and were called "standard OSW profiles" by the aircrews: four fighter aircraft would take off from Dhahran, fly north to the Iraq-Saudi Arabia border, refuel in flight from a KC-135R Stratotanker, and subsequently enter the no-fly zone, patrolling the area for approximately thirty to forty-five minutes before returning to Dhahran. Sometimes a flight would be ordered to overfly a specific area and observe any unusual ground activity, but its main purpose revolved around its presence on Iraqi radar displays—to let Iraqi president Saddam Hussein know that coalition air power, which had punished the Iraqi military so spectacularly during DESERT STORM, remained on guard.

On the morning of 27 December, Lt Col North led a flight of four F-16s on a typical Operation SOUTHERN WATCH mission. The pilots had just rejoined with the KC-135 tanker for refueling while monitoring the AWACS control frequency for an update

Original art of "Nordo's" kill titled "Benji four-one, Fox one...Splash One!" by Lockheed staff artist Price Randel.

on air activity when they heard urgent transmissions between a formation of four F-15s in the no-fly zone and AWACS controllers. An Iraqi MiG-25 had crossed the border into the no-fly zone, flown within lethal range of the F-15s, and was speeding north to safety with the F-15s in hot pursuit. One F-15 had been close enough to gain visual acquisition on the MiG and confirm it as a "Foxbat," and it had requested clearance to fire in accordance with the standing rules of engagement. By the time the clearance was coordinated, the Foxbat was safely north of the thirty-second parallel, and the F-15s, now low on gas, prepared to leave the area.

Wanting to avoid further delay, North and his wingman refueled with only enough gas to allow them to cover their assigned on-station time in the no-fly zone, and crossed the border into southern Iraq while the third and fourth aircraft in their group continued to refuel. They established a rotating orbit in the north-central area of the zone in accordance with their assigned tasking. Within minutes, AWACS radar detected an Iraqi aircraft heading south toward the thirty-second parallel. The Iraqi aircraft approached the border, safely remained several miles north of the line, and flew east before turning back to the north. AWACS controllers ordered the two F-16s toward the aircraft to ensure it did not cross into the no-fly zone. As the F-16s were terminating the intercept and returning to their orbit point, AWACS radar reported another high-speed contact originating in the north and crossing into the no-fly zone, approximately thirty miles west of the F-16 formation. Again, AWACS controllers directed the F-16s to intercept the trespassing aircraft, forcing the Iraqi fighter to turn north to safety before the F-16s, armed with two AIM-120A Advanced Medium Range Air-to-Air Missiles (AMRAAMs) and two AIM-9M Sidewinder missiles, could engage it. As the F-16s returned yet again to the orbit point, AWACS radar monitored another aircraft, northeast of the F-16s, flying south toward the no-fly zone, following almost the exact same ground track and flight profile as the first MiG. As the F-16s again flew to intercept the aircraft, an Iraqi surface-to-air missile (SAM) radar site began tracking the aircraft. Although the Iraqi jet never crossed the line and the SAM radar indications disappeared, this mission had very rapidly turned into "not your normal day in the sandbox."

As North was returning to the orbit point for a fourth time, he ordered the third and fourth aircraft in his group, now with a full load of gas and approximately sixty miles to the south, to fly north at their best speed. At this time, AWACS radar again reported a radar contact entering the no-fly zone to the west of North's formation at high speed at 30,000 feet. The aircraft was

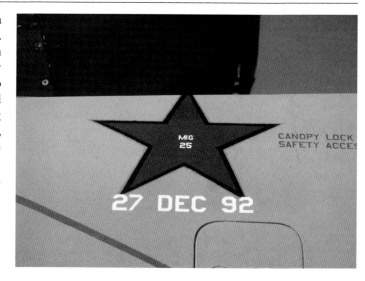

Close-up of the kill marking on North's F-16D. *David F. Brown.*

flying directly toward them on an easterly heading. Calling for a tactical offset to the north to "bracket" the F-16s between the MiG and the thirty-second parallel, North created a blocking maneuver, trapping the Iraqi intruder in forbidden airspace. It was quickly apparent that the MiG could not escape back into Iraqi territory without a fight. North knew at that point that, "someone was going to die within the next two minutes, and it wasn't going to be me or my wingman."

Requesting clearance to fire, the two F-16s continued to close on the trespassing aircraft, lighting their afterburners and climbing toward the Iraqi jet. North visually identified the aircraft—a MiG-25 Foxbat, typically armed with AA-6 "Acrid" radar guided missiles—and directed his wingman to employ his electronic jamming pod. Again, he requested clearance to fire. The MiG began turning to the north directly in front of North's jet, when finally he heard, "BANDIT-BANDIT-BANDIT, CLEARED TO KILL" over his head set. At fifteen degrees nose high and fifteen degrees right bank he fired an AMRAAM. Impact with the Iraqi aircraft occurred twenty miles inside the no-fly zone, and was easily seen by the F-16s. North later commented, "I saw three separate detonations. The nose and the left wing broke apart instantly, and the tail section continued in to the main body of the jet for one final, huge fireball." The entire episode, from the time North left the tanker until he shot down the Foxbat, transpired in less than fifteen minutes.

This engagement marked both the first U.S. F-16 kill, and the first kill for the AIM-120 AMRAAM. Lt Col North went on to command the 35th Operations Group, Misawa AB, Japan, the 8th FW "Wolfpack" at Kunsan, and the 18th Wing at Kadena AB, Okinawa. After some more time on the Joint Staff he assumed the position of Director of Operations (J-3) for Pacific Command, and is currently the Commander, 9th Air Force and U.S. Central Command Air Forces (USCENTAF), having attained the rank of Lt General. "Nordo" has over 4,100 hours in the F-4, F-15C, and F-16.

1 Lt Craig "Trigger" Stevenson (USAF)
"Cleared to lead and kill MiGs"

23rd FS, F-16C
Operation PROVIDE COMFORT
MiG-23
17 January 1993
Call-sign: DEVIL 01

Craig Stevenson enlisted in the Air Force shortly after high school in 1981, and was trained as an Air Traffic Controller at Spangdahlem AB, Germany. After finishing his degree from ERAU in 1988, he was selected for OTS, UPT, and F-16 RTU before returning to Spang in 1991. Total Viper time when the shoot-down occurred was 450 hours. The following account was written by "Trigger" for this publication.

Original art of "Trigger's" kill titled "Slammer Kill No. 2" by Lockheed staff artist Price Randel.

In December 1992 the atmosphere around our squadron, deployed to Incirlik Air Base, Turkey, felt something like a reunion. Six months earlier our squadron, the 23 FS "Fighting Hawks" at Spangdahlem AB, Germany, had been a mix of Wild Weasel F-4G and F-16s in a hunter/killer role. The F-4Gs and crews were reassigned stateside, and we became an F-16 only squadron, with Close Air Support (CAS) as our primary mission. However, due to increasing tensions in Northern Iraq and the need for dedicated Suppression of Enemy Air Defenses (SEAD) experts the Phantoms returned, and our mixed squadron was once again united as part of Operation PROVIDE COMFORT (OPC), 7440 Combat Wing (Provisional), Incirlik AB, Turkey. Needless to say, I remember being very happy to see our old Phantom-driving friends and former squadron mates again.

Because we were all well versed with mixed element hunter/killer operations and tactics, we began flying combat sorties together almost immediately. The rules of engagement for the F-4Gs were pretty straightforward, and it read something like this: "If it's a military ground radar radiating in the no fly zone, kill it." And they did quite frequently, using their sophisticated APR-47 equipment and HARM (high speed anti-radiation) missiles. The F-4s also carried AIM-7M Sparrow radar guided air-to-air missiles to deal with possible air threats. Their F-16 wingmen typically carried a pair of HARMs that the F-4Gs could target to a specific threat, or a pair of CBU-87 cluster bombs to "hard kill" a threat after the F-4Gs had taken out the radar. This, is in addition to the F-16's normal compliment of AMRAAM and Sidewinder air-to-air missiles. Tensions in Northern Iraq were fairly high in December 1992 as we approached the 2nd anniversary of the beginning of Operation DESERT STORM. The Iraqi forces seemed much more aggressive in their flying style and tempo south of the 36th parallel, their frequent targeting of coalition aircraft with SAM radars, and the occasional barrage of anti-aircraft-artillery fire (AAA). We responded with equal aggressiveness.

I was a 1Lt at the time, happy to be back with the same Weasel group with whom I'd cut my teeth as a fledgling fighter pilot in Germany. Like any young fighter pilot, I was anxious to upgrade to flight lead. Our squadron's flight lead upgrade program consisted of ten graded training flights and a check ride given by a squadron supervisor. This allowed you to brief and lead a two-ship of F-16s performing any mission the aircraft is capable of, anywhere in the world. Interestingly enough, our upgrade program contained a requirement to satisfactorily lead a dissimilar type aircraft sortie (F-4, A-10, F-15), probably a leftover requirement from when F-4Gs were still a part of our squadron six months previous. The fact that this requirement existed is the only reason I'm writing this story today.

The standing rule at OPC was "No upgrade sorties in the Area of Responsibility (AOR)." In other words, no training flights in combat. Sounds reasonable enough, until you realize we spent more time supporting OPC than anything else, and if any upgrades at all were to be done, we would have to find a way to bend the rules in our favor a little. Because I was in the middle of my two-ship flight lead upgrade when I deployed to Incirlik, it seemed natural to "knock out" my dissimilar lead requirement once we got

settled into a comfortable routine with the F-4G Wild Weasels. I was scheduled to fly this sortie on 17 January 1993, the two-year anniversary of the start of Operation DESERT STORM.

The sortie was scheduled for mid-morning takeoff: fly approximately 50 minutes to the AOR, rendezvous with aerial refueling tankers, conduct reconnaissance operations, provide Wild Weasel SAM suppression for British Jaguars photo-reccing a newly discovered SA-6 SAM site, a second aerial refueling, and Combat Air Patrol (CAP) operations until relieved by another F-4/F-16 Wild Weasel team and return to base. Total sortie length was scheduled for just under five hours. The F-4G Instructor crew who would be giving me my evaluation was pilot Lt Col Steve "Sieg" Heil and EWO Capt Rich "Casper" Pearcy. I would brief, lead, and debrief the sortie, but would assume the wingman role and responsibilities during the Jaguar recce run due to the F-4Gs' need to conduct random and dynamic maneuvering necessary to triangulate, range, and kill an enemy radar site.

The night prior to my sortie, over a few beers at the British hospitality tent I engaged Capt Dave "Logger" Rose in a strategy discussion of exactly *how* to employ the AIM-7 air to air missiles carried by the F-4G in the event this became necessary. "Logger" flew F-15s at Soesterberg AB, Netherlands, had killed an Iraqi MiG-23 Flogger during Operation DESERT STORM, and was very familiar with the tactics to successfully employ Sparrow missiles. Little did I know I would accomplish the same feat the very next morning with a different type of missile. I remember "Logger" impressing upon me two things that evening: first was to make sure, above all else, that before you fired an air-to-air missile you were absolutely positive it was a hostile aircraft, and not a friendly (copy, don't kill the good guys). Second was the need to formulate, brief, and execute a simple and easy to understand air-to-air game plan because, as he put it, "when it really happens out there, your IQ will drop to about 10." I appreciated the advice, and incorporated it into my briefing the next morning.

The morning briefing, takeoff, and tanker rendezvous of DEVIL 01, our call sign that day, were uneventful. After topping off our tanks, we relieved another mixed Weasel pair who began their return-to-base (RTB). The F-16 wingman of that relieved flight, Capt Jim "Dome" Mastny, a friend and Flight Commander, called me over the VHF secure radio to request I fly to a specific location to determine battle damage assessment (BDA), where they had earlier attacked an enemy radar site with HARM missiles. After locating the site I was unable to determine the success of the attack, and continued with the pre-planned mission. After about another 30 minutes or so of general reconnaissance, it was time to refuel once again in preparation for the SAM suppression portion of the mission; the low altitude British recce run on the very lethal and highly mobile SA-6 surface-to-air missile site. It was after this refueling the F-15 Eagles would begin their RTB, and we would assume air-to-air CAP responsibilities in addition to the Weasel duties for our fearless British friends. After the Eagles departed there would only be four aircraft in the Northern No-Fly Zone. That would soon change.

The rules to engage an enemy fighter were also pretty straightforward. An enemy fighter visually identified north of the

36th parallel dies, plain and simple. To shoot an enemy fighter beyond visual range (BVR) in those days was a little more complicated, and required an E-3 Sentry aircraft declaration of hostile and a few other things to avoid the possibility of fratricide, something every fighter pilot dreads.

I turned over the lead of the formation to "Sieg" and "Casper," while I flew a wedge formation about a mile off the F-4's left hand side. We were at 25,000 feet, and approximately 20 miles west of the last known location of the SA-6, a position where we could quickly employ HARM missiles to shut down the enemy radar should he start radiating, tracking, or engaging the Brit Jaguars. My job as a Weasel wingman was deeply engrained by the veteran Phantom crews: keep sight, stay in position, and keep a good visual lookout for any possible threats. As part of my pre-flight briefing, I had told "Sieg" and "Casper" that in the event of an air threat while I was in the wingman role, I would immediately reassume the lead of the formation and use the F-16's APG-68/

AMRAAM combination to defeat the threat, with "Sieg" as my wingman. He agreed. Also included in my air-to-air briefing was the use and employment of a Desired Engagement Zone (DEZ), a single-side-offset to maximize the sun's advantage and set up a low to high intercept geometry to minimize the threat from the Iraqi AA-7 radar guided Apex missile, contracts, ID/ROE review, fuel tank/bomb jettison criteria, and shot doctrine, among other things. Following "Logger's" advice, I did my best to keep things as simple as possible for my wingman and me.

We had only been in our Weasel Cap for a few minutes when it happened; in fact, the Jags had not even reached their target yet. While "Sieg" and "Casper" searched for signs the SA-6 was coming to life, I scanned the skies and my radar for signs of enemy activity. The only game in town were a few non-threatening MiGs boring circles in the sky south of the 36th parallel, over 40 nautical miles away. Then, at a known active enemy airfield south of the 36th parallel codenamed "Caddy," I saw the unmistakable radar

"Trigger" Stevenson on the boom of a KC-135 after the engagement; notice the missing AIM-120 and external tanks. *via Craig Stevenson.*

return of an enemy aircraft rolling down the runway and heading in our direction, about 30 nm away. Now, that in itself was not unusual; they flew from Caddy regularly, and I followed the normal procedure of radar locking and broadcasting the contact to my wingman and the AWACS controller. As briefed, I took the tactical lead of the flight and, due to orbit distance, the AWACS radar had not yet detected the threat. To manage the DEZ, I initially turned the flight cold while AWACS then detected the MiG and began broadcasting threat information. With the relatively short distances involved between the MiG and our flight, we essentially did a continuous 360-degree turn. "Sieg," as DEVIL 02, deployed to the proper position as we turned hot, and I reestablished a radar lock on the bandit. We began to offset slightly west. Shortly after turning hot, with the MiG continuing toward the No Fly Zone, AWACS gave our flight the "commit" call. As planned, I jettisoned my two nearly full external 370-gallon fuel tanks, selected afterburner, and began a combat descent to manage the AA-7 Apex Weapons Employment Zone (WEZ). The plan was to basically get well below the bandit's altitude, forcing his radar into a look-down mode, and thus reducing its already limited capabilities. At .95 Mach I was well above the selective jettison design limitation for the fuel tanks, and the aircraft quickly let me know. The jettison was so violent I remember looking back at my horizontal stabilizers to make sure they hadn't been damaged by the fuel tanks.

The MiG's flight path remained predictable. He accelerated to supersonic speed, climbing straight toward us, attaining an altitude of approximately 17,000 feet. We began a combat descent in afterburner and leveled at 4,000 feet, over Mach 1.2. In the debrief, "Sieg" and "Casper" told me that from their position, over 1.5 nm away, my falling tanks looked similar to a missile being fired from my aircraft. The MiG crossed into the No Fly zone, and when AWACS gave the "cleared kill" call, the now supersonic MiG was only 12 miles ahead. My Radar Warning Receiver (RWR) was quiet, meaning the enemy's radar had not found me yet. Concurrent with the AWACS "cleared kill" call, the enemy began what's known as a drag maneuver; a high performance, normally energy-depleting turn 180 degrees in the opposite direction. This maneuver broke my radar lock (although I visually acquired him during the drag), and left me in a "tail chase" position, with the MiG slightly above me at 6000 feet. Although supersonic and "tally-ho" with the bandit, I was slightly outside of the maximum aerodynamic launch range of the AIM-120A missile. Since I only had 50 knots of overtake velocity on the MiG, my only hope was the bandit would maneuver toward me before I came within range of the numerous fixed SAM sites ahead, near the 36th parallel. Meanwhile, off to my west "Sieg" and "Casper" were unable to acquire the MiG with their air-to-air radar, so they simply concentrated on becoming the best wingmen they knew how. You see, sometimes it's difficult to make the transition to being a wingman when you're so accustomed to flying the lead position. Not these guys, though. Not only did they keep sight, stay in position, and clear my six, they began to target various nearby fixed SAM sites *in the event* they became active and threatened us. All the while searching for the MiG, keeping track of fuel, and communicating which airborne and ground radars were emitting. A real lesson in wingman role assumption and a total class act.

The MiG realized he couldn't escape; I had almost closed to within maximum aerodynamic launch range when he began a left turn reversal to re-engage. This turn immediately brought him within max launch range, and I attempted to fire my first AMRAAM. After several seconds, with no indication of the telltale "whoosh" of a fired missile, I looked out to my left wingtip and saw the AMRAAM that should've been gone still there. "Not good," I thought, and used the missile step button to switch to the

"Trigger" Stevenson immediately after landing at Incirlik after the shoot-down. Due to the misfire of the port AIM-120, he was directed to the hung ordnance area after landing. Weapons troops are disarming the remaining weapons, while the team chief is warning off the photographer, who happens to be standing directly in front of a live, hung AIM-120! *via Craig Stevenson*.

"Trigger" Stevenson with his F-16C after it was towed to the shelter. *via Craig Stevenson.*

"Trigger" Stevenson with his crew chief (holding forms) and various 23rd FS personnel, including Capt Jim "Dome" Mastny (blue T-shirt). *via Craig Stevenson.*

AMRAAM on the opposite wingtip and fired. The feedback of a fired AMRAAM is immediate. It rocketed from my right-hand missile rail like it was angry I'd shot it. The only thing to watch after that was about a second or two of red rocket motor, and then it was gone. The MiG continued its turn toward our flight and, with information displayed in my Heads Up Display (HUD) indicating the missile was active (operating without guidance from my onboard radar), we began a northbound turn to avoid nearby SAM sites. Shortly after turning northbound I checked over my right shoulder for evidence of a "splash" and saw the MiG continue to turn into the missile until impact. The only thing that emerged from the big fireball was a smaller fireball, slowly descending; there was no chute observed. I called "splash one" to AWACS as we continued north away from the fireball, and looking left, there was "Sieg" right where he had been briefed to be.

I needed some gas, and I needed it quick. I spent some time running around in afterburner, and barely had enough to make it home to Incirlik. "Sieg" didn't jettison his externals, so he had enough gas to stay on station while I made a trip up to the orbiting KC-135s. The details of my rendezvous with the tankers could be a story in itself, but suffice to say, my mind was far, far away from thinking about aerial refueling as I finally pulled up below the tanker. We won't mention the possible hazards my hung AMRAAM missile presented to other aircraft in my vicinity. After refueling, I proceeded back to the CAP location and passed "Sieg" on his way to refuel. South of my CAP, I could clearly see the pillar of smoke from where the MiG-23 Flogger had crashed. In fact, the smoke could clearly be seen from Caddy, his base of departure. I silently wondered if perhaps some of his squadronmates might see this and launch their fighters for retribution, and exactly what my game plan would be with only a pair of Sidewinder missiles remaining, and my Sparrow equipped wingman on the tanker. I must admit my heart skipped a beat when, a short time later, I once again acquired a radar contact departing Caddy airfield. "Here they come," I thought. Fortunately for them, it turned out to be a low and slow rescue helicopter on its way to the crash site.

You gotta love the fact that the Eagles are always looking for a fight. When this engagement happened, the F-15s had been headed home to Incirlik for the better part of thirty minutes. After the shoot down the AWACS must have turned them around, because it wasn't long before I kept hearing repeated, frantic calls on the Guard frequency, calling for some flight to "turn North immediately, you're in Syrian airspace" over and over again. Any guesses who that was? Our Eagle brethren, of course. God bless 'em, they thought somebody might need help, and they flew through 100 miles of Syrian airspace, going just as fast as that Eagle would go, ignoring calls from AWACS. Why? Because it was the shortest way to the fight. I'm happy there are guys out there like that.

"Sieg" wrote a grade sheet for that sortie, and needless to say I passed with an overall grade of "4," the highest possible. His final written comments were, "Cleared to lead mixed Wild Weasel sorties and kill MiGs."

This was the 65th worldwide F-16 kill, and the second USAF F-16 victory.

After his Viper tour at Spangdahlem, "Trigger" went on to teach on AT-38s at Randolph and Moody AFB. Major "Trigger" Stevenson retired from the Air Force in 2003, and currently flies for a major airline.

Captain Bob "Wilbur" Wright (USAF)

526th FS "Black Knights," F-16C
Operation DENY FLIGHT
3 x J-1 Jastrebs
28 February 1994
Call-sign: BLACK 03

After graduating the U.S. Air Force Academy in 1984, a sports injury delayed Lt Wright's assignment to pilot training. After a five year wait, Capt Wright graduated UPT at Columbus AFB, Mississippi, in class 90-09. Upon completing F-16 training at McDill AFB, Florida, he spent a year in the 80th TFS ("Juvats) at Kunsan Air Base, Korea. He was then assigned to the 526th FS of the 86th Fighter Wing, Ramstein Air Base, Germany. Wilbur had been in the squadron for two years, and had over 700 hours in the Viper prior to this engagement. This event marks the first triple-kill since Randy "Duke" Cunningham's in May 1972, and was also the first offensive use of NATO airpower. The following account is from a taped telephonic interview with Col Wright.

This was one of my first rotations down to Aviano Air Base, Italy, for Operation DENY FLIGHT. I was assigned to the 526th Fighter Squadron at Ramstein AB, Germany, but we were spending a lot of time TDY (Temporary Duty) to Italy. We were patrolling the airspace over Bosnia to prevent the Serbs from conducting any military air operations. On this day we had a couple of two-ships airborne. I was paired with my wingman, Scott "Zulu" O'Grady (BLACK 04), and Steve "Yogi" Allen was checking in as KNIGHT 25. I can't remember who his wingman was. We were flying Block 40 Vipers configured with two AIM-120s, two AIM-9s, and a couple of General Purpose (GP) bombs. We didn't have LANTIRN pods yet.

"Wilbur" Wright's F-16C 89-2137 seen several years later at Aviano after being reassigned to the 31st Operations Group, 555th Fighter Squadon – "The Triple Nickel." *Stefano Antoniazzi.*

Original art of "Wilbur" Wright's kill titled "Triple over the Balkans" by Lockheed staff artist Price Randel.

We left our rooms at about 11:00 pm and took off at about 0100. Weather had moved in, so they could not launch our replacements, so we were staying in the CAP until they could launch. We were getting low on gas, and getting ready to go for the tanker. We had been monitoring a helo out in the western part of the airspace near Mostar, in southern Bosnia, but it had not crossed the border, so we were just watching it. The weather had finally gotten better at Aviano, which allowed the launch of KNIGHT 25 on their CAS mission over Sarajevo. "Yogi" was the unsung hero of all this, because as he was checking in with AWACS, he picked up the contacts outside of the airspace and pointed them out to AWACS. The contacts were between Split and Ubdina airfield, and since they were still outside the airspace we were only monitoring. After making the radio call pointing out the contacts, they vectored "Yogi" on down to Sarajevo. As I said before, we were just getting ready to go to the tanker because we had high joker and bingo fuels based on the weather back at Aviano.

AWACS then asked us to take a look at those contacts. The weather was clear above, with some haze and fog down low. The sun was just getting ready to come up, so the sky was getting light, but you still really couldn't see the ground. As we pressed north my wingman was searching high with his radar, and I was "burning worms" looking low. I picked up a two-ship and called them out to AWACS. We "greened 'em-up (master arm on)," since they were fast-movers. They were fast-movers (fighters), but slow, going about 250 knots.

They were heading south-southeast, and I couldn't see them visually, so I knew that I would have to go down to ID them. I kept my wingman high to cover, and because I didn't want to drag him down into any small arms fire. We knew that if anyone on the ground saw someone fly by, they would shoot at us. We did a high to low conversion. The two-ship was running down the valleys as I converted below and behind them. When they crossed a ridge I was able to identify them at first as Galebs, but actually they were J-1 Jastrebs, the single-seat version. The Galeb is a two-seat training version that looks like a T-33, and these were the single seat versions. But I called the ID into AWACS as "Galebs."

To stay behind them, I started to jigsaw behind them while I read them U.N. Resolution 816 off of my kneeboard on Guard (243.0, frequency). This instructed them to exit the airspace, or they would be engaged. I saw no reaction from them. So now, here we were all set up, after flying a great intercept, and in a position to carry out the mission, and what I got back from AWACS was "Standby." This was followed by the instructions to "shadow" those aircraft. Since the aircraft were going only 250kts, my plan was to spin my wingman and set up a race track to allow us to maintain a more tactical airspeed and "shadow" the two-ship.

In the meantime my wingman lost track of my exact posit, so we were working hard to get him back on me. This was really difficult for him, since he was high looking into a black hole. I was doing a jigsaw maneuver to stay behind the two-ship, since I was going faster than them. At this point they must have visually picked me up, because they started to jigsaw also, making it a little more difficult. I was at about 1,500-2,000 feet, and the two Jastrebs were slightly below me.

Capt Bob "Wilbur" Wright. *via Bob Wright.*

At this point I got a tally on an additional four-ship, way above me. They were about 8,000 to 10,000 feet above and to our southeast. I was padlocked on this new four-ship as we all proceeded roughly south down the ridgelines. I still had the original two-ship on radar. I made a call to AWACS that I wanted KNIGHT 25 to come up and assist. Right now I was feeling very offensive, being 1 vs. 6, and working my wingman, and all I needed these guys to do was scatter. So I called "Yogi" Allen to come up from Sarajevo and help me corral these guys.

As my wingman was getting situated and "Yogi" was on the way north, the original two-ship started to climb to join the four-ship. I was thinking this is great, since it helped me keep my visual on both flights. It had been a little easier to see the four-ship since I was looking up into the blue sky, but I had needed the radar to keep track of the lower two-ship. I was just maintaining trail, and my guess is that at least the two-ship knew I was there. But if you look at the recent history, we had not engaged anybody. The helos had been flying in there, so they were kind of scoffing at the "no fly zone" by that point.

The flights joined into one six ship, and I was feeling VERY offensive, sitting behind six aircraft. I think if I had squeezed the trigger and kicked the rudder, I would have shot down six aircraft, but I didn't have clearance to do so. The two-ship had joined to the right of the four-ship to make a six ship line-abreast wall formation, and I was about 4,000 to 6,000 feet behind—close enough to be ready to engage if necessary. I queried AWACS again. Their reply was, "Not cleared." I think that "Not cleared" was an answer to "Yogi's" request to jettison his external fuel tanks. After talking with "Yogi," "Yogi" had requested to jettison his tanks, to help him get to us faster. At that time we didn't want anything falling in Bosnia, so I think that "Not cleared" was telling him to hang on to his tanks. At the time, I found this all very confusing.

In the meantime, they began to do a "Pappy Boyington" roll-in on a munitions factory, and I was rolling in as number seven. Here we go! When the first bombs started going off they had fulfilled a hostile act, and I could start to engage them. The bad news was that I started to see stuff coming back up, and I was "tail-end Charlie." I decided that this was not the best place to be. I couldn't tell if it was secondaries going off or people shooting at me, but it was time to get out of there, so I broke off to the southeast to extend and get some distance between myself and the six-ship.

As I pitched back in and pointed, I reported to AWACS that I had lost the visual, but still had them on radar, and that they had committed a hostile act. I queried AWACS again, "Am I cleared to fire?" That's when they came back with, "You're cleared to engage." What I painted on my radar was basically a ladder, and they were heading back to the northwest, kind of where they had come from. I got my wingman turned around back to the north, since we had made this big turn, and he was back on board. KNIGHT 25 was behind us, so I had the good guys in trail of the bad guys, and we were all running back north.

I engaged the closest contact with an AMRAAM. I hammered-down, and there was a time delay for the missile to come off the rail. After I hammered-down, I remember thinking that it didn't work, and I looked over at the rail, and the missile came off the rail like a freight train. I was at about five thousand feet (~2,500 AGL) and descending. I had seen the aircraft as he crossed another ridge (that's how I ID'd him again), then I hit the pickle button. The missile jumped out there, and the explosion was huge. I'd seen missiles shot at drones during WSEP, but this explosion was huge. In fact, you can see on my tape where I kind of flinch from the explosion—Holy Cow, that was a big explosion! There were no chutes from any of the aircraft. I came off of him, and I picked up a two-ship on my radar, close-aboard, and I was running them down. I locked the guy on the right; I'm not sure if he was the wingman, but he was slightly aft. I used a heater on that aircraft, thinking that I wanted to save my last AMRAAM for a "fade-away jump shot." I shot the heater, and it came off the rail like a bottle rocket and BOOM, that aircraft blew up. At that point, the flight lead knew that his wingman had exploded, so he was up and over a ridge, and I was trying to run him down.

I was low when I crossed over the ridge and started pulling lead for guns when I saw a town in the background. I realized two things: one, there was a town there, so if I missed I'd be throwing "BBs" through the middle of town. Also, I was pulling lead in about 135 degrees of bank and I was low, and I didn't want to pull lead into the ground. So I decided not to go for guns, and pulled up and did a spacing maneuver, then came back in for the second heater. That was also an AIM-9M. My wingman was coming up on my right five o'clock for about three miles, supporting. As the target went over the next ridge, beyond him was nothing but fields, so I fired my last heater, and it tracked the aircraft all the way, and again, BOOM, explosion. The missiles all did a great job.

My wingman was onboard now, and he locked the next aircraft and called "Engaged." He fired an AIM-9 and pulled off, but the missile was just a little out of range. I watched it and it did detonate, but not quite on the aircraft. I did a fuel check; my joker/bingo was 5,500 pounds, and I had 3,700 and my wingman had 3,000. Time to go. "Yogi" was coming up behind us; my wingman came off his target and kind of pitched into "Yogi," so "Yogi" saw this and locked us up. I told "Yogi" that he was buddy-spiking us, that we were going to the tanker, and the bandits were out there

off his nose. I had my wingman reference the exit gate so that we could go get gas.

"Yogi" picked the aircraft up on radar, and I'll let him tell his story, but he fired an AIM-9 at the closest contact, but it didn't fuse. Actually, what had happened was that the missile took the umbilical with it and didn't fuse. His next missile got that victory.

We got to the tanker over the Adriatic, and we were obviously low on gas. Since there was the weather factor, I was thinking that we would go into Falconara Airfield if we couldn't get gas. It was our divert, down the east coast of Italy. I put my wingman on the boom first so he could get a couple of thousand pounds, to make sure he could get gas, then I would get some gas. Next thing I heard was "Yogi" checking in right behind the tanker with his gas state. So we went quick flow, and after Scott got 4,000 pounds I got on the boom and cleared "Yogi" to the tanker's right wing. After I took gas I cleared up to the tanker's left wing. While "Yogi" was on the boom, the CAOC was trying to decide who they could send back in to clean up. Based on our missile states "Yogi" won, so he went back in to see if he could find them, and we RTB'd (went home to Aviano).

The weather still wasn't good, but it was above our minimums, so we recovered to Aviano. It was one of those "don't mess it up now" things. It really hadn't sank in yet. With the training we get, I had just reacted. It wasn't until I was on the boom and the boomer asked me how many I had shot down. I said "Three," and he said "Awesome," and it was not until that point that it hit me. Once on the ground "Zulu" pulled in first, and the squadron was all there, then I pulled in and got the same reception. But I was rushed to debrief, and I didn't even get to see my tapes, because within twenty minutes of landing my squadron commander and I were on a plane to Naples to brief General Ashey and Admiral Borda on what had happened.

I didn't get back to the squadron until after midnight, and it was just "Yogi" and I left in building. Everyone else had already left. I guess the squadron had a great celebration without us, because there was barely one beer left for the two of us. So we drove back to the hotel together and talked over what had happened. But the guys were great, and you know, people say you did awesome, but I didn't. I just did what I was trained to do. I don't normally like talking about this, because anybody could have done the same or better. I just happened to be the lucky one there at the time. The credit for the victories goes to our training, such as the Red Flags and the WSEP shoots. It's all of that and the luck of the draw. Everyone involved in this engagement followed their training, and did a superb job in a tough visual and terrain environment.

Shortly after this engagement, the 86th FW moved permanently from Ramstein to Aviano AB, Italy. Capt Wright's 526th FS reconstituted as the 555th FS "Triple Nickel" under the 31st FW. After completing his tour in the Nickel, Capt Wright attended Intermediate Service School, and then served on the staff at the Pentagon. He went on to be the Operations Officer of the 522nd FS and the Commander of the 523rd FS at Cannon AFB, New Mexico. He is currently the Operations Group Commander of a large fighter group.

"Wilbur" Wright seen in F-16C 89-2137, which displays the three kill markings, plus one bombing mission credit under the boarding ladder. *via Bob Wright.*

Captain Steve "Yogi" Allen (USAF)

526th FS, F-16C
Operation DENY FLIGHT
J-1 Jastreb
18 February 1994
Call-sign: KNIGHT 25

Steve Allen commissioned via Officers Training School in 1985, and went on to graduate UPT at Laughlin AFB, Texas, in 1987. He remained as a T-38 FAIP until 1990, when he was selected for the F-16. Upon completing F-16 training he got to Hahn Air Base, Germany, just in time for it to close. He then transferred to the 526th FS of the 86th Fighter Wing, Ramstein AB, Germany. Yogi had been in the squadron for almost three years prior to this deployment. "Yogi" wrote the following account for the first time for this publication.

My nickname is "Yogi." How did I get that name, you ask? Well, "Fat F$%&n' Dork" was already taken. Just kidding...as far as you know. I like to tell people that I'm smarter than the average bear, but then even the above average bears aren't all that bright. I'll probably wake up someday in Jellystone with a radio collar and a tag in my ear. But I digress. I'm supposed to tell you a war story. I'll start it with how every good war story begins. There I was, and this is no shit.

I was a member of the 526th Fighter Squadron from Ramstein Air Base, Germany, deployed to Aviano Air Base, Italy. We were there to enforce Operation DENY FLIGHT. This involved enforcing a no-fly zone over Bosnia. The running joke was, they fly—we deny it. This no-fly zone was the result of one of the numerous resolutions being puked out of the U.N. like pizzas from Dominos. The *theory* of a United Nations working in harmony to alleviate global suffering is laudable. The reality is an extremely parochial organization incapable of concrete action. Rwanda (800,000 dead), Srebrenica (8-10,000 dead), and Darfur (still ongoing) are recent examples. The bureaucrats issue resolution after resolution, then stand back and wring their hands while nothing happens. It

"Yogi" Allen's F-16C, seen later on final approach at Aviano, now assigned to the 510th FS "Vultures." The LANTIRN Targeting pod is visible just below the intake. *Stefano Antoniazzi.*

reminds me of the movie "Monty Python and The Holy Grail"— "Stop, or we will be forced to taunt you a second time!" Or maybe the frazzled mom at the Chuck E. Cheese who tells junior, "If you don't stop that right now, you're going to be in trouble!" Of course the little brat doesn't listen. He's used to the empty threats. Just another squallin' young 'un to get on everybody else's nerves. Now don't get the idea that I don't like children, because I do. Love 'em in fact. They taste like chicken. But I digress again.

Back to the story. Since there were no quarters on base, we were "forced" to spend our time at a local hotel enjoying the alpine ambiance. Tough duty, but our country called. The actual missions were routine, if not downright boring. We would depart Aviano, and with the magic of air refueling, would cover four hour vulnerability (vul) periods over the area of responsibility (AOR). Most of us had experience drilling holes in the sky over northern Iraq enforcing that no-fly zone, so we were familiar with the mission.

The day before the shoot down, my scheduler asked if I wouldn't mind leading an early flight in the morning. I said it would be fine. That's when he tells me, "Oh, by the way, you'll be flying with a Colonel from Spangdahlem." I had never met the man. It turns out that Colonel "Jace" Meyer was a good aviator, fine officer, and an overall good shit. Sometimes a perceived bad deal ends up paying huge dividends.

We arrived at the squadron the next morning around 0330-0400 for a takeoff sometime around 0630 with a call sign of KNIGHT 25. It was dark as we crossed the Adriatic Sea. Bob "Wilbur" Wright and Scott "Zulu" O'Grady, call sign BLACK 03/04, were already established in the AOR. There was an airspace corridor

"Wilbur" Wright (left) and "Yogi" Allen. *via Wright.*

that extended from the Adriatic Sea across Croatia and terminated in Bosnia. Approximately ten miles west of the Bosnian border and slightly north of that corridor lay Ubdina airfield. This airfield, though in Croatia, was occupied by Serbian forces. Dawn was breaking as we transited the corridor, but the sun had not actually broken the horizon. I had the low search, with my wingman looking high.

About halfway through the corridor, I got radar contacts 20 degrees left at 15-20 miles—right about where Ubdina was. It was a fairly large "blob," indicating multiple contacts. They were heading east at low altitude, indicating 250-290 knots. This would have them entering Bosnia in a matter of minutes. We pushed it up to 400 plus knots. I called out the contacts to AWACS, and they responded that the bogies were in Croatia. I emphasized that they were heading east, and they told us to continue to monitor the situation. Once the bogies were clearly in Bosnia we were given clearance to intercept. We ran them down from behind and closed to four nm when AWACS told us to "skip it," meaning terminate the intercept. I couldn't believe it. Here I was with a large group of four to six bogies violating the no-fly zone on my nose for four miles, and I'm supposed to just leave? After haggling back and forth on the radio, they responded more forcefully, "CHARIOT says skip it."

CHARIOT was Major General James "Bear" Chambers at the CAOC in Vicenza, Italy. He was a gruff, straight shooter type of leader, hence the nickname "Bear." I had flown with him many times. He was one of the most competent, mission oriented generals that I had ever had the privilege to fly with. So when he said "skip it," I figured there was good reason. It turns out that the "skip it" did not come from him. They had called him, and he was still on his way into the CAOC. Someone else at the CAOC saw that my flight was scheduled as a close air support mission (CAS) and made the call. It was never clear to me where the breakdown occurred. That's when they called "Wilbur's" BLACK flight and started bringing him in on the bogies, even though BLACK flight was low on fuel. I turned my flight south and climbed. I told AWACS to call me on Guard if they needed us. We would be on a different frequency working CAS with French Forward Air Controllers (FACs) in Sarajevo.

We never made it to Sarajevo. AWACS called on Guard. They said to turn northwest and switch to the air-to-air freq. Before I even checked in I heard "Wilbur" calling "Splash three!" There was a huge furball on my radar about 15-20 miles away. I couldn't believe I was witnessing an actual air-to-air engagement, much less about to join the fray. One of the contacts was separating from the engagement and coming towards me. I locked on to it and made a "Raygun" call. This call is for friendly aircraft to check their threat warning receivers to determine if they are the ones being targeted. "Wilbur" replied that he was "Buddy Spiked." He was leaving the fight due to his low fuel situation. I dropped my lock on him and continued to sort among the various contacts. His wingman, "Zulu," was still somewhere in front of me, and fratricide was my biggest concern.

After all the debris from "Wilbur's" kills faded off the radar, I was able to break out two distinct contacts flanking north with

Soko G-2 Galeb (Serbian for "Seagull"), which is a two seat trainer version of the single seat J-1 Jastreb ("Hawk"). This example is seen in 2001, after having been shipped to the United States. *Author.*

about five to seven miles between them. They were approximately 12 miles off my nose. I had a good rate of closure due to my airspeed and intercept geometry. A third contact popped up closer than the others, so I retargeted. I made another "Raygun" call and got no response from "Zulu." This was the bogey I was going to prosecute. I was not going to shoot, though, until I made a visual identification (VID). The bogey was indicating 320-350 knots. I remember noting that it was faster than their ingress. I didn't know then that they had delivered bombs. The reduction in drag helped them fly faster. I suppose a few F-16s on their ass may have been a motivating factor as well.

I closed to about one mile, and was positioned at the bogey's dead six. I had my low altitude warning set at 500' AGL, and it was going off. Bitchin' Betty was serenading me with calls of "Altitude, Altitude," which meant I was below 500' AGL. Normally I wouldn't be down there in the weeds, especially with the poor light conditions, but I couldn't yet get a tally on the bogey. I was impressed with the bogey's low altitude skills. He was *well* below me, probably flying close to 75-100' AGL. We were flying over low rolling mountains that were well forested with bare trees. There was also snow cover on the ground, which provided enough contrast that allowed me to safely fly that low. We approached a small ridge that the bogey had to climb over. He crested the ridge with a direct bunting maneuver that allowed me to see a perfect wings level silhouette against the gray sky. I could clearly see the distinctive wing tip fuel tanks of the Jastreb/Galeb. It resembled a T-33. This was the last piece of the puzzle I needed to engage—a positive VID.

I bumped my altitude up as well so I wouldn't lose line of sight, and thus my radar lock, when the bogey descended down the backside. I selected the AIM-9 Sidewinder missile from my left wingtip station. The high pitched tone indicated a good track by the missile. I mashed down on the pickle button, and the missile shot off the rail. It sounded like a pop bottle rocket going off. The missile plume was easy to track in the dim light. The missile shot out straight, then took a bid right for the target. I lost sight of the missile plume when it was about halfway to the target. I mentally

counted down the few seconds it should take to get there, but nothing happened. It occurred to me that I might be experiencing temporal distortion, and that if I was patient I would see a fireball momentarily, but nothing happened. I selected the AIM-9 from my right wingtip rail. It went off exactly like the first one. I again lost sight of the missile plume about halfway to the target. This time, however, the missile found its mark, and I was rewarded with a tremendous fireball 4,000 feet off my nose. The size of the fireball surprised me. I wouldn't have imagined a relatively small aircraft torching off like that. The fireball was still expanding as the debris descended into the treetops and began to tumble across the snow covered ground. The contrast of a bright orange fireball tumbling across the monochromatic landscape is indelibly imprinted on my diminutive, alcohol damaged brain. I didn't know how many bogies there were, so I climbed the flight for a better radar picture.

"Zulu" had left the fight by this time due to his low fuel state. I put my flight into a slow orbit, since the bogies could have run in any direction. We did several orbits, but couldn't find any more targets. The magnitude of what just transpired hadn't sunk in yet. I pointed the flight towards Sarajevo, because I figured somebody still wanted us to do CAS. We were trundling along towards Sarajevo when my wingman pulled up next to me about 500 feet off my right wing. He was giving me an incredibly enthusiastic two thumbs up. That's when it started to sink in. I was getting anxious to get back to Aviano and start celebrating with my buds, but the CAOC had other plans. All launches had been stopped, and we were to re-role to a counter-air mission. We were the only fighters left over Bosnia, because BLACK flight had returned to base. All the airborne tanker assets now belonged to us, and we ended up logging over six hours that day (along with filling several piddle packs).

We eventually recovered to Aviano, but there was hardly anybody to meet us. There were just a handful of crew chiefs that we shared high fives with. I went into the squadron and found myself alone. My wingman had gone to the base command post to meet the wing leadership. I called my wife and told her the news. Then I read the paper and did the crossword puzzle. I waited

An example of a 512th TFS F-16C seen at RAF Mildenhall in 1991. *Michael Baldock.*

Cockpit view of the Soko G-2 Galeb. Except for a few different armament switches, the Galeb front cockpit is identical to the J-1 Jastreb. *Author.*

around, thinking somebody was going to show up for a formal debrief. It was incredibly surreal. Eventually, my boss called and told me to go to the command post to conduct a phone interview with the press. What a bunch of biased dickheads! One guy asked me if I felt like I was "shooting fish in a barrel," insinuating that we were some sort of bullies picking on the little kids. I told him to interview the victims of the bombing raid, and ask them how it felt to be fish in a barrel. He got even snottier, and asked me what I thought about it "not being a fair fight." I told him, "That's what your tax dollars are paying for." I was glad to get off the phone. My advice—never argue with an asshole.

I bear no animosity towards the Serbian pilots that flew that day. In fact, I sort of admire them, all politics aside. They had a lot of balls. Big *cajones*, if you prefer. They executed a well planned low level ingress in less than optimal conditions, and conducted a successful attack. "Wilbur" turned out to be the monkey wrench in their gears, the fly in their ointment. His handling of the ROE and VID were the most important factors in this entire engagement. I have no doubt that if he had had more fuel, he would have mopped up all the bogies. It is incredible to me how the whole event seemed like just another training mission. We had flown countless training scenarios that were very similar. Obviously, the fireballs were a new twist.

Anyway, I feel honored to have been a part of it. And that's all I have to say about that.

The 86th FW transferred all assets to the 31st FW at Aviano Air Base, Italy, and "Yogi" was part of this move. In 1997 it was decided that it was finally safe enough to return "Yogi" to the States, and he was assigned as the Active Duty Advisor to the South Dakota Air National Guard (ANG), the 175th Fighter Squadron. In 1999 "Yogi" separated from active duty, and is a part-time ANG member and flies for a major airline.

Lt Col Cesar "Rico" Rodriguez (USAF)

493rd EFS "Grim Reapers," F-15C
Operation ALLIED FORCE
MiG-29
24 March 1999
Call-sign: KNIFE 13

Lt Col Rodriguez's ALLIED FORCE kill marked the first of the conflict and the third in his career. It also made him one of only two pilots to shoot down two MiG-29 Fulcrums. The following account is from a taped interview with Col Rodriquez.

In January 1999 I was assigned to the 493rd Fighter Squadron, known as the "Grim Reapers," stationed at RAF Lakenheath in the United Kingdom. We were the only F-15C squadron left in Europe; Spangdahlem had recently closed its Eagle squadron, and sent some of their jets to us. This enabled us to "plus-up" from an 18-jet squadron to a 24-jet unit. Several squadrons in the states were also to plus-up at this time. This made us the "pro's from Dover," the only unit dedicated to providing air supremacy in the European area of operations (AOR).

Whereas my unit in DESERT STORM (58 TFS) had wingmen with over a thousand hours in the Eagle, the 493rd Fighter Squadron had wingmen showing up straight from the training course at Tyndall as recently as a month prior to the deployment. Some were finishing their Mission Ready (MR) check rides the week before we left for Italy. We had some very, very young aviators with us, and that's not to say they didn't perform admirably. On the contrary, they did incredibly great work. In particular was one of

these young troops, "Wild Bill" Denim, my wingman on the night of 24 March.

We left Lakenheath and deployed un-refueled, but fully loaded, to Cervia, Italy. Cervia is an Italian base 80 miles south of Aviano, on the east coast of Italy. This gave us the capability to take off in full afterburner, turn due east, and within eight and a half minutes be on station to monitor Yugoslavia, or provide support to anyone that needed it. We were the only U.S. presence at Cervia, which was a huge advantage over being deployed to the "USS Aviano." We did not have to compete for runway, ramp, or weapons storage space, so we had a pretty good deal set up for us. The Italians were phenomenal hosts, not only on base, but also downtown, in the restaurants and hotels we frequented. They were equally determined to see this conflict ended as rapidly as possible with as minimal impact on the communities involved.

On 24 March we prepared for the first mission of this conflict. There were two missions on this first night, both spearheaded by

F-15C 86-0169 used by "Rico" Rodriguez to shoot down the first Serbian MiG-29 of Operation ALLIED FORCE, seen on final at RAF Lakenheath in August 1994. This aircraft was later lost on 26 March 2001 in a tragic mishap in the mountains of Scotland, claiming the life of the pilot of 86-0169, and that of another 493rd F-15C. *Bas Stubert via Pieter Taris.*

F-15s of the 493rd Fighter Squadron. The first was a U.S.-only mission that went north through Hungary to act as the northern arm of the assault. They focused on Belgrade and the SAM threat, employing F-117s and EA-6Bs. Our mission, on the other hand, was a coalition-centric mission, with a strike package made up of most of the coalition members. We refueled with the package over the "boot" of Italy, and then pushed north up the eastern shore of the Adriatic. The targets were primarily in Montenegro; radar sites and SAMs positioned to deny access to Pristina. The strike was designed to break a hole in this SAM belt, and to open access for the close air support (CAS) assets that needed to get into Kosovo from the west.

Our four-ship of F-15s proceeded north, consisting of the flight lead "Cricket" Renner, and his wingman "K-Bob" Sweeny. I was number three, with my wingman, "Wild Bill" Denim. We were positioned with "K-Bob" on the far left to the west, then to the right was "Cricket," then myself, and "Wild Bill" was on the far right. As I mentioned, "Wild Bill" was one of our youngest members in the squadron, having just completed his MR check, and barely had 100 hours in the jet. In fact, he would finish the war with more combat time than peacetime flying in the F-15 and, like all our young aviators, he did just phenomenal work.

As we did our pre-strike sweep heading north, we got an initial radar contact about 25 miles north of Montenegro's airfield. At first it appeared to be a CAP, as the contact was orbiting; however, the slow speed and lack of any jamming led me to believe this might not be a fighter CAP. We were now thinking our element of surprise had been compromised. Lead and two focused on this contact as we closed the range, while "Wild Bill" and I kept our focus on Pristina's airfield. We knew this was their primary MiG base, with extensive underground shelters. This was our briefed primary threat axis, and our main task was to insure that nothing took off from Pristina heading towards Montenegro that might attempt to intercept our strike.

I got an intermittent contact out of Pristina, moving at high speed through the mountains. As the contact climbed above the mountains (about 10,000 feet) I was able to maintain a solid track, and I called him out as being on a bearing from our noses of 030 degrees for 70 miles. I started my ID matrix, and asked AWACS to do the same so that we would all be on the same sheet of music when the time came. Once I had determined my contact met "hostile" criteria, I handed him off to my number four to monitor, and I began monitoring the original contact, which was slightly west of our nose, to assist the lead element as needed. Lead then advised me that it appeared that this contact was landing, so I switched back to the eastern contact and asked four what its status was. Number four came back with a bearing, range, and altitude (BRA) on the contact that allowed me to put my radar right there. Four also had gotten a positive ID on the contact as a MiG-29, and it was pointed right at us.

I directed my element to start a climb, jettison tanks, and push it up. This would give our AMRAAMs greater range and, since we were on the front edge of the strike package, I wanted to shoot as soon as possible, to start the shooting match on our terms, not the MiG's. I asked AWACS if they had an ID on the

contact, but they were unable to provide any information. Since both jets in my element had a positive hostile ID, I took it upon myself to declare "Hostile," and I shot one AIM-120 at about 25 miles. I didn't realize we had accelerated to about 1.3 Mach, so as I shot the missile I looked to my left, and it appeared to be flying alongside of me. The missile took a couple of seconds to build up momentum and accelerate out in front of me, and during that time I thought I might have a bad missile. As it pulled away from me towards the location of the MiG the motor appeared to be a small glow, about the size of a dime.

I had a good radar track and did not see any jamming, so I opted to fire only one missile. I also was concerned with managing my missiles, as we had a long way to go, and a long time period to cover, so I didn't want to waste any. I also checked my element a little more to the east to avoid some of the SAMs that were starting to become active. My RWR was indicating that the SAM radars were starting to acquire us, so I wanted to stay away from them.

At about 15 miles to the MiG, I directed the element to come left and go pure, or point at the target. I did this for a couple of reasons. First, I had gotten a little too far east to be able to meet my contract of holding the east-west, counter-rotating CAP after this engagement was complete. Our four ship had briefed the strike package that we would hold our CAP between Montenegro and Pristina, and I needed to be in a position to uphold my responsibility. Second, I wanted to get an eyeball check on the missile and the threat. As I looked through the TD box in the HUD, I could not see the MiG, as it was pitch black out, but I was counting down the seconds left for the missile to impact.

As the counter reached zero, a fireball erupted in my HUD. Because the western mountains were still covered in snow, the fireball literally lit up the sky as it reflected off of the snow-covered mountains. The only thing I had ever seen like this was when they turn on all the lights at an NFL stadium, except this was like five times that bright; it really lit up the whole sky. In fact, an F-15E WSO about 85 miles to the southwest of the fireball heard my "Splash" call and simultaneously saw the bright glow. He became suspicious of what might have detonated up there, since the glow was so bright! As it turned out it was just that MiG-29 exploding.

Wreckage of MiG-29, serial number 18112. This is the MiG-29 downed by "Rico" Rodriguez. An AA-11 heat-seeking missile is in the foreground, and an AA-10 radar guided missile can be seen under the wing. *USAF.*

There were a total of six aerial victories during ALLIED FORCE, and four of these were credited to the "Reapers," so we were very proud of our squadron's performance. One of the other kills was accomplished by a Dutch F-16, and the Shaw F-16s also got one.

Operation ALLIED FORCE represented a turning point in the understanding of warfare by the average fighter pilot. As one of a few DESERT STORM veterans in our squadron, I kind of felt it was my responsibility to help the guys understand their role in actual combat, and the impact of combat on our squadron, our base, and our families back home. I also made a point to help the young guys understand the political ramifications of being armed with an air-to-air machine, and that you are sending a political statement anytime you hit that pickle button.

ALLIED FORCE represented a political tightrope, where U.S. forces and NATO forces were coming together for a political objective. We realized at that point that NATO had fallen behind in its training and technological investment. As a result, some of the tactics that were employed had to be "watered-down" significantly so that other partners could play completely in the entire operation. We also had the unique scenario where, as the U.S. leadership from SHAPE was directing airpower, they were not always airmen, and hence sometimes that direction was poor. It was common to go after targets that had already been struck, or going after targets that had no impact on forcing Yugoslavia to surrender. Even the youngest Lt in the squadron could tell that we were not doing things as well as we could have.

I say it was a turning point because, unlike DESERT STORM, where we had no idea what was going on, and we were just the execution element, we were actively involved in planning the air campaign over Yugoslavia. Unfortunately, when these recommendations got to SHAPE, they were often changed, and airman were put into harm's way striking targets that had no significance, and in some cases had already been destroyed. But that's a whole other aspect of this battle space. The actions of the 493rd were significant in developing tactics for both day and night employment that are still used by the F-15 community, and also by the F-22 as it becomes operational.

The investment in technology also paid off, as we were finally equipped with a missile that had the range to kill the enemy well beyond visual range, and was lethal enough to insure a kill. The investment made after DESERT STORM was made on the recommendations of the Captains, Majors and Lieutenants that fought in STORM, and much of the credit for the success in employing these new systems in ALLIED FORCE goes to them.

So to wrap it up, I ended up with three MiG kills. Three kills by a fighter pilot who I consider to be average; I was by no means

Lt Col Rodriguez with his crew chief, "Bull," on the ramp at Cervia. *via Rodriguez.*

the golden boy, and never had golden hands. What I had were great instructors and commanders who forced me to achieve higher levels of performance through dedication and hard work. They allowed me to experience failure, but they were also there, 100% of the time, to get me back on my feet, and help me to achieve new standards. Those three MiG kills are also a reflection of the dedication of the men and women who fix the F-15, and all those that supported the combat operations we were in. The men and women in today's maintenance world make success possible in the battle space. When it comes right down to it, every time you enter an engagement, the enemy has an equal opportunity to employ his weapons against you, so your aircraft and your weapons are the tiebreaker. In both STORM and ALLIED FORCE the troops that worked the jets, loaded them, fueled them—you name it, they were phenomenal. As were the support folks that take the creature comforts of home and deliver them to the forward edge of the battle space. They knew the mission, and supported it in every detail.

Also, a large part of this true success story is the family members, the spouses and the children left behind. I've been blessed to have my wife, who has endured three full-up combat deployments with what I would call the heart of the envelope; being involved each time in the night one operations, which are always the most challenging in combat. She has had to endure three of them, and she's been a true trooper. The same goes for my two great kids, who supported me and my wife during these deployments, and allowed me to do my job. When you look at the total amount of sacrifice it takes to accomplish the mission, even though my name appears on these kills, it should appear at the bottom of a very long list!

"Rico" recently retired from active duty as a full Colonel.

Captain Michael "Dozer" Shower (USAF)

493rd EFS "Grim Reapers," F-15C
Operation ALLIED FORCE
MiG-29
24 March 1999
Call-sign: EDGE 61

\Mike Shower graduated the United States Air Force Academy in 1990, and attended UPT at Vance AFB, Oklahoma. In 1993 he completed F-15C training, and was assigned to the 43rd Fighter Squadron, Elmendorf AFB, Alaska. Following this tour he was selected to attend the F-15C Fighter Weapons Instructor Course at Nellis. Upon graduation, "Dozer" was assigned to the 493rd Fighter Squadron, RAF Lakenheath, United Kingdom, in the summer of 1997.

Besides the multiple deployments to Incirlik to support Operation NORTHERN WATCH, I had also been on the ADVON (Advance Team) to Cervia AB, Italy, for one false alarm. On that trip in October 1998 I went with an out-going weapons officer, Maj Stu "Razor" Johnson. The entire squadron deployed; we had no idea if a war would kick off. In fact, the Serbians backed down, partially due to winter conditions in theater. The deployment only lasted a little over a month, and when they backed down everyone

Original art depicting "Dozer" Shower's MiG-29 Fulcrum kill by noted aviation artist Ronald Wong.

redeployed to their home bases. On February 19, 1999, I had just completed a BFM hop with another IP, Capt Ken "Heater" Griffin, when the Operations Officer (Ops O) met me at the door and told me to get my bags packed; we're going back to Cervia. Four hours later I was on an airplane for Italy, ADVON for the 2nd round.

A couple of days later the first 12 jets arrived from Lakenheath (we still had six jets deployed to Incirlik performing Operation NORTHERN WATCH; they would show up to Cervia a week before the war), and I assumed my flight commander duties; I was still helping our brand new weapons officer get up to speed, so I was fairly busy. The experience level in the squadron was very low, and there weren't many IPs; in fact, we had several brand new wingman, and even worse, several of our most experienced instructor pilots, including "Razor," "Heater," "Tonto," and a few others, had just PCS'd (Permanent Change of Station), leaving a big hole in our experience level. In one unusual aspect we were lucky; since we had just deployed to Cervia for the same drill, there weren't many unknowns to deal with. As the weeks wore on I shuttled back and forth between Cervia, the CAOC at Vincenza, and the planning cell at Aviano doing the mission planning for F-15Cs. It was obvious that things were getting more serious, and the prospect of actually going to war was looming near. As we stood-down from training sorties a few days prior to the start of hostilities everyone knew that the time was close. Still, it was difficult to come back to the squadron and have to pretend that nothing was going on, or at least that I didn't have any "gouge."

One of the more interesting things from my perspective as the weapons officer was how much more attention the squadron was paying to academics during the last couple of days. Instead of the usual "oh well" attitude, guys were on the edge of their seats to learn more about SAM breaks, the survival radios, you name it; everyone knew their lives depended on this information, so it was a great time to be a weapons officer. Another very important factor was the great leadership we had in "BillyMac," our Squadron Commander, who was also a Weapons School Graduate; he too had been there for the first deployment. He was a superb pilot, and incredibly calm throughout the entire deployment, and I was able to share details, ideas, and thoughts with him as we made plans, prepared, and flew missions—that was a great benefit, and made things much easier.

The day of 24 March was very surreal. Most of us tried to sleep until about noon, most couldn't. Since it was March, and still pretty cold and not yet tourist season, our little resort town of Cesanatico on the beach was empty. The guys were bummed, since it's a nude beach in the season! The pilots were in a four star hotel with a four star restaurant with outstanding per diem; all I can say is, if you've got to go to war, this was the way to do it! Everyone was restless, so about 20 of us head down and play beach football. In hindsight, this was pretty stupid, as any one of us could have broken something and been off the schedule, but it *was* a blast, and was all about relieving the stress that we were all feeling. We played for a good hour and a half, got cleaned up and in uniform, got in our cars, and went to war. Strange how that stays so vivid in my memory.

The flight line was completely still and quiet when we stepped to the jets—it was a somber moment. I'll always remember handing my nametag to Sgt Donald Green, aircraft 159's crew chief; I really don't remember much of what was said—it was pretty emotional—but I think it included, "bring my jet back and you with it!" I taxied and took off first, since I was leading the first four-ship out; our package had a greater distance to travel before our push time. We took off at sunset, one at a time (it was a tiny runway), and I'll never forget it, because there must have been 100 personnel lined up along the infield down the runway standing at attention when we took off—it sent chills down your spine. The line-up was myself as EDGE 61 and "Man-O" Steele as my number two. The second element consisted of "BillyMac" as number three, with "Dirk" Driggers on his wing. We used most of the squadron during the first 24 hours, including our newest wingmen. "Dirk" was one of these, with only a few hours of night flying in the Eagle, not long out of RTU, and here he was in the first four-ship, at night, and at war over hostile territory—it was great! While they were nervous, they did a fantastic job hangin' in there. In fact, I was most impressed throughout the entire conflict by how well our young pilots performed. They followed their training to a "T," and in many ways performed better than "us" more experienced pilots did.

Capt Michael "Dozer" Shower. *USAF via Mike Shower.*

One of "Dozer" Showers' F-15C flight taking off from Cervia on night one of Operation ALLIED FORCE. *via Mike Shower.*

"Cricket" Renner was leading the 2nd four-ship to takeoff. My four-ship was tasked to protect a "U.S.-Only" package consisting of ten F-117s, two B-2s on their combat debut, four F-16CJs, and two EA-6Bs over northern Serbia. "Cricket" had a coalition package of aluminum (non-stealthy) aircraft pushing first into the Kosovo province and southern Serbia. In his flight were "K-Bob" Sweeney as number two and "Rico" Rodriguez as number three, with "Wild Bill" Denham on his wing. Both "K-Bob" and "Wild Bill" were also very inexperienced in the Eagle.

The northern push was considered the "low-observable stealth" package, and since it was U.S.-Only, the NATO AWACS was not well informed of its presence, purpose, or composition. This was not great planning or coordination on the coalition leadership's part. Out of many painful lessons learned, a few were that you might not want to plan that the war will only last a few days, and it might be wise to bring in everything you need to fight—like a U.S. AWACS to control your U.S.-only packages! In fact, when I checked in with the AWACS, they said in effect "Who are you?," so we were off to a rough start, and this had a significant impact on our mission. The package marshaled over Hungary, and then was to push south through Serbia towards Belgrade. The B-2s were moving from south to north throughout the country, so they were really under everyone's protection during the mission. The F-117s were doing their "spider routes," going all over to their various targets in north Serbia. Our plan was to sweep the area as two two-ships separated by about 25 miles, then set up two CAPs just north of Belgrade facing south. This would keep us out of the SAM rings, but give us good coverage of their known MiG bases. I was holding down the western CAP with two, while three and four held the east CAP. With all this going on, and NATO AWACS not being in the loop, it made for a real mess.

Since we didn't have night vision goggles (NVGs) yet, our formation within the elements was about a five mile trail for the wingmen. They maintained this using the radar, air-to-air TACAN, and the IFF (Identify Friend or Foe) interrogator, as well as having built in altitude deconfliction between aircraft. Since we were a little short of AIM-120s, some of the aircraft had six AIM-120s, and some had four -120s and two AIM-7MHs. All had two AIM-9Ms, three bags of gas, and full chaff and flare. My aircraft had the two AIM-7 configuration, along with the AMRAAMs. The heavier AIM-7s were on the front stations, with the AMRAAMs behind them and on the inboard wing stations.

We pushed first, about two minutes in front of the CJs as planned. This gave us room to pump cold once, and not run over the CJs. It was a crystal clear night; we could see all the way to the southern end of Serbia. The lights of Belgrade were right there to the south. Since we knew the timeline, as the Time On Target (TOT) for the initial wave of cruise missiles came close, I had the whole flight look south at Belgrade. We could see the orange glow of the explosions as they hit various targets. Then it was our turn, and we pushed south.

We were in the mid- to high 30s, and the CJs were in the 20s. The F-117s were below them, and the B-2s came through WAY above everyone. This gave us some concern, having JDAMs (GPS-guided bombs) coming down through us, but it was "big sky theory" in such a tight airspace. We were really stuck; we didn't know where they would be, we had no way to see or avoid them, and we had to stay close to the MiG bases. I had briefed the F-117 weapons officer that if we engaged low targets we would shoot and dive through their block. He said he was fine with this, after all, it's a Big Sky Theory—you'll hear more about this later!

We had just gotten to the southern end of the CAP point and were getting ready to set up our counter-rotating CAPs when I hear the call "Splash one MiG in the south" relayed via AWACS. This was the luckiest guy in the world, "Rico," who now had his third MiG kill (two in DESERT STORM); he had just killed a MiG-

29 that drove right at him—single AIM-120 to a fireball about 10 miles from Kosovo's capitol, Pristina. So we were pretty fired up now, as we knew they were flying. We had questioned whether they would fly or not, and now we knew the MiGs were up. We were running 10 mile legs in the CAP, and we had been in country for roughly 6.9 minutes. I turned south again for the first time and, just like that, at 35 nm, there's a blip on the radar. I lock him up, and he's doing 150 knots at 1,500 feet, climbing out from their airfield in Belgrade, Batajinica. I call everyone, "Heads up, contact out of Batijinica." There's no ID or AWACS calls yet, and I break lock and go back to search. A short time later the radar shows him northbound, so I lock him again at 25 miles, our briefed lock range. Now he's at 10,000 feet going 400 knots.

Unknown to me until after the sortie, most of my radio calls on my main radio were unreadable. The radio was jamming itself, but I didn't know it; there was no feedback in the headset, and all we heard when playing the tapes together after the sortie was silence on everyone else's tapes, while I was jabbering away on the radio on my tape. So almost all of my contact calls, IDs, shots, etc. were not heard by anyone but me. This will turn out to be a huge factor in the chaos that ensues.

By 17 miles I have an ID that this is a bad guy, and I call it out. I talk first and shoot second, just what you're not supposed to do. So I call, "Hostile, Hostile, FOX 3" and take my first AIM-120 shot at 14 miles. I made sure the AIM-120 was active, and then thumbed to and shot an AIM-7. No kidding, I've always wanted to shoot an AIM-7, and that big ol' Sparrow comes off, WHOOSH! I'm looking down into the lights of Belgrade so I can't see anything, but I was able to follow the missile motor for awhile. I'm ramping down from 37,000 feet the whole time. At about six miles, and just after the AMRAAM times out, the target turns right, directly into the beam. This could have been triggered by several things. He could have gotten indications of my radar lock. The AMRAAM could have exploded near him but not damaged him, who knows, but he does maneuver into the beam. So now he's maneuvering when the AIM-7 gets there, and it apparently misses also.

Now I'm at 5.5 nm, look-down, when I shoot another AIM-120 and call, "FOX 3 again." I'm at about 20,000 feet, and he's at about 10,000 feet and I'm diving. This missile comes off and goes about straight down, and I'm diving and turning left, looking down and trying to follow it. The MiG then comes out of the beam in a climbing left turn towards me, kind of breaking up and into me. Maybe he got spiked, got a call from his GCI, or just looked up into a dark sky and saw the missile, but we end up about eight or nine thousand feet apart, and he's almost directly under me, head to head aspect. I pick up a spike (I have no idea where it came from—I never looked), and at the same time I'm glued to the missile motor when it turns into a fireball. Of course, I'm supposed to be in AUTOGUNS and clearing for other bad guys. Instead, I'm in a steep left turn staring at the fireball, thinking, cool! I don't see an ejection, but there was a lot of stuff coming off the aircraft, and I watched it impact the ground. We found out later that the pilot actually survived, which I was really glad about. My goal was to shoot down the aircraft, to eliminate a threat to our aircraft; you really don't think about killing the other guy. In hindsight I was

glad to have only shot down the aircraft—he had a wife and kids, too.

The Yugoslavian press claimed that the only MiG pilot to be killed was shot down by their own air defense SAMs. There are a lot of conflicting reports, though. The pilot flying my MiG wrote a long article about his short flight, and it even had his picture. It's been "edited" by a very sarcastic U.S. fighter pilot, and it's hilarious. He claims to have had three missiles shot at him; how he figured that out I'll never know—maybe he guessed, but he was spot-on.

Remember what I said about the F-117s and the big sky theory? This is exactly where this proved false—as always, Murphy's is alive and well. Because we had spun once in the CAP prior to the commit, one of the F-117s was now in front of us, directly between us and the MiG during the engagement. He's flying along, looking through his NVGs when, WHOOSH-WHOOSH, two missiles go right over the top of his canopy. He looks back and forward and realizes he is sandwiched, smack in the middle of an air-to-air engagement. I'm 20 degrees nose-low, and about a thousand feet away from the F-117, pointed right in front of him, when I fire my third missile. I find out by talking to him on the phone later that he sees all this as the missile motor illuminates my F-15, and the missile, followed closely by me, flying right across his nose. I almost hit him. He turns and follows the missile's path, and sees the MiG turning left towards him, also! Then the MiG explodes, and he watches it crash, too. Another F-117, about 35 miles away, sees the explosion. With his NVGs he clearly saw the MiG, the Eagle, and the F-117 all together. So much for the "Big Sky Theory," and of course, I have NO IDEA this just happened!

While all this is going on, my wingman and other flight members are only getting bits and pieces of my radio calls. My wingman knew something was going on, but not the whole picture. Because of this, when he sees the fireball "Man-O's" first thought is, "Dozer just got shot down!" I then transmit on the other radio "Let's come off north," and he thinks, "Thank God it's not Dozer!" He did have an ID by then, and was ready to shoot, but held off on his shot trying to figure out what was going on—outstanding patience for a young fighter pilot at night, on his first combat sortie! The other element didn't realize what had happened until later (radio again). So that's the end of the first engagement.

We had just reset in the CAP when we turn south and see an exact repeat of the first radar contact, except at 20 miles this guy turns into the beam. I can't get an ID on him and AWACS is no help; not once did they call an ID on a real airborne contact that night in the north. I can't blame them entirely, because first, NATO AWACS did not train as focused on tactical engagements as U.S. AWACS controllers did, and second, they were not given our U.S. Only Air Tasking Order (ATO), so they didn't know who was where, at what altitude, times, etc. In addition, since they couldn't hear my ID and shot calls, either, there was no way for them to hold onto a contact and pass the ID back to us if we lost track or had to turn cold (again, a factor later on). At this point I end up right over the top of the contact—I'm at 30,000 feet, and he's at 10,000. I call my element out north, since I don't have an ID and no NVGs, so we're not comfortable running on him. In my heart-of-hearts AND based

"Dozer" Shower's jet, F-15C 86-0159, in the break at RAF Lakenheath in 2005. *Ian Nightingale.*

on information I had in front of me, I KNEW this was a hostile, I knew where everyone else was (Eagles and CJs, and I knew he wasn't a F-117 or B-2), but without the technical and "legal" ID I couldn't shoot. After the shoot-down of the Black Hawks, the F-15 community was so conservative and worried about doing something wrong that we missed an opportunity to do something right. While being conservative is a good thing, we completely removed the ability of a pilot to use common sense and situational awareness. I had no doubt who this guy was, I had tracked him off his airfield. So while I did the *right* thing, what if the MiG had gotten a lucky contact and shot one of *us*? I fully believe I would have been questioned for not shooting. In retrospect, and I teach this all the time now, under the same circumstances—SHOOT! If there's ANY doubt you *don't* hit the pickle button, but if there isn't, don't be a lawyer—*do what's right*!

Meanwhile, "BillyMac" and his element are running on this guy, who is now northeast of Belgrade, turning back to the north. "BillyMac" runs on him for 30 miles with a lock, and he can't get an ID. One of the problems is while I was directly over the top of the MiG, "BillyMac" gets a "Friendly" indication from our merged plot. I didn't think to call out that I was directly over the MiG, and he doesn't know to break lock and reacquire to clean up the picture—in those days we didn't have data link yet, so we didn't have great S.A. on where other people were. They go in to 10 to 15 miles and abort out for lack of ID. Meanwhile "Dog" Kennel, an F-16CJ pilot (CLUB 73), has a solid radar lock on the MiG but no ID. He asks me seven times to confirm "Hostile" on the target, but once again, because of my radio he can't hear me (I

respond five times to his calls!). In the heat of the battle he forgets to then get an electronic ID, so he holds his shot and comes off north with "BillyMac's" flight.

With no one able to get an ID we now have EIGHT fighters all running north away from ONE MiG-29 because we couldn't ID him, nor use situational awareness to shoot him. While we are bravely running away to the north, my two-ship is in a position to start a turn back to the south to look at Belgrade again. Right then AWACS calls out "MiG-29 CAPs airborne near Belgrade," so I'm thinking where did all these MiGs come from? We found out just before takeoff they had moved six MiGs well to the south (the ones "Rico" engaged), but what AWACS was calling was ground traffic. We flew south all the way to Belgrade looking for these MiGs that weren't there (they became somewhat infamous for this—and worse were those in charge at the CAOC that several times attempted to commit us through SAM rings throughout the conflict to attack MiGs that weren't there because they were ground tracks). Operation ALLIED FORCE took a big step (backwards!) towards centralized control AND execution.

A few minutes later the lone MiG-29 had turned south, so the other six U.S. fighters turn and start chasing this guy south. "Dog" calls me and recommends that I turn north. As soon as I do, I get an immediate radar contact with hostile ID at 16 miles, beak-to-beak. "Man-O" is with me and locked also. At exactly the same time that I call the bullseye position of the hostile contact at 10,000 feet, AWACS comes back with "Friendly there, 27,000 feet." So I start a steep dive from 37,000 feet trying to get below 27, all the while screaming for the position of the other Eagle element and CLUB flight, the CJs. Of course they can't hear me because of the radio issue, so I get no answers from anyone!

By the time I'm diving through 19,000 feet the MiG is now five miles off my nose, and I know I'm looking at a guy WELL below 270. I call "Hostile, FOX-3" and shoot one AIM-120. I make a cardinal mistake here, and it's something I always hammer guys on doing—take two shots! They are called "miss"iles, not "hit"tiles. So I hold the second shot, since I only have one 120 left and an old AIM-7. I should have cranked, which would have given me room to complete the intercept and be in a position to shoot again (another mistake), but I don't, so I'm in a right turn looking straight down when near time-out I see a small "pop." This could have been a proximity detonation of the missile, or it could have been the missile hitting the ground. Either way, it didn't down the MiG and there's no fireball, so my "one" shot didn't do the job. Now I'm too close to keep him on the radar, so he gimbals off my radar low; I'm looking all the way down, and he's got to be right under me, and I'm thinking this isn't a very good situation. So I've got to spin to get spacing, and hope he ends up in front of me again. I call for a 360 turn, or "spin," and around I go. I say "I" go because of the radio again, as two doesn't hear the call.

"Man-O" has been locked to this guy the whole time, but he doesn't hear my hostile call, my shot, nor the spin call; he also doesn't have his own ID, so he's not sure who this contact is. While I'm in my 360 turn I see the air-to-air TACAN range getting bigger, so I ask him for his heading in the other radio, and he says "south." I direct him to come north and spin to get back in formation, and being a good wingman, he drops the contact and turns north. Had I known he was tracking the same contact, and was in a position to kill this guy, I would have shouted, "Shoot him, he's hostile!" In fact, when we listened to his tape later there was broken but audible radio calls from "Man-O" about being locked to something—had I been able to process that and figure out what was happening, we might have been able to get this MiG.

Once I roll out southbound and "Man-O" is back behind me, we get more locks on a contact that we "KNOW" is the same guy; he's heading south towards Belgrade, same place we left him, same airspeed and altitude, but I can't get an ID, and AWACS

"Dozer" Shower at the unavoidable post-kill press conference. I think his look says it all. *via Mike Shower.*

keeps saying "friendly there," so I can't shoot. No kidding, this is the only radar contact in the area; everyone else we can see with radar and IFF is behind us (ie, it was only stealth aircraft in front of us and the MiG). He starts to slow and descend, so I secretly hope he has battle damage and is going to crash, but he was probably on approach to his field. We are coming up on the SAM threat rings around Belgrade, and I don't want to go from hero to zero by getting us shot down, so I drop the contact and call us out north. We missed killing this guy not once, but twice, for a variety of reasons. My radio problems, ID issues, not shooting two missiles, AWACS not hearing the hostile calls, and the reasons mentioned before all compounded in the "fog of war" to cost us this opportunity. And many of the issues were solvable at the time, had I just been able to process the information and act upon it.

However, at this point we just return to our CAP; the B-2s are nearly overhead based on timing, and it's time to egress and Return To Base (RTB). All said and done, it was still a pretty cool start for Eagle drivers on the first night of a war!

The Yugoslavian press later reported that the first MiG-29 to launch from Batajnica Air Base was Maj Nebojsa Nikolic in MiG-29 18111, followed shortly by Maj Ljubisa Kulacin. Nikolic was reported to have been shot down almost immediately, while Kulacin claimed to have evaded three missiles fired at him. Since Batajnica AB was under attack by NATO forces, he chose to land at Belgrade International Airport. Both pilots reported that the radars and SPO-15 radar detectors were inoperative on their aircraft. These reports match amazingly close to the NATO claims.

Capt (now-Lt Col) Shower went back to the F-15C Fighter Weapons School, this time as an instructor. Following this tour, he was selected in the initial cadre of F-22 Raptor pilots for the initial operational test and evaluation, and currently is stationed at Elmendorf AFB, Alaska, commanding an operational F-22 Raptor squadron.

Captain Jeff "Claw" Hwang (USAF)

493rd EFS "Grim Reapers," F-15C
Operation ALLIED FORCE
2 x MiG-29s
26 March 1999
Call-sign: DIRK 21

Capt Hwang Graduated UPT at Laughlin AFB in 1990. Upon completing F-15C training at Tyndall AFB, he spent six years flying the Eagle and T-37 prior to being assigned to the 493rd Fighter Squadron of the 48th Fighter Wing, RAF Lakenheath. "Claw" had been in the squadron for two years, and had flown one Operation ALLIED FORCE mission prior to this engagement. The following account is from an email he sent just days after the event to fellow Eagle Drivers.

Well, I'm finally back in England after being Temporary Duty (TDY) since the end of January—at least for two weeks anyway. Got sent direct to Cervia AB, Italy, from Operation NORTHERN WATCH in Turkey after being at Incirlik AB for over seven weeks ("Luv the 'Lik" no 'mo!). My house and yard are a total mess!

There doesn't seem to be an end in sight in the Kosovo situation, but the war is over for me, at least for a while. Some of you have probably already heard through the grapevine about what happened to "Boomer" and me. Here's the proverbial "Rest of the Story."

Original art of "Claw" Hwang getting the double kill by noted aviation artist Ronald Wong.

F-15C tail number 86-0156 seen landing at RAF Lakenheath in 2005. It was in this aircraft that "Claw" Hwang scored his double MiG-29 kills during Operation ALLIED FORCE. *Tony Silgrim.*

"Boomer" and I were tasked as Bosnia-Herzegovina DCA on 26 March 1999, Vul time (Vulnerability Time, or "station Time") from 1500Z to 1900Z. We were established on CAP over Tuzla for about an hour after the initial refueling. At 1602Z, while eastbound approaching the Bosnia/Yugoslavia border, I got a radar contact 37 nm to the east, 6K' (Altitude 6000' feet), beaming south at over 600 knots.

Of course AWACS had no clue, and did not have any inkling someone was flying on the other side of the border (although he was real good at calling out every single friendly WEST of us!)

I called out the contact, and "Boomer" was locked same. Without an ID, and not being tactically sound to cross the border at the time, I elected to pump our formation in a right hand turn through south and called, "PUSH IT UP, BURNER, TAPES ON!" (We were initially flying .85 Mach at 28,000 feet, and rolled out heading west/southwest.) At that time I didn't think anything much would happen. I figured the contact would probably continue south or turn east, and remain well on the eastern side of the border.

Nevertheless, I called the flight lead of the south CAP over Sarajevo and gave him a craniums-up on the position of the contact, altitude, and the heading. This entire time AWACS still had no radar contact, even after I called it out on the radio. Man, running away with the contact at our six o'clock with AWACS not having any clue was NOT comfortable!

"Boomer" and I continued west for a total of 60 seconds (about 10 nm) before I directed the formation to turn back hot, again turning through south in an attempt to get some cut-off. "Boomer" was on the north side of the formation (left side, as we rolled out heading east). We both got contact BRA 070 degrees for 37 nm, 23,000 feet, target now heading west (hot towards us). AWACS finally woke up and starting seeing the same thing. Now, I'm starting to think Sh!T IS GONNA HAPPEN (evident with the increase of about two octaves in my voice!).

It was fairly obvious this guy originated from FRY (Former Republic of Yugoslavia), and there were no OCA missions on at the time. We still needed to get clearance from AWACS to engage,

so I requested (codeword) and got no reply from the controller (pretty sure he had no freakin' clue what that codeword meant!). About this time both "Boomer" and I got good ID on the target in our own cockpits, and with threat hot towards us inside 30 nm I decided to blow off the AWACS/clearance to engage restriction and go for it!

Target was now inside 30 nm, and I directed "Boomer" to target the single group. I broke lock, and went back to search in 40 nm scope and 120 degree sweep. The target then check-turned to the right towards the northwest (about 14L aspect) and descended to high teens. "Boomer" and I checked about 30 degrees left to the northeast for cutoff. This check-turn slung me aft in the formation, so I stroke it up to full afterburner to get more line abreast. I called "COMBAT 1, ARM HOT," and saw "Boomer's" wing tanks come off with bright flames under the wing. Pretty impressive!

I was well over the Mach when I punched my tanks off, and the jet jumped up abruptly (you can see it in the HUD). I took a quick look back to check and see if my stabs were still intact... I rolled my radar elevation coverage down, looking from about 5,000 to 21,000 feet, and no kidding, stayed in search for at least one full frame (believe me, I wanted to go back to single target track SO DAMN BAD!). AWACS started calling out two contacts, lead - trail. Sure enough, I was starting to see the break out on my scope!

At about 20 nm "Boomer" called "FOX 3, 18K!" I saw the cons/smoke from his jet and thought "SONOFABITCH! I gotta get me some!"

I commanded miniraster on the leader, and as soon as the radar locked, I immediately thumbed forward to HD TWS. My first shot came off inside 16 nm from the leader. When I pressed the pickle button, it seemed like an ETERNITY before the missile actually launched, but when it did...WOW!!!! I have never shot an AMRAAM or AIM-7 before at WSEP (and I don't think I have a chance in hell of shooting more missiles at WSEP after this!). The missile came off with such a loud roar/whoosh, I not only heard it clearly in the cockpit above the wind noise, radio comm, ear plugs, and helmet, I actually FELT the rocket motor roar!

In the HUD, you can see the flames shooting out from the tail end of the missile, and the smoke and cons following it! I stepped immediately to the trailer in HD TWS, and pressed and held the pickle button for at least three seconds. Again, thinking "COME ON, DAMN IT! LAUNCH!"

The second missile came off just as impressively as the first after the same painful delay. I yelled, "Dirk 1, Fox six, lead trail!" (I was later critiqued on my comm as incorrect 3-1 terminology... WHATEVER!)

Since "Boomer" was the primary shooter I assumed he was locked to the leader, so I kept the trailer as the PDT. Didn't want to screw with a good thing, so I stayed in HD TWS inside 10 nm (our Weapons Officer promptly criticized me for NOT going STT inside 10 nm upon reviewing my VSD tape; thus, I still have to pass my IPUG Tactical Intercept check ride!). Both targets started a left check-turn to the southwest (14L to II to 16R aspect) and continued to descend to low teens. Approaching 10 nm, checking RWR to make sure we weren't targeted: "DIRK 1 naked !" "DIRK 2 naked !" "DIRK [flight], let's go pure!"

From 30K, both of us rolled our jets inverted, pointed nose low directly at the TD box on the HUD, and pulled throttles to idle. I think my heart rate at this time was reaching my aerobic limit for my age (you know, that formula: 220 minus age...)! Against a broken cloud background, I saw a tiny dot in the TD box about seven to eight nm out. I called, "DIRK 1, tally ho, nose seven nm, low!"

Realizing I saw the trailer, I was praying "Boomer" would soon follow up with a tally call on the leader. Approaching five nm, I'm scanning in front of the trailer for the leader, but no joy. Sh!t! The trailer continued his left turn to southwest, and I was looking at approx 14R aspect. Inside of five nm I thumb aft to AIM-9, and tried twice to un-cage, but the tone was not there.

Just then, between the HUD and the canopy bow (about right 12:30 to 1 o'clock position), I saw the leader explode! The best visual description I can think of is if you held a torch from one of those Hawaiian Luau parties and swing it through the air. The flame, with an extended tail trailing the torch, is exactly what I

USAF personnel inspect the remains of MiG-29 tail number 113. Wreckage indicates the MiG impacted with very little forward speed, and stayed relatively intact. *USAF via "Claw" Hwang.*

saw! Turning my attention back to the trailer, the trailer exploded into a streaking flame seconds later just as I tried to un-cage the missile the third time! Never mind!

"DIRK 1, SPASH TWO MIG-29s, B/E 035!!!" I'm ashamed... I was screaming like a woman! I didn't really bother to keep an eye on the fireballs, so I didn't see any chutes. Later reports confirmed both pilots ejected safely.

Anyway, I called for "Boomer" and me to reference 080

Another view of the inspection team going over the wreckage of the MiG-29. This was one of the two MiG-29 Fulcrums downed by "Claw" Hwang. *USAF via "Claw" Hwang.*

Close-up of the rudder of MiG-29 tail number 113. *USAF via "Claw" Hwang.*

heading and short range radar. Thumbed aft to AUTOGUNS, plugged in full afterburner, and accelerated to 460 knots at 20K (20,000 feet). My cranium was on a swivel, and I was breathing like I just ran a full sprint!

"DIRK 2, blind!" Crap!!!! I looked north, and it took me a few seconds to find "Boomer" (about 3.5 nm left and stacked high). I tried to talk his eyes back to me, but "Boomer" called out to west in a right turn. I waited a few seconds to sanitize, and turned west as well. During the turn I immediately pulled into double beeper due to airspeed and Gs (looking back, I should've over-G'd so the mission would've been more impressive...).

Rolling out, I was three nm in trail of "Boomer," so I had him shackled to the south to pick up line abreast. The fun wasn't over yet. "Boomer" got an AUTOGUN snap lock less than 10 nm south of us, low altitude, with no ID. I told him to press for VID while I followed him three nm in trail. We were diving back down to the low teens, and I saw ABSOLUTELY NOTHING on my radar!

"Boomer" all of a sudden pulls up and yells, "DIRK 2, unable ID!" That's BAD!!! I just about sh!t in my pants! I saw nothing, and after a few seconds I asked "Boomer" if he saw ANYTHING at all. "Boomer" said he didn't see anything, so we just stroked it up and separated to the northwest for a while, then came back for a second look. Nobody home! "Boomer" thought it may have been a bad radar lock. I sure hope so!

The rest of the sortie was one excitement after another. While on the boom, AWACS controller started calling out every single ground traffic as possible contacts crossing the border into Bosnia. For a while it sounded like a mass attack on Tuzla! By now it was night, and "Boomer" (in an offset 3-5 nm trail) and I were still running around with our hair on fire!

One time AWACS called out contacts very low alt moving towards Tuzla westbound. I didn't see squat on my tube, and neither did "Boomer." As the position of group started getting closer to Tuzla, I expected to see a burst of explosion from the airfield underneath! "Boomer" and I were gonna go from "heroes to zeros" real soon!

AWACS later called out MiG CAPs just 15 nm northeast of the border! "Boomer" and I were ready to "Pop a cap in their ass" across the border as soon as we got contact and ID! Again, nothing on the radar. We even did two iterations of a grinder with a two-ship of Vipers, and no one got a solid radar hit.

That night we committed and armed hot THREE MORE TIMES after the MiG kills based on ridiculous AWACS calls! No kidding, by the time our replacement showed up (four hours of vul time later), I was totally exhausted and drained!

The flight across the Adriatic was uneventful, and "Boomer" and I finally had a moment to think about what happened. After I landed and pulled into de-arm, I saw a freak in a flight suit wearing a reflective belt, jumping up and down. Sure enough, it was "Freak" welcoming us back!

Taxi back to the chocks was like having a bunch of kids following an ice cream truck! Everyone came running out, and waited at the parking spot for "Boomer" and me. "Boomer" taxied in front of me as I pulled into my spot. Losing all professionalism and radio discipline (yada yada...), I called out on Ops freq: "'Boomer,' You're the Sh!T!!!" Getting out of the jet and greeting all the bros and maintainers was THE GREATEST MOMENT OF MY CAREER!!! Our Ops Group Commander was first to shake my hand, followed by the mob!

We were laughing, shouting, hooting, high-fiving, and hugging! It was awesome! Couldn't wait to review the tapes, so we all piled into the "Turtle" (a deployable secure debrief facility, aka a small trailer) and watched my HUD tapes. Thank God it recorded everything clearly, including the fireball from the trailer.

More of the squadron bros almost knocked me over when they came storming into the Turtle! We were all screaming and jumping so hard in the Turtle I thought it was going to fall over! Too bad "Boomer's" VSD tape did not run, and his HUD tape was washed out due to a high aperture setting. "Boomer" and I were laughing and high-fiving the entire car ride home! We weren't even supposed to fly that day!

Some afterthoughts... No kidding, it took over a day for this to finally sink in. It felt almost surreal that day/night. Our Maintenance Officer said it best when he saw me hours after I shut down engines, "So 'Claw,' have you landed yet?" Only a few words can describe this event: F***ING unbelievably LUCKY! Not the fact we shot them down, but that they were airborne during our watch. Any Eagle driver could've easily done what "Boomer" and I did, but as one person said, "You guys won the lottery!"

The sequence of events happened in our favor like the planets lining up. The jets, missiles, and radar (well, at least mine) performed marvelously! Our Maintenance dudes deserve the bulk of the credit. We had no spares that day. The crew chiefs and the Pro Super absolutely BUSTED THEIR ASSES working red balls and launched us on time! "Boomer," my wingman—what can I say? Regardless of whose missile hit which MiG, WE shot down two Fulcrums that afternoon. We succeed as a team, and fail as a team (good thing it was the former)!

"Boomer" did an OUTSTANDING job of finding the group, working the ID matrix, and targeting according to plan. If I didn't have faith in him, I would not have broken lock and broken out the lead trail formation. Of course I'm proud of what we did, but there's one thing I'll really stick out my chest for: to everyone who taught me and influenced me on my tactical flying and gave me long debriefs (though painful at times), especially (names omitted), I DID NOT LET YOU GUYS DOWN!!! It doesn't get much better than this, guys! Well, maybe two more kills would be pretty cool... That's all I have to say.

Later analysis showed that even though "Boomer" shot first, it was "Claw's" two AIM-120s that destroyed both MiG-29s. Serb sources later stated that Major Peric and Captain 1st Class Radosavljevic were scrambled from Batajnica Air Base to intercept other NATO aircraft. After multiple malfunctions, to include both of the MiGs' radars, and some poor GCI directions, both MiGs were dispatched. While it appears that both pilots ejected, it is reported that Radosavljevic did not survive. Capt Hwang was awarded the 1999 Hughes Trophy for this double-kill.

F-15C 84-0014 was flown by "Boomer," and was incorrectly painted with a Serbian kill marking before it was determined that "Claw's" AMRAAMs were responsible for both kills. The previous Iraqi DESERT STORM kill belongs to "Nigel" Doneski. *via "Dozer" Shower)*

Lt Col Michael "Dog" Geczy (USAF)

78th EFS "Bushmasters," F-16CJ
Operation ALLIED FORCE
MiG-29
4 May 1999
Call-sign: PUMA 11

Lt Col Geczy graduated from Euro-NATO Joint Jet Pilot Training (ENJJPT) at Sheppard AFB in 1983. Upon completing F-4E training in 1984 he flew the Phantom II for two years, converting to the F-16C in 1986 while on his first operational assignment at Ramstein AB, Germany. He later graduated from the USAF Fighter Weapons School F-16 Division in 1992. Lt Col Geczy had approximately 2,300 flight hours (including previous combat experience in Iraq and Bosnia) in the F-16C (Blocks 15, 30, 42, and 50) before deploying to Aviano AB for Operation ALLIED FORCE (OAF). This MiG-29 kill occurred on his 115th career combat mission, and his seventh mission supporting OAF. The following excerpts were taken from a briefing that Lt Col Geczy gave about a year following the event.

We were tasked for what we call a "force protection" mission... loaded up with two High Speed Anti-Radiation Missiles (HARMs), two AIM-120A AMRAAMs, two AIM-9M Sidewinders, a full load of 20mm, and self protection assets (external jamming pod on the centerline, chaff and flares, and towed decoys). As there were no Eagles tasked as part of this daylight strike mission, our job was to protect the strikers from both the surface and air threats.

The jets were Block 50 F-16CJs. F-16CJs are configured with the HARM Targeting System pod on the side of the intake. The HARMs are those large white missiles closest to the external fuel tanks that home in on radar emissions from SAMs, AAA, or early warning radars. The other key part to our force protection mission was air-to-air, of course. On the wingtip missile stations are the AIM-120 AMRAAMs; we also carried the shorter range AIM-9M infrared missiles on the inboard stations, and the trusty internal, 20 mm Gatling gun for shorter range air-to-air engagements.

My flight included myself as number one (on my 12th contingency deployment), my wingman, who was a 1 Lt ("DBAL" Austin, with about 350 hours in the jet) on his third contingency deployment; the number three and element lead ("Hajii" Julazadeh) was an instructor pilot with about 1,200 hours (and on his eighth contingency deployment). The number four man, "Nut" Peterson, was absolutely critical to our success that day. Although "Nut" was flying as a wingman and number four, he was then a four-ship flight lead, and upgrading to instructor pilot with about 800 hours in the F-16. Operation ALLIED FORCE was "Nut's" second contingency deployment. This combat sortie was the seventh or eighth Operation ALLIED FORCE sortie for all of us, since Shaw

Lt Col "Dog" Geczy immediately after the mission; note empty AIM-120 rail.
USAF via Geczy.

Original art of "Dog" Geczy's kill titled "Snakebite over Serbia" by Lockheed staff artist Price Randel.

Block 50 F-16CJ showing the standard configuration used during Operation ALLIED FORCE. *USAF via Geczy.*

Left to right: "Nut," "Hajii," "Dog," and "DBAL" (in "wall" formation) following the mission. *via Geczy.*

AFB deployed our squadron into the theater about three weeks into the war as part of a NATO force structure plus-up.

I have to admit, my opinion is that the Serbian surface-to-air missile (SAM) battery crews were pretty darn good...well trained and coordinated during Operation ALLIED FORCE, and with some pretty creative and unpredictable tactics. They fired over 700 SAMs at NATO aircraft during the war! Of course, the Serbian military had been watching NATO's operations over Bosnia for more than six years, and had been quick to modify their tactics during this operation to increase the probability of a successful kill against NATO aircraft. So frankly, since the Serbian MiG-29s had not faced NATO pilots for almost seven weeks at this point of the war—and we had just lost our second NATO jet a couple nights prior to a SAM—my biggest concern that day was the SAM operators. I was dead wrong, as the biggest threat that day would end up being one MiG-29 driver who would attempt to intercept "tail-end Charlie" during the egress phase of the strike.

On that day, NATO was conducting some of its first daylight strikes in central Serbia, near Belgrade. There were two flights of four F-16CJs, each dedicated to the force protection of these

Block 50 F-16CJ sheltered at Aviano AB during Operation Allied Force. *via Geczy.*

midday strikes. My flight, call-sign PUMA 11, was tasked to launch out of Aviano, pre-strike refuel, enter Serbia, protect Strike "Alpha," egress, refuel again, re-enter Serbia again, and then protect Strike "Charlie." Strike package "Alpha" that day included Dutch, British, and French strikers. Another flight of four F-16CJs (PANTHER 21) were from Spangdahlem AB (but also launched out of Aviano), and were protecting strikes "Bravo" and "Delta" in the same manner.

Keep in mind that, since the F-15Cs were dedicated to protecting the tankers and AWACS that day, they only had CAPs up in Bosnia and Hungary. The other players that day included EA-6Bs, a French AWACS that controlled all of the activity in Bosnia, and a British AWACS that controlled the strikes in Serbia.

Let's get on to the details of that day. First of all, the weather was poor. The clouds were layered to broken up to almost 30,000 feet. Our flight had some difficulty finding good, clear airspace to CAP to do the best job protecting against the air and surface threats during the strike period. In fact, the British and Dutch strikers ended up weather aborting their attacks completely. On the other hand, the French strikers, or KNIFE 61, were working overtime trying to deliver their bombs between holes in the weather in their target area.

Near the end of the strike period, KNIFE 61's flight lead requested that we stay on station another eight minutes or so until they finished their attacks. I agreed, but of course, was concerned that we might end up stretching the flight's fuel before we could get back to the tanker. Since my fuel state was actually the lowest in the flight, I made a mental planning note that I was the most "skosh" on gas.

Later, I heard the next set of F-16CJs for Strike Bravo, PANTHER 21, check in on the strike frequency. Well, the French finished their attacks after about 12 minutes of "overtime," and we started to escort them out of Serbia. Keep in mind, it had been a very quiet mission up to this point. Although we had done some preemptive SAM targeting, we had not fired any HARMs at active SAM sites during this first strike period. I was probably a bit too casual finishing up this "walk in the park" strike package, and too anxious to get air refueled and back on station for the next one.

It is near the end of this "ho-hum" egress that the AWACS controller calls out that a "bogey" is airborne in Serbia. I completely missed this call! Fortunately, our trusty number four man, "Nut," saved the day, and piped up on our discrete, intra-flight frequency with a "head's up" call and the bogey's position. We immediately turned the four F-16s around, and we faced the bogey in a wall formation. During our turn to face down track, NATO AWACS called out the track as hostile for the first of what would be a total of seven times during the intercept.

We simultaneously pushed it up to supersonic, climbed up into the high 30s (forgot to jettison our tanks!), and pressed right on into the SAM threat rings. Shortly thereafter, "DBAL" called out that he was bingo fuel...since I knew that I actually had the lowest fuel in the flight, I "copied" his call, and decided that all of us would most likely need to recover into Sarajevo after the engagement.

About this same time, the AWACS controller made some calls that made the NATO-required beyond-visual-range (BVR) rules of engagement (ROE) matrix damned confusing, and uncertain in my mind. As I was working through this dilemma, both in my head and with some calls back to AWACS, I tried to get PANTHER 21 flight's radars looking for the target (who were actually trailing us by quite a bit). I frankly started to have my doubts that we were going to finish this intercept with the little fuel remaining. Also during this final period of the intercept, the MiG-29 driver illuminated me with his radar a couple times, which definitely got my attention.

Fortunately, yet uncomfortably late in the intercept, and at range much less than we all wanted, I finally worked through all the ROE rules with AWACS... I got a chance to put my thumb on the weapons release, or pickle button—one of my last thoughts as I was mashing down on the pickle button was, "if it's important enough to shoot, shoot two. So, 'Dog,' fire these two off as rapidly as possible!"

Well, it seemed to take FOREVER for that first missile to come off—must have been time compression! I actually had second thoughts about whether I had properly armed-up or not. I just started to glance in the HUD to confirm the arm status, and then I saw the first missile come off from the left wingtip. I mashed the second AMRAAM off as quickly as I could after that first one launched. It didn't seem to take nearly as long for the second AMRAAM to blast off the right wingtip!

Although I had already fired an AIM-9 in training and HARMs in Bosnia during Operation DELIBERATE FORCE, and earlier in Operation ALLIED FORCE, I had not YET had a firsthand appreciation for what an AMRAAM live-fire looked like. Those two AMRAAM launches were EXTREMELY impressive, and continue to amaze me even today!

Since the MiG was at short range and maneuvering at this point, the line-of-sight of the target was changing rapidly across my nose and well below me—those missile fins obviously dug-in immediately after launch and dove with rapid, arcing attacks through the HUD field-of-view with breakneck speed (kind of like a pitcher throwing a curve ball)! It was a true testament to American technology that the AMRAAM performed so well at close range, and with a fantastically high line-of-sight! I am not sure any other radar missile out there could have hacked the square-corner that the AMRAAMs made that day!

Descending quite a bit after the launches, I noted on my radar that the missiles were preparing to impact, and made a mental note that in order to get credit for the kill, "I had better see this, as I may be the only one who witnesses it!" I rolled up in about 90 degrees of left bank, and then saw the aircraft exploding about six thousand feet below, and between scattered cloud layers (basically underneath my left knee). I made two, "Splash one with a fireball!" radio calls to AWACS—guess I knew that my chances of making that call again in my flying career were essentially nil!

"DBAL," on the other hand, reported after the mission that he watched both missiles all the way into impact. Fortunately, the weather had scattered out somewhat at the point of intercept, so

78 EFS "Rainbow" jets from the 77th, 78th, and 79th FS' getting armed at Aviano AB prior to an Operation ALLIED FORCE sortie; "Dog" Geczy's jet (91-0353) from the engagement on 4 May is the furthest to the right. *via Geczy.*

today "DBAL" has a "nanosecond by nanosecond" recollection of how the aircraft defensively maneuvered to a near perfect beam, the missiles' impacts, how the MiG started to burn, and what parts came off first!

Following the engagement, as we were all "skosh" on fuel, we immediately started our climb and egress to the west, towards the tanker tracks in Bosnia. I requested that the AWACS controller vector our tanker due east and directly back to us.

Now the real difficult part of the mission began! As it turned out, and as was frequently true during Operation ALLIED FORCE, the hairiest part of the mission was just beginning: getting rejoined on a tanker that has been directed to retrograde to a safer area, in the weather, while other F-16 and F-15 flights are rejoining on it simultaneously to do their refueling, in the weather. When we crossed into Bosnia, we discovered that our tanker was over 120 miles away and going further away!

I then set a divert bingo for the flight for Sarajevo, and had to call the tanker crew directly to get them to turn around for an in-the-weather tanker rejoin. In the end, we were able to refuel and get back on station for Strike Charlie. Shortly thereafter Strike Charlie was weather cancelled. With a full load of fuel, we flew back to Aviano "as the crow flies"—supersonic in the low 40s across the whole length of Bosnia, and across the Adriatic Sea—breaking all kinds of rules, I am sure!

It was raining like cats and dogs when we finally got back to Aviano; of course, I insisted upon bringing the four-ship up a combat, tactical initial after the mission (pretty dumb decision, as the rain storm was almost directly over the air base)—the guys did a marvelous job getting the jets on the deck, despite my stupid act!

We all lined up in the de-arm area, and a crew chief hooked up on the head-set communications cord during the aircraft de-arming. Since my HARMs were still loaded, I guess he thought that we had a "ho-hum" mission; he asked me in a real low key

voice, and obviously not really pleased to be in the pouring rain, "Well, Sir, how did your mission go?"

I replied, "Pretty good...Shot a MiG down."

He yelled back, "You got to be sh!ting me...Sir!"

I yelled back at him, "Look at the missile rails!!!" I looked at the rails too, at that point, and saw the other guys in the de-arm crew doing pull-ups on the missile rails in the rain! They were really psyched up, and came up later after shutdown to give me the AMRAAM umbilical cables that remained—perfect mementos for that mission!

"Nut" showed exemplary flight discipline that day. First, by succinctly and promptly advising the flight about the AWACS call that a "bogey" was approaching during our egress. And second, by employing his radar as directed to confirm that no other threats were airborne. Also, unlike other "yahoo-cowboy radio calls" that you hear sometimes during MiG kills these days, my flight members did not say ONE word after the MiG-29 was splashed. They maintained the strictest discipline throughout the egress, on to the next AWACS controller in Bosnia, to the tanker, and on the boom taking fuel. Only after the air refueling was complete, and when we were preparing to return for the next strike period, did "Nut" say on the discrete frequency "PUMA 1, PUMA 4, request?"

"Go ahead with your request, PUMA 4"

"Sir, can we go back there and do that again?"

By the way, last month "Nut" Peterson was selected to go to F-16 Fighter Weapons School for the class starting this summer.

There were some internet claims immediately after the war that this MiG-29 was mistakenly shot down by a Serbian SAM battery. That is absolute, complete, and pure BS! You can actually see the aircraft break up on my radar tape after the missile's impact!

I cannot speculate upon the Serbian Air Force single ship tactics that day, or why someone would make such a claim, other than to perhaps save face for the Serbian MiG-29s that performed

"Dog" Geczy at the obligatory interview with the Armed Forces Network the day after the mission. *via Geczy.*

so poorly during the war against NATO pilots (for lots of reasons, I am sure: weak equipment, poor aircraft serviceability, lousy Soviet-style training and flying currency, etc). Lately, more and more of the Serbian internet sites acknowledge that this MiG-29 was downed by an F-16CJ.

But what I can say is that the four of us that day were employing fully mission capable F-16CJs with 100% of our jets and avionics operational (thanks to our maintenance technicians), fully armed with a variety of operational weapons ready to handle all kinds of threats (thanks to our munitions, armament, and weapons technicians), and were fully trained to handle the events of that day (thanks to the USAF training and readiness model).

You bet, there are decisions and tactics that I would do differently if I had a chance to do that mission again. But any of my flight members could have ended up firing those two AMRAAMs and getting a MiG-29 kill that day. I was fortunate to have been the leader and targeted the group, and thankfully supported by a great flight of Viper drivers, particularly "Nut" Peterson, who really got the "light bulb turned on" during our egress.

Authors note: Although Lt Col Geczy deployed to Operation ALLIED FORCE as part of the 78th Fighter Squadron, the deployment included jets from other squadrons at Shaw AFB. The aircraft during Lt Col Geczy's MiG-29 engagement (91-0353) was actually from the 77th FS "Gamblers." Lt Col Geczy went on to command the 77th Fighter Squadron, and made F-16 91-0353 the squadron flagship during his two year command, as seen in the photo above.

Two F-16CJs from the 77th Fighter Squadron fly in formation over South Carolina during a training mission. The aircraft in the foreground wears the markings for the Commander of the 77th FS, Lt Col Michael Geczy. Note also the small green star under the canopy, indicating that this is the aircraft flown by Lt Col Geczy in which he shot down a Serbian MiG-29 Fulcrum during NATO Operation ALLIED FORCE. *USAF Photo by SrA Greg L. Davis.*

Appendix:
USAF Official Credit Orders

Source: USAF History website, Maxwell Library
Southwest Asia War (Gulf War) Victory Credits.

Name	Rank	Unit	Credit	Date	Position	Enemy	Aircraft	Weapon	Order
Bakke, Daniel B.	Capt	4 TFW	1	910213	WSO	MI-24	F-15E	GBU-10	USCENTAF SO GA-022, 15 Jun 1991
Bennett, Richard T.	Capt	4 TFW	1	910213	Pilot	MI-24	F-15E	GBU-10	USCENTAF SO GA-022, 15 Jun 1991
Denney, Jay T.	Capt	36 TFW	2	910127	Pilot	MiG-23	F-15C	AIM-9	CCAF SO GA-1, 1991
Dietz, Thomas N.	Capt	36 TFW	2	910206	Pilot	MiG-21	F-15C	AIM-9	CCAF SO GA-1, 1991
Dietz, Thomas N.	Capt	36 TFW	1	910322	Pilot	MiG-21	F-15C	AIM-9	CCAF SO GA-1, 1991
Dingee, Steven S.	Capt	36 TFW	0.5	910211	Pilot	Mi-8 Hip	F-15C	AIM-7	CCAF SO GA-33, 1995
Doneski, John T.	Capt	36 TFW	1	910329	Pilot	SU-22	F-15C	AIM-9	CCAF SO GA-33, 1995
Draeger, Rhory R.	Capt	33 TFW	1	910117	Pilot	MiG-29	F-15C	AIM-7	CCAF SO GA-1, 1991
Draeger, Rhory R.	Capt	33 TFW	1	910126	Pilot	MiG-23	F-15C	AIM-7	CCAF SO GA-1, 1991
Graeter, Robert E.	Capt	33 TFW	1	910117	Pilot	F-1 Mirage	F-15C	AIM-7	CCAF SO GA-1, 1991
Graeter, Robert E.	Capt	33 TFW	1	910117	Pilot	F-1 Mirage	F-5C	Maneuver	CCAF SO GA-1, 1991
Hehemann, Robert W.	1 Lt	36 TFW	2	910206	Pilot	SU-25	F-15C	AIM-9	CCAF SO GA-1, 1991
Hehemann, Robert W.	1 Lt	36 TFW	1	910322	Pilot	PC-9	F-15C	Maneuver	CCAF SO GA-1, 1991
Kelk, Jon K.	Capt	33 TFW	1	910117	Pilot	MiG-29	F-15C	AIM-7	CCAF SO GA-1 1991
Magill, Charles	Capt	33TFW	1	910117	Pilot	MiG-29	F-15C	AIM-7	CCAF SO GA-1, 1991
Masters, Gregory P.	Capt	36 TFW	1	910202	Pilot	IL-76	F-15C	AIM-7	CCAF SO GA-33, 1995
May, Randy W.	Maj	36 TFW	1	910207	Pilot	Helo	F-15C	AIM-7	CCAF SO GA-33, 1995
McKenzie, Mark T.	Capt	36 TFW	0.5	910211	Pilot	Mi-8 Hip	F-15C	AIM-7	CCAF SO GA-33, 1995
Murphy, Anthony R.	Capt	33 TFW	2	910207	Pilot	SU-22	F-15C	AIM-7	CCAF SO GA-1, 1991
North, Gary L.	Lt Col	363 TFW	1	921227	Pilot	MiG-25	F-16D	AIM-120	CCAF SO GA-1, 1993
Parsons, Rick N.	Col	33 TFW	1	910207	Pilot	SU-7	F-15C	AIM-7	CCAF SO GA-32, 1995
Pitts, Lawrence E.	Capt	33 TFW	1	910119	Pilot	MiG-25	F-15C	AIM-7	CCAF SO GA-1, 1991
Powell, Benjamin D.	Capt	36 TFW	1	910127	Pilot	F-1 Mirage	F-15C	AIM-7	CCAF SO GA-1, 1991
Powell, Benjamin D.	Capt	36 TFW	1	910127	Pilot	MiG-23	F-15C	AIM-7	CCAF SO GA-1, 1991
Prather, David S.	Capt	36 TFW	1	910119	Pilot	F-1 Mirage	F-15C	AIM-7	CCAF SO GA-33, 1995
Rodriguez, Cesar A.	Capt	33 TFW	1	910119	Pilot	MiG-29	F-15C	Maneuver	CCAF SO GA-1, 1991
Rodriguez, Cesar A.	Capt	33 TFW	1	910126	Pilot	MiG-23	F-15C	MiG-23	CCAF SO GA-1, 1991
Rose, David G.	Capt	33 TFW	1	910129	Pilot	MiG-23	F-15C	AIM-7	CCAF SO GA-1, 1991
Schiavi, Anthony E.	Capt	33 TFW	1	910126	Pilot	MiG-23	F-15C	AIM-7	CCAF SO GA-1, 1991
Sheehy, Todd K.	Capt	10 TFW	1	910215	Pilot	Mi-8 Hip	A-10	GAU-8	CCAF SO GA-1, 1991
Stevenson, Craig D.	1 Lt	52 FW	1	930117	Pilot	MiG-23	F-16C	AIM-120	DAF SO GB-386, 1993
Swain, Robert R., Jr.	Capt	926 TFG	1	910206	Pilot	Helo	A-10	GAU-8	CCAF SO GA-1, 1991
Sveden, David G., Jr.	1 Lt	36 TFW	1	910119	Pilot	F-1 Mirage	F-15C	AIM-7	CCAF SO GA-33, 1995
Tate, Steven W.	Capt	1 TFW	1	910117	Pilot	F-1 Mirage	F-15C	AIM-7	CCAF SO GA-1, 1991
Tollini, Richard C.	Capt	33 TFW	1	910119	Pilot	MiG-25	F-15C	AIM-7	CCAF SO GA-1, 1991
Underhill, Craig W.	Capt	33 TFW	1	910119	Pilot	MiG-29	F-15C	AIM-7	CCAF SO GA-1, 1991
Watrous, Donald S.	Capt	32 TFS	1	910128	Pilot	MiG-23	F-15C	AIM-7	CCAF SO GA-33, 1995

USAF Aerial Victory Credits During OPERATION ALLIED FORCE
March-June 1999

Name	Rank	Unit	Credit	Date	Position	Enemy	Aircraft	Weapon	Order
Rodriguez, Cesar A.	Lt Col	493 EFS	1	990324	Pilot	MiG-29	F-15C	AIM-120	16 ASETF SO#GF-024, 23 Aug 1999
Shower, Michael K.	Capt	493 EFS	1	990324	Pilot	MiG-29	F-15C	AIM-120	16 ASETF SO#GF-024, 23 Aug 1999
Hwang, Jeffery C.J.	Capt	493 EFS	2	990326	Pilot	MiG-29s	F-15C	AIM-120s	16 ASETF SO#GF-024, 23 Aug 1999
Geczy, Michael H.	Lt Col	78 EFS	1	990504	Pilot	MiG-29	F-16CJ	AIM-120	16 ASETF SO#GF-024, 23 Aug 1999

EFS: Expeditionary Fighter Squadron. ASETF: Air and Space Expeditionary Task Force.

About the Author

Craig "Quizmo" Brown graduated Southern Illinois University with a degree in Aviation Management in 1987. He immediately entered the United States Air Force, and after completing pilot training at Vance AFB, Oklahoma, was selected to fly the F-111. His first assignment took him to RAF Lakenheath, where he flew in Operations DESERT SHIELD, DESERT STORM, and NORTHERN WATCH. While instructing in the F-111 Fighter Training Unit (FTU) he was selected for the F-111 Fighter Weapons School. He was asked to return as an instructor to the Weapons School. Upon the retirement of the F-111, then-Captain Brown was assigned to the F-15E "Strike Eagle," where he participated in Operation SOUTHERN WATCH, and instructed in the F-15E FTU. After September 11, 2001, Major Brown was involved in the Air Defense of the East Coast of the United States (Operation NOBEL EAGLE). After serving 15 years on active duty, and flying over 2,600 hours in fighter aircraft, he joined the Air Force Reserve, participating in both Operations ENDURING FREEDOM and IRAQI FREEDOM. He is currently a Captain for a major airline, and resides with his wife and two sons in Washington, D.C.

Original art by noted aviation artist Ronald Wong, commissioned by Capt Cesar "Rico" Rodiguez depicting the end of "Rico" and "Mole's" 2-v-2 against Iraqi MiG-29s. Here, "Rico's" MiG-29 commits a fatal error, and tries to split-S at too low of an altitude, with the resulting fireball extending nearly a mile across the desert. This was the second maneuver kill of Operation DESERT STORM.

Patch Gallery

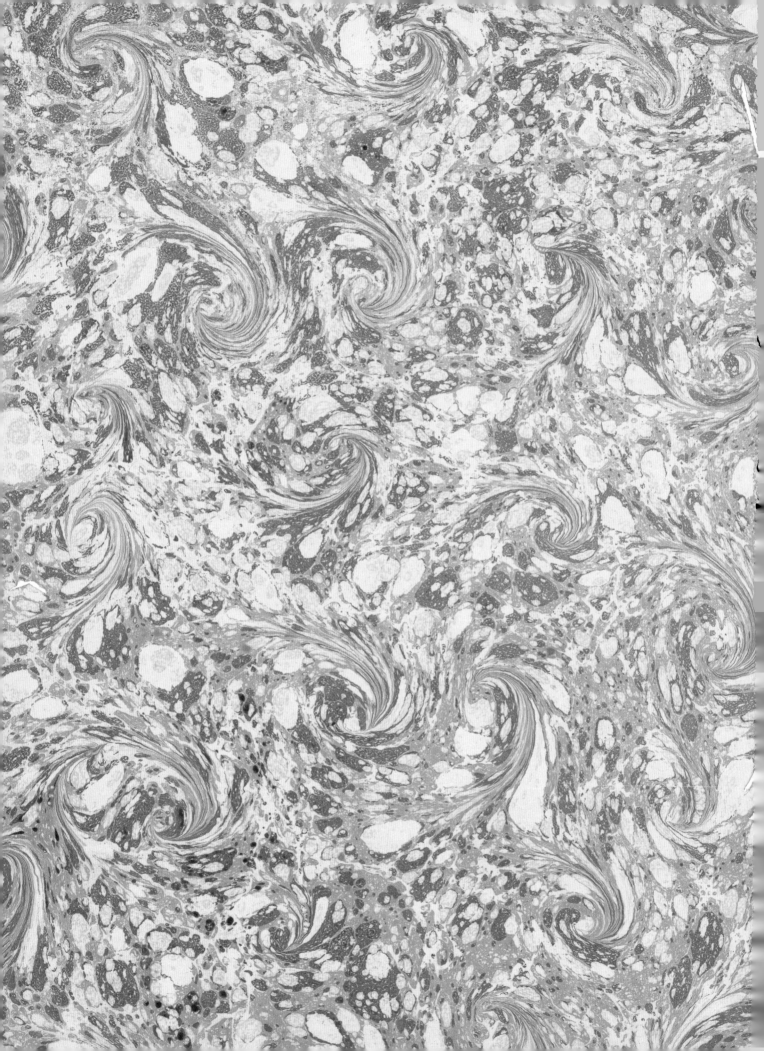